KV-638-301

THE STORY OF SKI-ING
AND OTHER WINTER SPORTS

THE STORY OF SKI-ING AND OTHER WINTER SPORTS

by Raymond Flower

with a foreword by Jean-Claude Killy

Angus & Robertson · Publishers

Preceding page Nineteenth-century reconstruction of the rescue of the infant Haakon Haakonsson by the 'Birchlegs' during the Norwegian civil war in 1206

Angus & Robertson · Publishers
London · Sydney · Melbourne · Singapore · Manila

First published by Angus & Robertson (U.K.) Ltd 1976

This book was designed and produced by London Editions Ltd, 30 Uxbridge Road, London W12 8ND

ISBN 0 207 95704 5

D. L. S. S.: 494/76
Printed and bound in Spain
by TONSA San Sebastián
and RONER Madrid

Contents

Foreword by Jean-Claude Killy

I was delighted when I heard that Raymond Flower had written the first history of all the winter sports because it seemed to me to fill a curious gap. Of course I always enjoy reading about the early days of skiing, particularly when the text is as lively and informative as this, but the history of skiing cannot be considered in isolation. The pioneers who first started Alpine skiing were usually keen skaters and tobogganers as well, and even though today the various snow sports are strictly divided into specialist events, like ski-jumping or ice-dancing, they still have one important thing in common – their main thrill is that they all pit individual skill and speed against snow and ice.

Looking at those fascinating pictures of Davos and St Moritz in the early years of the century, I felt tremendous admiration for the early ski fanatics. They certainly had to be fanatics, and it says a lot for my favourite sport that a single skater or tobogganer could be persuaded to slog slowly and laboriously uphill, unaided by lifts or tow ropes, simply to slither hazardously down again on short Norwegian skis that were totally unsuited to the steep Alpine scene. What a contrast they make to the pictures at the end of the book showing my own era, with all its super-specialized equipment and technical know-how.

I thoroughly enjoyed reading about the personalities and the inventions which made these changes possible, and about the development of all those other winter sports in which I have only participated as a rank amateur, or just as an onlooker.

I wish this book great success and I recommend it to everyone who enjoys any or all of the snow and ice sports.

LUB DES SPORT
MARTI
4
VAL D'IS
MARTI

To

DOROTHY AND GUNNAR SCHJELDERUP

for whom

Kindness and Good-fellowship

are a way of life

Author's Preface

Chesa sur l'En, St Moritz – Holmenkollen, Oslo November 1974–April 1975

Many people helped me to write this book, unwittingly as it happens, long before Hugh Begg of London Editions asked me to do it. To a few of them I am especially grateful. 'Lanty' Dixon, for instance, taught me as a schoolboy how to schuss and to christie. Maribel Vinson and Gretchen Merrill, whose fortunes I followed around Europe and the States, introduced me to the charismatic world of championship skating. The Oxford University ice-hockey team welcomed me as a camp follower during their highly successful Swiss tour in 1939, and my old friend William Broadhead, as Anglo-American captain of the Oxford ski team in 1951, infiltrated me into some skiing company that was far above my station. Bill Bracken and James Riddell managed to coax me through some hairy Ski Club of Great Britain tests at Zermatt, and both Sir Arnold Lunn and T. D. 'Tyke' Richardson took the trouble to discourse for many a pleasant hour on the early days of skiing and skating. Too many of them, alas, are no longer with us, but I am glad to have the chance of recording my appreciation for the friendship they so warmly offered.

I owe a debt of gratitude, likewise, to Peter Kasper of the St Moritz Kurverein, and to Anikò and Hans Jorg Badrutt who own the Palace Hotel; but above all to Eliane and Dieter Schwarzenbach for having made their splendid cuckoo-clock castle, the Chesa sur l'En, a home from home for an ever-widening circle of *aficionados*, so that it has now become more of a club than a hotel.

Generous, too, has been the help and advice given me by Rudi Matt at St Anton; Ernst Scherz, Paul Valentin and Doris Duke-Bally at Gstaad; Erna Steuri, Hansueli Seiler and Hans Rudolf Steller at Grindelwald, and Bruno Courteaud at Megève.

Since 1956 I have hardly missed a season in Oslo, where Norwegian hospitality is so overwhelming that to the large circle of friends who have introduced me to every corner of their marvellous country I shall always be indebted. But in particular I would like to say 'Tusand takk' to Jeanette and Finn Søhol, Eva and Gunnar Sjøwall, Kåre and Hans Sartz-Knudsen, Else Wike and Kåre Erik Gullwåg, Lisa Nielsen, and Dorothy and Gunnar Schjelderup, to whom this book is dedicated. It is the least that I can do.

My thanks go also to the Editors of *Ski Magazine* for having commissioned (and paid most handsomely for) my first published article back in 1962, and to the Ski Club of Great Britain for so enthusiastically helping in every possible way.

Last, but certainly not least, my very warm thanks are due to Elizabeth Hussey and Jane Monro of *Ski Survey*, who edited and captioned the skiing pictures, and to Howard Bass, who did the same for the ice sports pictures.

Raymond Flower

Two seventeenth-century Dutch skating scenes by Anthonie Beerstraten *(above)* and Hendrich Avercamp *(right)* emphasize just how much social life in Holland once took place on skates – a commonplace form of early transport as well as a popular pastime

From Bones to Beau Monde

Left Skating has been popular on Dutch canals since the late Middle Ages, when speed skating began to evolve. This Dutch wood carving, printed in 1498 and showing early evidence of female participation, is the first known picture of the sport. It shows St Lydwina of Schiedam who, in 1396, at the age of sixteen, fell and broke a rib while skating. She entered a convent where she died in 1433 and later became known as the patron saint of skaters

Right The ice must have been thin on this canal. The scene was captured for posterity by H. Cock and one hopes that St Lydwina came to the aid of the hapless individual on the extreme right

> When the great fenne or Moore (which watereth the walles of the citie on the North side) is frozen, many young men play upon the yce, some stryding as wide as they may, doe slide swiftly . . . some tye bones to their feete, and under their heeles, and shoving themselves by a little picked staffe, doe slide as swiftly as a birde flyeth in the aire, or an arrow out of a crossbow. Sometime two runne together with poles, and hitting one the other, eyther one or both doe fall, not without hurt; some break their armes, some their legs, but youth desirous of glorie, in this sort exerciseth it selfe against the time of warre.

Thus wrote Thomas-à-Becket's secretary, Fitzstephen, in 1180, but in many ways the scene is timeless. The old Norse sagas, indeed, are full of allusions to skating, and primitive bone runners from as far back as neolithic days have been found in various parts of Northern Europe. At some point, it would seem, the early lake dwellers discovered that their boats could be used as sledges to slide across the frozen lakes, and that a flat piece of wood on each foot enabled them to get through the snow without sinking. In due course they found that bones, however crudely shaved to form an edge, ran better over the ice than wood did.

And so the first skates came into being.

'Ull, god of winter, runs on bones of animals over the ice,' sang an Icelandic poet, and significantly the word *schenkel*, meaning a shank or leg-bone, is still used in Holland for a modern steel skate. Dutch paintings, of course, abound in skating scenes, the earliest of which – a wood engraving in Brugman's *Vita Lijdwine* – portrays a luckless girl called Liedwi after a bad toss on the ice. (As a result of this mishap she apparently retired to a convent, and later became the skaters' Patron Saint.) Skating seems to have been practised to some extent in Scandinavia during the Middle Ages, despite the blankets of deep snow that covered both rivers and lakes. In Holland, however, where the canals froze over

Left Another Dutch skating scene by Hendrich Avercamp catches the atmosphere of colourfully-dressed crowds enjoying their skating on the frozen canals of the Netherlands during the hard winters of the early seventeenth century

but snow was not a problem, it became the quickest way of getting from place to place.

By the seventeenth century, in fact, it had grown into a national pastime enjoyed by every class of society. But while the peasants, hurrying along the frozen canals to market, were eager to get there as fast as they could, such emphasis on speed was hardly to the aristocrat's taste. Elegance and good manners required him to glide gracefully over the ice like a dancer, with one foot high behind and hands delicately poised. Treated in this fashion, skating became something of an art, and when during Cromwell's Protectorate the Stuarts were exiled to Holland, they too learnt the intricacies of 'outside and inside edges' and how to list neatly over into a 'Dutch roll'. Even the Princess of Orange took to the ice on the Duke of Monmouth's arm, causing the French Ambassador to comment tartly, in a despatch to Louis XIV, that

> 'Twas a very extraordinary thing to see the Princess of Orange clad in petticoats shorter than are generally worn by ladies so strictly decorous, these tucked up half-way to her waist, and with iron pattens on her feet learning to slide sometime poised on one leg, sometime on another.

Thus the seeds of both speed skating and artistic skating were sown in Holland, and when the Stuarts returned to England they carried the fashion back with them. Pepys, needless to say, was one of the first to comment on the new pastime:

> Ist December 1662: To my Lord Sandwich's, to Mr Moore and then over the Parke where first in my life, it being a great frost, did see people sliding with their skeetes, which is a very pretty art.

And Evelyn, not to be outdone, recorded on the same day that he saw

> The strange and wonderful dexterity of the sliders on the new canal in St James's Park, performed before their Majesties by divers gentlemen and others with Scheets, after the manner of the Hollanders, with what swiftnesse passe, how sudainly they stop in full carriere upon the ice . . .

The Great Frost of 1683, when the Thames froze hard from early December until 5 February, gave a notable boost to the new sport. A vast fair was constructed on the ice-bound river, and King Charles II arrived with Queen Catherine on a sledge pulled by a skater to watch a programme of bull and bear-baiting that included skating as well. They were particularly fascinated, it seems, by the Dutch sailors who performed intricate movements on the ice. A

Bottom Early Dutch wooden skates, from a print dated 1570. The oldest known skates were made from the shank or rib bones of the elk, ox, reindeer, or other animals. The earliest of these to have been discovered were found bound to the skeleton of a Stone Age man in Friesland, Holland, and were made from a horse's cannon-bone during the second millennium BC. Early skaters ground the bones down to make a flat surface and travelled with added propulsion from spiked poles. Wooden skates, because they were easier to shape, superceded bone before wood and metal combinations began to be developed around the mid-1500s

Left A contemporary drawing of the frost fair on the river Thames in 1683. Charles II visited the fair with Queen Catherine, and Samuel Pepys claimed to have danced on the ice with Nell Gwynn. Below the letter 'L' on the drawing is a man 'slyding upon skeats'

Right Skating attire has certainly changed – and so have the skates – since this glimpse of seventeenth-century Dutch ice fashions, drawn by Jan Peter Saenredam

contemporary ballad describes how

> The Rotterdam Dutchman, with fleet-cutting scates
> To please the crowd shows his tricks and his feats;
> Who, like a rope dancer (for his sharp steels),
> His brains and activity lies in his heels.

The craze for sliding over the ice with iron skates quickly caught on, and many Londoners (Pepys included) became reasonably proficient at it. All the same, their repertoire was limited to what would now be called 'plain skating' – that is to say, outside and inside edges, and the Dutch Roll, of course. It was not until the foundation of the Edinburgh Skating Club in 1742, the first ice club in the world, that figure skating began to be developed, and skaters who wished to join were required to pass a qualifying test. Amongst other things, they had to demonstrate the ability to brake. At that time this was a hazardous procedure: you leant well back on your heels, bringing your entire weight on to the back of your skates, with the toes pointing up into the air.

In due course an artillery subaltern named Robert Jones wrote a text book on how to skate, propounding for the first time the theory that to stop, the skater should turn sharply to the right or the left and press hard on the inside of the leading foot – more or less the modern method, in fact. He also described the execution of what he called the 'figure of a heart on one leg'. His book included a number of illustrations of beautifully dressed skaters in elegant attitudes that were clearly inspired by the Greeks.

What the Dutch had invented as a pastime, the British transformed into a

HG. Inuet. J. S. sculp.
4
Accumulant homines totum quęcunq per ,annum ,
Hęc ego consumo, soli hęc mihi cuncta parautur.
C.S.

stylish sport which soon spread over into France and Germany. At Versailles, the court took it up, and ladies of fashion appeared on the ice in a swansdown-draped sleigh, while their *beaux* glided round and courted the delicate figures that hid behind snow-white masks. Marie Antoinette herself ventured out, and is said to have become one of the best skaters of the time.

Goethe also became a passionate enthusiast for what he called the 'poetry of motion', sometimes circling on and on in the moonlight. It was an exercise, he thought, 'which brings us into contact with the freshest childhood, summoning the youth to the full enjoyment of his suppleness, and is fitting to keep off a stagnant old age.' Lamartine and William Wordsworth were keen skaters too – in fact, Wordsworth boasted (rather egregiously) that he could cut his name on the ice with his skates.

For the French, above all, it was an agreeable *divertissement* in which the natural grace of the dandy – his poise and his elegance – was transplanted on to the mirrored ice. An élite little group, known as the *Gilets Rouges* because of the brilliant red waistcoats they sported, widened the field of action to include skating backwards on both outside and inside edges, and evolved a repertoire of pirouettes and jumps.

Up to this point skating (with notable exceptions, such as Marie Antoinette) had been an essentially male preserve, especially in England. But by the end of the eighteenth century, ladies of fashion began to show their prowess too. What appealed to them, perhaps, was not only (as Robert Jones put it) that 'no motion can be more happily imagined for setting off an elegant figure to advantage, nor does the minuet itself afford half the opportunity of displaying a pretty foot' but also, as a contemporary chronicler reminded them, that 'a lady may indulge herself here in a tête-à-tête with an acquaintance, without provoking the jealousy of her husband; and should she unfortunately make a slip (sic), it would at least not be attended with any prejudice to her reputation'.

Poor Liedwi might turn in her grave, but skating, without doubt, had come a long way.

Right One of Germany's most illustrious skating enthusiasts – Goethe – skating in Frankfurt, and about to be brought down to earth by a snowball

Below Elegance might be the ideal of the English school of skating but the comic possibilities of the fashionable sport soon caught the eye of Andrew Cruickshank

The Origins of Skiing

Above This ancient rock carving, found in the northern part of Norway in 1931, near the Arctic Circle, has been dated to approximately 4000 years ago and must surely be the oldest representation of a skier

Top right An early Icelandic representation of the Norse god Ull shows him hunting on skis

Bottom right This drawing from a book published in Italy in 1555, shows how the northern peoples used skis for hunting and for fighting. By then Sweden had a trained corps of ski troops who could cover up to 100 miles a day

Skiing, meanwhile, was a non-starter so far as these elegantly pirouetting dilettantes were concerned. Few people outside the snowbound north had even given it a thought, if the truth be told, and yet for all this ski-running is one of the oldest of all human activities. At Rødøy, Tjøtta, in Northern Norway, a Stone Age rock carving depicts two men on skis hunting elks; while the petrified ski which was dug out of a bog at Hoting in Sweden has been dated by archaeologists back to 2,500 BC.

Since the earliest times, to be sure, Scandinavians had used skis as a means of getting from place to place across the snow that covered their land for so much of the year, and some of them, surprisingly enough, are not so very different from the wooden skis that are still in use today. Those found at Kalvträsk in Sweden were about eight feet long and fairly narrow, whereas the Hoting ski was shorter and broader, rather like a snowshoe, with fur fixed to the sole to prevent it from slipping backwards on uphill treks. Others from Østerdal in Norway were of unequal length – a long left ski and a shorter right one with which, helped by a long pole, it was possible to get along quite quickly with a sort of skating step, something like riding on a scooter. Usually they were fastened to the feet with straps.

What the archaeologists have discovered, moreover, has been backed up by historians. The earliest written reference to skiing occurs in Procopius (526–559 AD) who mentions a race of Skridfinnar – that is, sliding Finns – as the Lapps seem to have been known as to the Ancient World, and the old Norse sagas abound with tales about ski-running. Ull, the winter god, for instance, may have skated on bones up in Iceland, but he is always portrayed on skis with curved tips; while Skadi, the giant goddess who married Njord is said to have left her husband to return to the slopes. (Not surprisingly, she was adopted as the goddess of the skiers.) Then again, in a ninth-century saga, King Harald the Fair-haired sang the praises of Vighard, who apparently skied straight down a mountain that nobody had ever dared take straight before; while six years before the battle of Hastings, King Harald 'Hardrada' wagered a well-known Norwegian named Heming Aslaksen, that he could not schuss a steep slope on Bremanger Island, off Bergen, and stop before the edge of the cliff. Aslaksen, it appears, won the bet by driving his stick into the snow and swinging himself so high round it that his skis flew off into the void (which raises an interesting point about the bindings he used).

Indeed whether Norwegians (as they will tell you) are born with skis on their feet or not, they have certainly made use of them both for hunting and for war. During the Battle of Oslo in 1200 AD King Sverre of Norway sent his scouts off on skis to reconnoitre what the Swedes were doing; and six years later, during the Norwegian civil war, another king's son, Haakon Haakonsson, was carried to safety over the mountains in the dead of winter by two of his aides (called

Right This drawing from *The Lapps in Finmark,* written by Knud Leem in 1767, shows one of the earliest types of ski race. The course would be set down a steep slope and competitors had to pick up objects (in this case a cap) as they went

Bottom This English picture shows Norwegian ski troops exercising near Trondheim in the winter of 1822

'Birchlegs' because they wrapped their legs with birch bark against the cold) a feat that is still commemorated by an annual langlauf race, known as the 'Birkebeinerrennet', over the route that they took.

That the Russians also used skis in military campaigns is apparent from a pleasant old legend that describes how a Lapp, who had been pressganged into guiding the Russian ski troops against his own people, led them with a torch to the edge of a precipice and threw himself over, followed by the Muscovites who crashed into oblivion. On the other hand a small Swedish army that moved into Norway in 1718 was annihilated by the Norwegian ski battalions largely because it was *not* equipped with skis. (The Norwegians, incidentally, were fitted out in white uniforms lined with green so that in summer they could be reversed and worn inside out.)

Although skiing was more or less confined to the Nordic countries, it seems to have been brought to Scotland by the Vikings. Certainly it is recorded that Ragnvald Kale, Yarl of the Orkneys, was skiing up in his domains in the twelfth century. Later we hear of miners going to work on 'skees' in Weardale, and in *Lorna Doone* there is a description of skiing in Devonshire in the sixteenth century. Francesco Negri, an Italian from Ravenna, seems to have been the first southerner actually to have attempted to ski up in Norway in 1663, and it seems likely that some form of skiing was practised in the Black Forest and in some of the valleys of Austria a century or two ago, but then died out.

Up to comparatively recent times, however, skis served a utilitarian purpose. They were to move about on, not for fun. Admittedly Knud Leem, a professor at the University of Copenhagen, described in 1767 how the Lapps skied steep slopes without sticks, picking up pieces of clothing that had been put around in the snow, which certainly has a sporting flavour about it. But the emergence of skiing as a sport really dates from the time that Sondre Norheim and his friends skied from Telemark to Christiania (now Oslo) in 1868 and gave a new look to both running and jumping.

For one thing, Sondre Norheim had designed a more maneuverable ski with binding straps for toe and heel. For another, he had developed the telemark turn (taken, in a kneeling position, with the toe of the inside ski touching the boot of the outside foot) that was streets ahead of the skidding movement practised in Christiania. Elegantly performing S-turns with outstretched arms, the young men from Telemark caused a sensation at an official jumping competition held on Huseby Hill, just outside the capital. Crichton Somerville describes how the others grasped a long, stout staff, as if (he thought) their lives depended on it:

> Starting from the summit, riding their poles, as in former times, like witches on broomsticks, checking the speed with frantic efforts, they slipped

A skiing competition in Finland in the 1880s. The 'quick stoppage', top left, looks rather drastic and some artistic licence seems to have been used in the way the snow spurts up in the lower drawing. The ski dividing the pictures shows a curious narrow piece before the front spatule, and a platform to support the boot. There are plenty of judges at work on these Helsingfors slopes, no doubt because the competitors were given points for style and speed as well as length of jump

Above Nansen with members of his 1888 expedition. They crossed the country from east to west, dragging their sledges 500 kilometres and reaching a height of 2,700 metres. Nansen's subsequent book had a great influence on other ski pioneers

Left Fridtjof Nansen was already a keen skier at the age of nineteen, when this photograph was taken. Seven years later, in 1888, he became the first man to cross Greenland on skis

> downwards to the dreaded platform or 'hop' from which they were supposed to leap, but over which they but trickled, as it were, and, landing softly beneath, finally reached the bottom somehow, thankful for their safe escape from the dreaded slide. But then came the Telemark boys, erect at starting, pliant, confident, without anything but a fir branch in their hands, swooping downwards with ever increasing impetus, until, with a bound, they were in the air, and 76 feet of space was cleared ere, with a resounding smack, their ski touched the slippery slope beneath, and they shot onwards to the plain, where suddenly they turned, stopped in a smother of snow dust, and faced the hill they had just descended . . .

In Sweden the first recorded race was held outside Stockholm in 1879. The downhill events appear to have ended on a frozen lake and the competitor whose speed carried him furthest was adjudged to be the winner. Modern slalom, what is more, was anticipated by the fact that the runners had sometimes to turn around poles or flags. (Slalom, incidentally, comes from the Telemark dialect, and referred to a 'style competition' and according to Arnold Lunn means a 'track left after something is drawn or dragged'.) Einar Stoltenberg mentions, indeed, that there were originally three types of course in Norway: *slalom* itself, which was run over slopes without sharp changes of

Far left The skis invented by Sondre Norheim had stiff osier binding around the heels, making them manoeuvrable. The skis in this picture, which he constructed in 1870, also had curved sides, varying in width from about 8cms in front to 7.2cms at the binding and 7.6cms at the back

Left Sondre Norheim, the father of modern skiing, was born in Morgedal, Telemark, Norway in 1825 and died in 1897

gradient or fences and walls; *villom* (literally, 'wild journey') which was a high speed descent over difficult terrain – corresponding, in fact, to the present downhill; and the *langrenn* (now more commonly known as *langlauf*), a long cross-country race. Be this as it may, these early contests in the hills behind Oslo led to the first Holmenkollen competition in 1892. It was the Norwegians, to be sure, who gave the first great impetus to the sport. The development of skiing outside Scandinavia itself, which began in the last years of the nineteenth century, was entirely due to Norwegians and enthusiasts who learnt to ski in Norway and then spread the gospel elsewhere.

Swiss skiing in its early days was given an initial boost by Odd Kjelsberg, who brought the first skis to Glarus, and not long afterwards another Norwegian, named Bjørnstad, opened a ski shop in Bern and became the unofficial leader of the Swiss skiers. But what really dramatized the sport was Fridtjof Nansen's celebrated crossing of Southern Greenland from east to west in 1888. For forty days his party dragged their sledges on skis over a distance of some five hundred kilometres, climbing at one point to a height of 2,700 metres. Wilhelm Paulcke, who first crossed the Oberland glaciers, and Mathias Zdarsky, who became the first unofficial ski teacher giving free instruction every Sunday near Vienna to all comers, were both converted to skiing by Nansen's exploit. Admittedly the technical level of their pupils was limited to stemming and floudering hopelessly in deep snow, to the huge amusement of onlookers, who considered that to get involved in such contortions one must be either a nut, or a clown. But at least it was a start.

Right With much of their land covered with snow every winter, Canadian trappers, loggers, and miners took to snowshoes even before they took to skis. The picture shows a hurdle race at the turn of the century

Left Even when the Alps in winter were shunned by all reasonable people as full of danger, discomfort, and mystical dread the lakes were popular in the summer with fashionable families

Right Later in the nineteenth century, when the warmth of the winter sun had been discovered at St Moritz, ladies learnt to take gentle walks among the snow-covered trees and fill their sketch-books with drawings of this romantic new landscape

Alpine Prelude

The Alps had for a long time attracted visitors, to be sure, but if they were regarded as the playground of Europe, it was an arcadia to be visited in summer only. No one ever dreamt of venturing into the winter snows. What appealed about them to Shelley, for instance, was the majesty of the scenery. 'Range after range of black mountains are seen extending one before the other, and far behind all, towering above every feature of the scene, the snowy Alps', he enthused. 'Their immensity staggers the imagination, and so far surpasses all conception that it requires an effort of imagination to believe that they indeed form a part of the earth.' His enthusiasm was shared by other devotees of the romantic movement, and the trickle of visitors to Switzerland became a steady flow after the end of the Napoleonic wars. Admittedly most of them had health rather than culture or sport in mind. It became fashionable to go to the mountains for a cure, and soon every other village had become a thermal spa, each with its *Kurhaus*, its waters, its doctors, its routine, its band, and its dedicated *Kuristen* (as the habitués came to be known.) Some of the visitors joined in the game with such fervour that, as Emile Souvestre remarked in one of his contemporary Swiss sketches, they proceeded from a *cure des bains* at Bex to a *cure d'air* on the Selisberg, a hot milk cure in the Gruyère, and ended up with a wine cure at Clarens.

A century ago you left London at 7.40 am and, crossing over from Dover to Calais, reached Paris at 6.0 pm. At 8.05 you caught the Basle express, which got you in just in time to have a shave and breakfast at the station before the train for Chur left at 10.30. It was all quite leisurely, and if you felt inclined you could take a side trip from Zurich across the lake by steamer as far as Rapperswil, recatching the train in time to run along the shores of Lake Wallenstadt. Next came Ragatz, where quite a few travellers stopped over to visit the baths of Pfeffers. After all this, you reached Chur at seven in the evening. Thackeray thought it the end of the world. 'I have seldom seen a place more quaint, pretty, calm and pastoral than this remote little Chur' he observed in one of the *Roundabout Papers*. 'There is nobody at the hotel, save the good landlady, the kind waiters, the brisk young cook who ministers to you.' Yet, he goes on to muse,

> Time there was when there must have been life and bustle and commerce here. These vast, venerable walls were not made to keep out cows, but men at arms, led by fierce captains who prowled about the gates and robbed the traders as they passed in and out . . .

Thackeray would be surprised to see the place now. Indeed by the time that Dr Burney Yeo, (a physician from 44 Hertford Street, Mayfair, London) reached Chur in August 1870 it was already so bustling that he was lucky to get the last

Hot springs at Leukerbad had already made this little Swiss village a fashionable watering place. Men and women could mix only because both wore all-enveloping clothing. Today, skiers still enjoy the thermal baths at Leukerbad

room in the Steinbock Hotel (which has only recently made way for a chain store). From Chur you took a diligence for the last lap of the journey. There was a reservation problem in those days, too, and those who hadn't had the foresight to telegraph ahead and book a place in the *coupé* or *banquette* were liable to find themselves squeezed into the inside of an excruciatingly narrow *omnibus* with little chance of seeing the scenery as they zig-zagged slowly up the Julier, en route for St Moritz.

Back in 1841, a French writer called Rodolphe Töpffer had described that now famous spot as

> . . . a little town composed of stables and billiard saloons where bearded bath-guests pass their time; one of those places that owe to the transient presence of invalids a little false vivacity, much cigar smoke, and a grotesque mixture of busy peasants, idle gentry, tipplers, makers of cheese, and of cannons at billiards.

Thirty years later it had grown into a flourishing spa, packed with *Almanach de Gotha* characters and with accommodation very much at a premium.

For by then the same visitors were returning year after year to their favourite

Peter-Taugwalder sohn
Nov. 1843–1923.

Edward Whymper
1840–1911.

Peter Taugwalder
Vater, 1820–1888.

Lord f. Douglas
1847–1865

Rev. Chs. Hudson
1828–1865

D. Hadow
1846–1865.

Michel A. Croz
1830–1865.

Die ersten Besteiger des Matterhorns 14 Juli 1865

in der Reihenfolge des Abstieges, nach zeitgemässen Aufnahmen.
Oben die drei damals Ueberlebenden. (Zusammengestellt v. P. Montand

Left Edward Whymper made his ninth attempt on the Matterhorn in July 1865. On the Italian side he met Lord Francis Douglas, who suggested trying the Swiss route, so they went round to Zermatt to pick up the Taugwalders, father and son, as guides. There, too, they met the Reverend Charles Hudson with his young friend Douglas Hadow, both guided by Michel Croz. The parties combined and reached the summit on 14 July. On the way down the rope broke and Douglas, Hudson, Hadow and Croz all fell to their deaths

Right Earlier that year Whymper had climbed Dent Blanche with Croz. The face was separated from the glacier by a deep crevasse across which lay a fragile snowbridge. They negotiated this safely, reaching the summit in a blizzard. They had a gruelling journey down over ice-covered rocks but reached Abricolla in safety

Far right The previous year, in 1864, Whymper had climbed in the Dauphiné with Jean Reynaud (whom he had previously described as a jolly fellow), Michel Croz, Walker, Moore and Aylmer. On this occasion, on the way down from the Col de Pilatte, Reynaud was out of condition and laden with books, instruments, food and drink. He fell but was luckily not badly hurt, getting no sympathy from his companions, who were only concerned that the bottles he carried were broken

Alpine haunts, some to take the waters, others, more athletically, to climb the mountains. Mountaineering, if you like, was the first of the Alpine snow sports. As far back as 1786 Jacques Balman and Dr Paccard had conquered Mont Blanc. But the golden age of mountaineering really began in 1854 when two Englishmen, Blackwell and Wells, made the first ascent of the Wetterhorn, and in 1865 Charles Hudson and Edward Whymper finally scaled the Matterhorn. And indeed before long most of the peaks in the central Bernese alps had been climbed by men like Mummery, Whymper, Geoffrey Winthrop Young, W. W. Graham and Sella of Italy.

Yet all of these were summer activities, to be sure. Winter sports on snow and ice were still a little way off. They began, if you like, with a bet that was made in St Moritz one autumn evening of 1864.

On the last night of their stay (the tale goes) four Englishmen sat around the fire in the lounge of the Engadiner Kulm having a farewell drink with their host, Johannes Badrutt. Not unnaturally, a touch of nostalgia crept into the conversation as they lamented that the summer season was over and long winter months had to be endured before they could return to the sun of St Moritz. 'But don't you realise that it's even sunnier here in winter than in summer?' remarked the hotelier. 'Winter may be cold in London, but here in the Engadine the sun shines so brightly that we can go round in shirt-sleeves.' When his guests pointed out that there was already a nip in the air and that one would surely freeze to death during an alpine winter, he passed round the Kirsch bottle and went on with a proposition. 'Why don't you come and see for yourselves? I tell you what: I'll make you a sporting bet. Come back for Christmas as my guests, and if it's not as warm and sunny as I say, I will pay all your expenses.'

Whatever their misgivings, the offer was too good to be refused. They shook hands on it, and in the middle of December set off back to St Moritz with various members of their families. At Chur they had to hire sleighs for the last part of the journey and wrapped themselves up from head to toe in furs. They had brought everything they could think of against the cold. But one thing they had forgotten. They had no sun-glasses. The Julier was ablaze with sun and instead of getting frozen as they had expected they reached St Moritz covered in perspiration and half blinded by the sunlight on the snow. Johannes Badrutt was waiting for them in shirtsleeves at the entrance of the Kulm. He had won his bet, and they stayed until March.

Mythical though the story may sound, when the pillars of the old porch of the Kulm were knocked down in 1954 for remodernization, a case was found containing documents that confirmed the old tale of the wager. And the hotel records show that fifteen English guests, Lord Shrewsbury among them, stayed at the Kulm that winter. What's more, an entry in the visitors' book justifies Herrn Badrutt's confidence in the St Moritz sun:

> We spent five and a half months at Herr Badrutt's and feel ourselves much indebted to the great kindness of himself, his wife and his family. They made our winter quarters so comfortable, that we were loathe to leave them when the spring came . . . on an average we were out four hours daily, walking, skating on the lakes, sleighing, or sitting on the terrace reading . . . Far from finding it cold, the heat of the sun is so intense at times that sun shades were indispensable. The brilliance of the sun, the blueness of the sky and the clearness of the atmosphere quite surprised us. The lake affords the opportunity to those who love the art of skating, without interruption for five months . . .

The concept of a winter sports holiday had been born.

Above A lady alpinist in 1885. Despite their hampering clothes ladies did make considerable climbs. Some were known, when out of sight of prying eyes, to take their skirts off and tuck them away in their guides' rucksacks until the climb was over. Others evolved a complicated system of strings running through curtain hooks to hitch their skirts up at tricky moments

Right More lady mountaineers, on Fuorcla Surlej, near St Moritz. In the background are skiers. Today the great cablecars at Corvatsch whisk thousands of skiers a day up to the glacier slopes above Surlej

Above Skating fashions in 1870. The skirts are slightly shorter than was normal at that time but the skates are still a somewhat primitive strap-on version, with unnecessarily ornate curves

Right Davos, Switzerland, is the setting for this vivid glimpse of speed skating in 1894. This rink opened in 1877 and Davos has been the headquarters of the International Skating Union ever since its formation there in 1892

The Oldest Winter Sport: Skating

STAND
5000 Mts

Skating, of course, was the principal draw. In the middle of the nineteenth century people brought out their skates whenever a sheet of ice could be found. Come a frost, and the question shot round: 'Will the ice bear today?' As far back as 1830 some dedicated enthusiasts had founded the Skating Club in London. A grand and exclusive affair, with the Prince and Princess of Wales as patrons, it had a special marquee on the bank of the Serpentine where, sporting the club badge (a miniature silver skate hanging from a ribbon in the button-hole), its members decorously performed their repertoire before the admiring eyes of ordinary mortals – who all too often invaded the sacred precincts of Long Water and crashed into the distinguished figures just as they were executing a masterly twiddle. For the general public at large, skating was still very much the thrill of sliding over a slippery surface.

Now, providentially, *aficionados* had the chance of going to an idyllic spot where they could skate to their hearts' content under a brilliant sun from November to March. The message got round and almost immediately the skating fraternity began flocking to the Engadine. In February 1870 the *Globe* reported that at Silvaplana 'a club of *patineurs*, mainly English, has been formed who practise daily on the beautiful surface of the Silzer See', which provoked a gentle correction from the President of the St Moritz Skating Club:

> The St Moritz lake is the scene of the Skating Club's performance and all the members reside at St Moritz and not at Silvaplana.

This unnamed correspondent told the editor of *The Times* on Monday 21 February that year,

> No skating is practised on the Silser See which, with the other lakes of the Engadine, has been covered with snow for the past three months. On a portion of the St Moritz lake we are able to produce artificially a 'beautiful surface' [he went on to explain] By proper appliances – viz, a sluice gate and guiding shoots – we divert the course of a stream on to the surface of the ice, having first surrounded that portion marked out for the skating with a low ridge of ice made out of wet snow . . .
>
> Sleighing [he added, getting down to the job] which is very enjoyable, is in vogue for about six months of the year, but nothing short of an actual trial would enable anyone to realise the pleasure of gliding along rapidly in a sledge under a brilliantly blue sunny sky with the crisp white snow beneath. Another favorite entertainment of the English as well as natives (and also practised in Canada and Russia) is sliding down steep inclines on small sledges constructed for this purpose. The speed attainable is almost incredible. In this sport both old and young join . . . There is every

Top right A party of Europeans holding what must have been one of the first skating parties in Japan, near Yokohama in 1865. Since then of course, Sapporo, in the northern island of Hokkaido, where the winter Olympics were held in 1972, has become one of Japan's main winter sports centres

Bottom right The Emperor Napoleon III skating in the Bois de Boulogne, Paris, in 1867. Skating appears to have been something of a family tradition: in 1791, when he was a student at the Ecole Militaire, Napoleon Bonaparte narrowly escaped drowning while skating on the thinly frozen moat of the French fort at Auxerre

Overleaf Americans have always been quick to skate in New York's Central Park when climatic conditions allow, as endorsed by this nineteenth-century scene. The first properly maintained American rink was organized in Central Park in 1858. The New York Skating Club was founded in 1860 and two years later it organized a skating carnival on the frozen Union Pond in Brooklyn

DANGEROUS

Skating in the low-lying Fenland districts of Lincolnshire and Cambridgeshire has long been a prominent pastime during hard English winters. Much of the 2,000 acres of shallow water which froze there during the nineteenth century has since been drained by pumps. The two drawings *(left)* show a speed skating competition in 1869, with a beer barrel for the winning post. Since the National Skating Association of Great Britain was formed on 1879, officially recognized outdoor championships have been decided over a distance of one-and-a-half miles each year that ice conditions have been suitable. The photograph on the right shows the Lincolnshire Amateur Champion of 1907 at full speed

inducement to tempt a lover of winter pastimes to spend the winter, or part of it, here.

Reading this over breakfast on a dull English day (along with intelligence to the effect that the Emperor Napoleon III had decreed that Prince Pierre Bonaparte should be tried for killing M. Victor Noir in a duel, that the *Bourse* was dull, and that police in Rome had found placards ridiculing the question of Papal Infallability) it is hardly surprising that well-heeled gentry began flocking to the Alps. Despite the war between France and Prussia, the flow of tourists to places like St Moritz and Davos increased year by year. Whereas Davos had only two winter visitors in 1866, five years later the number had reached ninety. In 1875 the Hotel Belvedere opened and was immediately filled with English guests, bent on skating rather than getting cured from tuberculosis. The newcomers immediately set about planning an ice-rink. But there must have been something rather daunting about their combination skating, and the disdain with which intruders were regarded (the Victorians could be stuffier than most when they chose) because a rival rink was quickly opened for the German and Russian skaters. Nevertheless, they joined forces in 1880 when the first Davos skating club was formed, which, with its giant rink flanked by a pavilion along the whole north side as a protection against the often bitter north-east wind, its buffet and its band, soon became the best address in the skating world.

Yet for all this apparent chumming up, the two different schools of skating kept ostentatiously at a distance from each other. On the one hand, decked out

Top left and right By the turn of the century skating in Switzerland had become the chief winter sport of the fashionable set. Nobody would have believed then that electrically frozen rinks would eventually be installed at leading Swiss mountain resorts, but this coals-to-Newcastle trend ensured the present-day reliability of good skating conditions all the year round at many recreational centres in the Alps

Below The Royal Albert skates, to the left, were made for Queen Victoria, each blade being decoratively extended at the toe in the shape of a swan's head. The skate to the right, designed in 1890, by which time metal skates were well in vogue, is an early example of the special skating boot to which the blade was screwed, a forerunner of the present-day type

in top hats, frock coats, sponge-bag trousers and white ties, exponents of the 'English style' focussed their efforts on the accurate execution of set figures. No hint of frivolity was permitted to intrude into the demanding science of cutting microscopically accurate traces on the ice. As good Victorians they insisted on a rigid deportment, with arms and free leg held woodenly to the side of the body, and all movements carried out with the stiff snap of a drill squad turn. For them the apotheosis was combination skating, when several correctly-attired members went through the austere cadences of their routine for all the world as though they were changing the guard at Buckingham Palace.

Breezier, in contrast, was the artistic skating of the 'Viennese' school. Predictably, a city that was waltzing to the tunes of Waldteufel, Lehar and Johann Strauss brought some of its elegant fizz to the ice. Skating, after all, should be fun, and even the most intricate figures were absurd if awkwardly executed. Easy and harmonious movements required a relaxed deportment with the free leg poised and the arms gracefully outstretched.

As it happens, this free and often theatrical style was largely inspired by an American. Skating seems to have been introduced to North America by British officers stationed there during the eighteenth century (Colonel Howe, brother of the general of revolutionary fame, was an early exponent) and was soon taken up in the States as an agreeable and fashionable winter recreation,

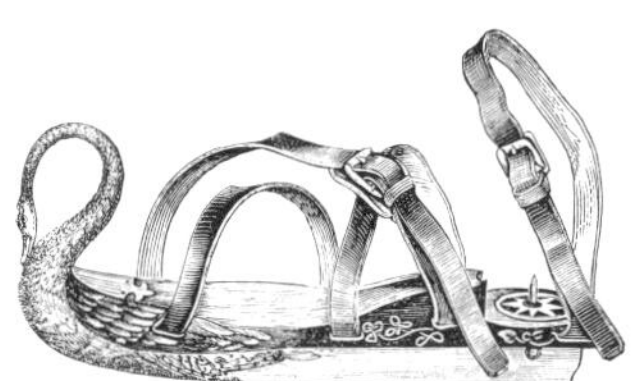

particularly in Philadelphia where the Schuylkill river had some good stretches of ice. There the 'Skating Club of the City and County of Philadelphia' was founded in 1849. Before long its members, as correctly attired as their English counterparts (but with wooden reels containing a length of strong thin rope attached to their left wrists in case the ice should break) were executing a repertoire of forward and backward 'threes', the grape-vine, the cross-foot spin, variations of the 'Q' figures, and a complicated movement known as the Philadelphia twist.

In due course the craze spread to Washington, New York and wherever there were ponds and rivers on the East Coast that froze. Along with the traditional figures, what's more, they began tracing intricate designs of stars, half-moons, flowers and even people's names on the ice, some of which required fairly acrobatic contortions.

Against this background, a young dancer was struck by the affinity between skating and ballet, and began to apply the techniques of ballet-dancing on the ice. Instead of concentrating on set figures, he experimented with dramatic poses, spectacular jumps, and the sitting spin. At the same time he invented a turned-up skate that could be screwed directly on to the sole and heel of the boot.

Traditionalists in both the USA and England may have scoffed at Jackson Haines's revolutionary interpretation of sliding over the ice as 'fancy skating' and gimmicky, but the general public lapped it up. Haines appeared in a variety of theatrical costumes – such as a Russian, a pearly prince, a bear, and even a ballerina – and went so far as to do stunts on stilts. Gyrating at high speed he culminated graceful spirals with lightning leaps. Such poise and sureness had never been seen before. His stagey exhibitions were applauded throughout Europe, and turned him into an international celebrity.

Nowhere was he more warmly acclaimed than in Vienna, where under his lead the dancing city took its waltzes and mazurkas on to the ice. A school of show-skating was founded and pupils of his such as Belazzi, Diamantidi, Von Korper and Max Wirth, evolved a new international style called *Sturm auf dem Eise* that was the forerunner of modern free skating.

Thanks to Jackson Haines, skating became an art rather than a science. Yet the old, academic 'English' school, developed by H. E. Vandervell and his pupil, T. Maxwell Witham, continued its meticulous quest for glacial perfection, gradually evolving the Counter, the Rocker and the Bracket to complete the range of set figures.

So Olympian was their attitude that a 322 page dissertation on skating by Maxwell Witham and others published by the Badminton Library in 1892 made not the slightest mention of either Jackson Haines or the innovators on the other side of the rinks at Grindelwald, Davos and St Moritz. Nevertheless, the advice given to their contemporaries has a certain period interest:

> The best time to go to Grindelwald is about the middle of January, as before that period the rink from its situation gets practically no sun, and the cold in the morning is consequently unpleasantly severe . . . [advises Witham] The only hotel open in winter is the Bear, owned by the Boss family. It is one of the best in Switzerland . . . the cost of boarding at the Bear is nine to ten francs a day, including bath, fire, lights and four o'clock tea, which is not to be despised after a day in the mountain air . . .
>
> The leading hotel at St Moritz is the well-known Kulm, the property of the Badrutt family . . . other good hotels are the Casper Badrutt, the St Petersburg, and the Beau Rivage . . . [which was to become the famous

An ice hockey match at Grindelwald at the turn of the century. Guests frequently organized light-hearted competitions, such as wheel-barrow races on ice, but this seems to be a relatively serious game

Palace] . . . The Kulm has, however, the great advantage of having the rinks in its grounds. It is also the centre of the social life at St Moritz, and all the balls and private theatricals take place there . . .

The school of skating at St Moritz is a very severe one: great size, and power and perfect quietness and control of the body and limbs are what is aimed at, and the object throughout is rather to do everything that is attempted in the best possible style than to do a great many different movements moderately.

The unemployed leg is 'kept in its proper place' and the skating at St Moritz is probably the strongest and at the same time the quietest and most accurate that exists. The few accomplished *habitués* of the rink have taken the early teaching of the Skating Club as their starting point and availing themselves of the long period during which they can practise, have perfected it in a really astonishing manner . . . When we see here in England a young skater who may not be able to skate a great many movements, but who does everything he can skate in perfect form, it will generally be found that he has been educated at the St Moritz school . . .

The Roaring Stones

An outdoor curling match in Montreal, played in the earlier days of the game's development in Canada. Curling was introduced to Canada by the Scots in 1807. Now Canada is the sport's dominant nation and Air Canada sponsors the annual World Championships, first held in 1959

Above The Royal Caledonian Curling Club was founded in 1838 and nine years later, in 1847, Scotland's first large-scale outdoor Grand Match tournament *(bonspiel)* was held. This painting shows the second Grand Match, which took place at Linlithgow the following year

And then, of course, there was curling. No one has much doubt that this is Scotland's 'Ain Game', except, perhaps, for the Germans and Dutch who both, when the spirit moves them, have laid claim to its invention. Be this as it may, the game was certainly played in Scotland at the beginning of the sixteenth century using smooth boulders taken from the river bed with holes cut out for the finger and thumb. (One of them, dated 1511, can be seen in the Macfarlane museum at Stirling.) Tradition has it that James IV of Scotland (1472–1513) not only curled himself, but also presented a silver replica of a curling stone to be played for annually in the Carse of Gowrie. Certainly Camden, when describing the Orkney Islands in 1607, noted that one of them supplied 'plenty of excellent stones for the game called curling'. An old Scottish family, the Drummonds of Carlowrie, went so far as to incorporate what appears to be a curling stone in their coat of arms, and George Graham, Bishop of Orkney, was severely censored for being 'a curler on the ice on the Sabbath Day'.

In 1838 the 'Grand Caledonian Curling Club' was founded and received its royal imprimatur after Queen Victoria and the Prince Consort had been initiated into the mysteries of the game on the polished floor of the Palace of Scone. Thereafter the Royal Club grew so quickly that within fifty years there were no less than 481 affiliated clubs in Scotland with 18,800 members, as well as 128 in Canada and a sprinkling as far away as Russia and New Zealand. Curlers in the United States, what is more, were organized in 1867 under a national club with its headquarters in New York. For all this, the mother body in Scotland kept a firm grip on deportment and ceremony, so that any curler who put a foot wrong was liable not only to go sprawling on the ice but to invite a fine for his solecism; and indeed even today the game has a sort of muted, well-heeled heartiness, somewhere between the golf club bar and a Rotary luncheon.

Basically, it is *boccia*, or if you prefer, bowls on ice. At each end of the 46yd rink there is a tee with a 6ft radius marked round it. Four players a side make up what is also (rather confusingly) termed a 'rink', each playing two stones against the opposing team, so that sixteen stones are delivered in the course of a 'single end'. The object is to lay the stones as near as possible to the tee, and to knock away those of the adversaries. At the conclusion, points are scored for each stone of one side that lies nearest to the tee.

All of which sounds simple enough. Yet in fact curling bristles with as many technicalities and subtleties as the game of chess. For one thing, considerable skill is needed in the actual dispatch of the stone – nowadays sent off with a graceful 'sliding' delivery which has the player slithering along in its wake like a ship going out to sea. For another, it must be directed according to precise instructions given by the leader of the rink, known as the 'skip', who controls operations from up by the tee.

As in bowls, to be sure, a 'bias' can be achieved by twisting the handle of the

'Soop her up!' is the title of this early drawing of Scottish curlers. Sooping is the legitimate curling art of sweeping rapidly and skilfully with special brooms just ahead of the moving stone – but without touching it – in order to influence its pace and direction as required. 'Soop! Soop!' is thus a familiar cry to be heard during any and every curling game

stone at the moment of delivery. But on top of this, its speed and its course can be influenced after it has been played. Even on the highly polished ice, the smallest particle of dust can affect a stone's progress. Hence all the business with the brooms. 'Sooping', as it is called, can often add a yard or more to the stone's trajectory. Brisk sweeping warms the ice momentarily and knowledgeable players can marginally (but significantly) improve a stone's final lie.

Curling joined the Swiss winter sports scene when the St Moritz Curling Club was founded on 20 December 1880. The club's minute book lists sixty members who in Victorian times began curling around the middle of November and played steadily until the end of March. In due course the game spread to other resorts and today there is hardly a place in Switzerland that does not boast its own electrically frozen rink. At the last count, indeed, there were no less than 150 throughout the country, of which eight were in Lucerne. The same is true in Germany and Austria, where ice-stick shooting (a variation of curling invented in Bavaria) is growing in popularity. The only difference is that iron plates with steel handles are used instead of the traditional smoothly-curved stones, which naturally involves a modified style of delivery.

All the same, the Engadine players always managed to keep a slight edge over the others. According to the club records, Archduke Franz Ferdinand of Austria delivered the first stone in a match (or rather, *bonspiel*, to use the correct term) held at Celerina in 1908, which, needless to say, the St Moritz rink won, and even if kilts are less in evidence now that it has been taken under the wing of the Swiss Engadine Club, the curling is just as sharp as ever, though rather less hilarious. Nonetheless, it can no longer compete with the professional skill and accuracy of the Canadians who since 1959 have had a near monopoly in the World Curling Championship.

What is more, the old image of elderly folk capering ludicrously about with brooms and funny badge-bedecked hats will quickly be dispelled by a few minutes' visit to a modern bonspiel where the action hums along as crisply as the stones. If outdoors these seem to move with a marbled murmur, more like the purr of a Rolls-Royce engine, the indoor rinks are full of the traditional roar – and cheering too, as 10,000 spectators follow a world event. 'Just as the distinctive sounds of acceleration and gear changes thrill the motor enthusiast, so the curler derives his own particular pleasure from the roaring made by the stones as they speed and veer towards the tee' explains Howard Bass. Today it is far from being an old fogies' pastime. The young are taking to curling with such gusto that the average age of a recent Swiss national team was under twenty, and, in 1974, the veteran Hec Gervais of Canada found that he was almost three times as old as the teenage members of the Norwegian champion rink. If the skaters don't look out they may soon find, with dismay, that their favourite drop of ice has been pinched by the roaring stones.

Top left This is not ordinary curling, but a variation of the game called *Eisschiessen*, or Bavarian curling, dating from the nineteenth century and played primarily in Germany and Austria

Middle and bottom left *Eisschiessen* is played with a wooden, iron-ringed disc *(middle)* weighing between 11 and 13lbs. The normal curling stone *(bottom)*, which weighs up to 44lbs, could not be lifted like the *Eisschiessen* disc in the top left picture

Above Bud Somerville, of Superior, USA, twice winning skip in the World Curling Championship – in 1965 and 1974

The Early 'Plank-Hoppers'

Top left John A. Thompson was born in Telemark in Norway in 1827 and moved with his parents to California at the age of ten. He made skis from his recollections of those he had seen in Norway and earned the name Snowshoe by carrying mail across the Sierra Nevada at two dollars a letter in the

1850s. The loads he carried were between 60 and 100lbs and he made the eastward trip of 90 miles in three days, and the return journey, on account of long down grades, in two days, sleeping in caves or abandoned cabins en route

Bottom left Another Norwegian who spread the gospel of skiing over the world, Søren Gregoriussen, one of Australia's skiing gold miners, photographed in Kiandra, Australia, in 1870

Above By 1892 the Engadine area in east Switzerland was attracting a considerable proportion of winter sporters and to this day the Engadine ski marathon holds its own as a unique competition of its kind, with thousands skiing the fifty or so kilometres and the ages of those taking part ranging from seven to seventy

Left Roald Amundsen, the famous Norwegian explorer, taken in 1893 when he was twenty. In 1911 Amundsen and his party, travelling on skis, became the first men to reach the South Pole. If anything had still been needed, by that time, to emphasize the advantages of ski travel, it would have been the contrast between Amundsen's successful venture and the tragic fate of Scott's expedition, which relied on dog teams

They skated, they curled, they played bandy. They tobogganed down the slopes and (if they were English) they went head-first down the Cresta at St Moritz. They sat in the sun reading Ouida and Mrs Belloc Lowndes, took four o'clock tea, changed into black ties for dinner, played whist, had pillow fights, got up amateur theatricals and made off with each others' wives. The one thing our winter-sporting forbears didn't do was ski.

True, in the winter of 1883 those sitting round the rink at Davos may have spotted some of the village lads staggering about with curious wooden planks on their feet. Wilhelm Paulcke, a German schoolboy, had been given a pair of skis by his Norwegian tutor for Christmas and the village carpenter had copied them for a few of his friends. But none of the kids had any idea of how to set about skiing, of course. Not until Norwegians like Odd Kjelsberg appeared on the scene and demonstrated how to use the maddeningly unmanageable boards could any serious progress be made.

Skiing had been used as a means of locomotion in the hinterlands of Scandinavia for thousands of years, and appropriately it was the Norwegians who first saw the fun that it could mean. Once Sondre Norheim had finally broken with tradition and evolved something very much like a modern ski at Morgedal in 1868, the youngsters of Telemark quickly astonished their compatriots with a dazzling display of jumping and downhill running. Until then skis had been as cumbersome as sleighs and confined, on the whole, to straight running across the valleys. For anything but the simplest of turns the skier had stopped with the help of a long pole and then stepped round. Now, suddenly, the Telemark boys, thanks to their new skis with heel and instep

Right Mathias Zdarsky did more than perhaps any other single person to develop the techniques of Alpine skiing. His low crouch was far more suited to negotiating Alpine terrain than the traditional Norwegian upright posture, and although he is seen here with the old single pole, he later started using two poles for better balance

Overleaf The first Holmenkollen competition, which took place in 1892. Before this, from 1879, the Christiania Ski Club had organized competions on Huseby Hill. In 1952 this historic jump was used once more when the winter Olympics were held for the first time in Oslo

St Moritz, a health spa before it became famous as a winter sports centre, was one of the first Swiss places to which Nordic skiers introduced their sport: ski jumping in Graubunden (St Moritz area) in 1890 was still quite a novelty to the locals

bindings, were gracefully curving down the slopes in elegant esses and practising that most graceful of turns, the telemark (which was named after them), as often as not without sticks.

During the next two decades they were the pace-makers, winning every local competition in sight. And gradually the Norwegians who emigrated took their exciting new sport with them. This skiing 'diaspora', in truth, had begun as early as the mid-century when a Norwegian named Möller appeared in Germany, and Knut Bjerknes showed his paces first in Australia and then in New Zealand. Gold had been discovered up at Kiandra in New South Wales and the Norwegian miners there got about on skis when the place was snowed up in winter. But, perhaps inevitably, what began for a utilitarian purpose was soon turned into a pastime. The *Sydney Morning Herald* reported on 6 August 1861 that

> Kiandra is rather a dreary place in winter, but yet the people are not without their amusements. The heaven-pointing snow-clad mountains afford them some pleasure. Scores of young people are frequently engaged climbing the lofty summits with snow-shoes (sic) and then sliding down with a velocity that would do credit to some of our railway trains.

Soon afterwards a club was formed so that Kiandra (now one of Australia's top resorts) can claim to have the oldest skiing organization outside Norway.

Across the Atlantic, too, in the gold camps of La Porte, Alturas and Onion Valley, Norwegian miners were skiing down the Californian Sierras to give the Americans their first sight of the Nordic sport. Big money (and plenty of beer) was wagered on their hair-raising schusses, by all accounts. More soberly, John Thompson, the son of Norwegian parents, earned the name 'Snowshoe' by carrying the mail across the Sierra Nevada for a number of years at two dollars a letter. And in due course these latter-day Vikings spread their doctrine of skis as far as South America and even into the tightly-closed islands of Japan.

Surprisingly enough Switzerland, the traditional citadel of winter sports, was slow off the mark and it was only in 1889 that Odd Kjelsberg is credited with having started things going by skiing down a small hill near Winterthur. The following season an Anglo-Norwegian named Knocker settled down as a farmer at Meiringen and began skiing in the neighbourhood, while Colonel Christoph Iselin (now regarded as the father of the sport in Switzerland) had to creep out into the moonlight at Glarus to experiment on some home-made boards without the benefit of ribald comment from his friends. But it was all very tentative stuff. No one took these early pioneers at all seriously. Many years later Dame Katharine Furse described how a Colonel Napier, who had rented R. L. Stevenson's old chalet above the Hotel Buol, had been one of the first to bring skis to Davos.

> He had a Norwegian man-servant, whose use of the ski gave rise to many myths. It was even said that he skied down from the chalet to the hotel carrying a tea-tray on his shoulder. I remember him flitting down in a miraculous sort of way, but the ski being out of my reach for personal use I never paid much attention.

When Colonel Napier left Davos at the end of the season he gave her the skis and she then wished that she had. It was all very mystifying since nobody knew how to use them. 'Though I often took them out for fun I never mastered the art of running or turning', she confessed. The bindings consisted of a loop over the toes and around the heels, and with her soft shoes she had no control. Another problem was that without wax the snow stuck to the skis. 'All this was somewhat discouraging and we tended to look on the ski as a toy rather than as a useful means of progression.'

Most people thought exactly the same at the time. Luckily a little group – among them Sir Arthur Conan Doyle, the author – persevered with the awkward business the following season. A long pole was used. 'It was very heavy and unwieldy' Mrs Furse remembers, 'but it helped one remain upright while running slowly.' They practised on the slopes behind Davos Dorf, but with no one to teach them progress was slow and turns were not attempted.

> We simply went straight up and down slopes, not even realising the possibility of traversing. Going uphill was of course a great difficulty, until someone having heard of the use of sealskin to prevent back sliding, we all had strips of sealskin nailed to our ski, which was a great help. It wore out quickly, however, going downhill, necessarily retarding our progress, of which we were rather glad, as we fell less. And so it went on till the Richardsons came to Davos, in 1901, and various keen skiers took up the sport seriously.
>
> Bobbing and tobogganing were serious rivals, and I never looked upon skiing as an attractive game until after the [1914–1918] war, when it had begun to replace tobogganing, and the fine art of skiing had still to be learnt.

Katharine Furse, who won a number of tobogganing awards at Davos in her youth, nevertheless was one of the first women to pass the Ski Club of Great Britain's First Class test, and in 1925 became president of the Ladies' Ski Club. So these early tribulations were obviously worth while.

Meanwhile, even before the arrival of the Richardson brothers who were to propagate the expertise that they had learnt up in Norway, Sir Arthur Conan Doyle had made enough progress to be able to tackle a mountain tour. The creator of Sherlock Holmes became the first Englishman to do so, in fact, when on 23 March 1894 he crossed the Maienfelder Furka from Davos to Arosa in the company of two Swiss guides. For a novice it must have been a daunting experience. 'You come to a hard ice-slope at an angle of 45 degrees, and you zig-zag up to it, digging the side of your ski into it, and feeling that if a mosquito settles upon you, you are gone,' he wrote afterwards in the *Strand Magazine*. All the same he suggested, somewhat prophetically, that hundreds of Englishmen would one day come to Switzerland for the spring skiing season.

For if the Norwegians first developed skiing as a sport, to be sure, it was the British who introduced the new game to many parts of the Alps. Gerald Fox learnt to ski on a visit to Christiania (Oslo) in 1889, and two years later took his skis to Grindelwald. He used, it seems, to put them on in his room and then clatter down the corridors of the Bear Hotel, all of which was considered to be a bit of a joke; and indeed the activities of the dedicated little bunch of ski-runners, wallowing about in the snow with their ungainly boards, were dismissed as pure eccentricity right up until the early days of this century.

Apart from all else, there was the difficulty of equipment. The narrow Nordic skis (as any langlaufer faced with a steep schuss will agree) were adequate for cross-country running with gentle descents and sweeping telemark turns. But

Swiss children started skiing on barrel staves. The wide curved planks do not look too unlike the skis of today. A leather thong over the toe, two palings as ski sticks, and the equipment was complete

the Norwegian technique, evolved for the open countryside and long trails through the woods, ran into trouble when practised on the steep, hazardous Alpine terrain.

What with one thing and another, the pioneers had a far from easy time. They could put up, of course, with all the leg-pulling from their smart skating and tobogganing friends. But they found it hard to make much progress without any instruction manuals or teachers and with such rudimentary bindings. (There were still no toe-caps as such: two little rings were attached to the side of the ski through which a toe-strap was passed, while the foot was theoretically held in position by a cane heel-strap attached to a lace round the ankle.) It was difficult enough to run straight, far less make a turn. 'There was next to no lateral rigidity,' explains Sir Arnold Lunn, 'and when one tried to turn, one's heels simply came off in the snow.' In any case, he adds, he skied for three winters before seeing a stem turn, much less a telemark or christiania.

Sir Arnold was ten years old when he first put on skis at Chamonix in 1898. His father (who founded the travel agency that still bears his name) had organized a party there and engaged a Swiss guide who was supposed to know how to ski.

> About four or five Englishmen at Chamonix skied, but I cannot remember seeing any of the locals do so, with the exception of our instructor, who regarded his ski with obvious distaste and terror. He slid down a gradual slope, leaning on his stick and breathing heavily, while we gasped our admiration for his courage. Somebody asked him whether it was possible to turn. He replied in the negative, but added that a long gradual turn was just possible if one dragged oneself round on the pole. He claimed to have seen an expert perform this difficult manoeuvre, but modestly added that he was unable to demonstrate it himself.

Sir Arnold lived for another seventy-six years, and thus, unlike the other winter sports, the story of Alpine skiing at least is virtually encompassed within the span of a single lifetime (1888–1974). From the fumbling early days that he described, skiing gradually evolved until it exploded, after World War II, into arguably the most popular contemporary sport, enjoyed by something like 27 million people wherever snow is to be found around the globe.

Yet from these lumbering beginnings men like Wilhelm Paulcke, Henry Hoek, and Christoph Iselin, 'letting the ski carry them where it will until the air acts as a natural brake and brings them naturally to a rest' (as a German newspaper put it), pioneered touring expeditions into the high Alps. But it was above all Mathias Zdarsky, the Austrian, who evolved the technique of Alpine skiing. With the dedication of a one man guerrilla army he retired into the mountains at Habernreith and practised skiing alone for six winters, gradually developing skis and bindings that met with his requirements. He believed that the traditional Norwegian way of running was unsuitable for steep ground and that in order to cope with the Alpine terrain short skis were essential. Finally he settled for a five foot long grooveless ski with bindings that were made of steel and had a spring to prevent the foot from going forward too quickly. He advocated, moreover, a single diskless pole which, he wrote,

> . . . must never be used as a support but rather as an instrument to grope or feel. The weight of the body should never rest heavily on the stick. The trailing of the stick behind one produces in a short time a remarkably steady position. In emergencies the stick can be made use of.

His technique became known as the Lilienfeld school. Early skiing enthusiasts flocked to be instructed by him with military precision outside Vienna every Sunday. Basically what he taught them was to snowplough and stem, moving on to stem-christianias and telemarks.

Some two hundred years earlier an Austrian writer called Valvasor had published a book in which he described how the peasants in Carnolia used short skis to 'wind and twist about like a snake'. In his lonely experiments, Zdarsky rediscovered the lost art of S-turning by the process of a series of continuous stem turns – a thing that the Norwegians, for all their inborn knowledge, had never thought of doing. Vivian Caulfeild, who was perhaps the first Englishman to understand and explain the dynamics of skiing, considered that 'some of his analysis of technique was extraordinarily keen.' But he also thought that Zdarsky's system of relying on the snowplough position for turning and braking, often balancing with the help of the stick, was self-defeating in the end because it avoided difficulties rather than overcoming them. 'It turns out ski-runners quickly by allowing them to run badly,' he commented.

Wilhelm Paulcke (the small boy who had slithered so helplessly around in Davos but was now actively skiing in the Black Forest) so scathingly criticized the Lilienfeld method that the early development of Alpine skiing took place against animosities that were early Christian in their fury. For some of the pioneers, it seemed, skiing had become more of a religion than a sport. Paulcke, along with his Black Forest friends, upheld what they believed – somewhat erroneously – to be the pure doctrines of the Norwegian school. Zdarsky cracked back with such high-caloried venom against any slur on his system that thirty years later he was still carrying on the feud in the columns of *Der Schnee*. Professor Paulcke, he suggested, was the victim of a sadistic complex because as a small boy he squeezed his snowballs into ice before throwing them at the other kids. And when Colonel Bilgeri, who was responsible for introducing skiing

St Moritz has always been a fashionable winter resort from before the turn of the century and by 1906 special clothes for skiing were being advertized in the Ski Club of Great Britain Yearbook; for ladies, long skirts were de rigeur until the First World War and the glimpse of an ankle was considered rather daring. Only in the 1920s were breeches for ladies considered decent

into the Austrian army, gave his support to the opposition, he likewise became the victim of Zdarsky's acidic tongue. Describing how a stem-christiania should be done, he had inadvertently referred to the 'hind-leg', at which Zdarsky sneered in print that 'there would seem to be an officer in the Imperial Army who has four legs'. Bilgeri responded not with a libel suit but a challenge to a duel. But if passions ran high among those early pioneers, at least it showed that skiing had got off to a lusty start.

Above As a schoolboy, Wilhelm Paulcke was given skis for a Christmas present and soon became a convert to the sport, but he absolutely opposed Zdarsky's Lilienfeld method of skiing. He led the first great ski mountaineering expedition when from 18–22 January 1897 he made a partial traverse of the Bernese Oberland. The party seen here: Paulcke, V. de Beauclair, R. Mönnichs, Dr Ehlert and W. Loemuller, went from Meiringen across Oberaarjoch, Grunhornlücke, and Bel Alp to Brig. Paulcke's book *Der Skilauf*, the first in German on skiing, was printed in 1899

Right In these pioneer days the skiing season was mainly in the spring when the weather was more conducive to outdoor sports. Men could adapt their clothes more easily than ladies who remained decorously clad in ankle length skirts and, of course, hats, which were recommended to be not too large, although a wide brim would afford protection from the sun

Ski Mountaineering

Left A collection made at the end of the last century of skis, snow shoes, ice axes, and the all-important flasks. Skis developed individual features in different areas, hence the wide variety in length, tips, and bindings

Right Climbing used to be an integral part of skiing. This group of skiers in 1897 had climbed up to Corviglia, above St Moritz, and took their well-earned rest before embarking on the descent which, although considerably faster than the upward trek, would have involved sometimes hairy shusses, punctuated by falls

While Zdarsky was assiduously teaching people how to stem at Lilienfeld, his rivals in Germany and Switzerland were striking out into the great unknown. Or, to be more precise, the mountain tops. Even before Conan Doyle crossed the Maienfelder Furka from Davos to Arosa, Christoph Iselin had embarked, in January 1893 on what was probably the first genuine Alpine ski expedition, crossing the Pragel Pass from Glarus to Schwyz. Over Easter the same year four of its members celebrated the formation of a ski club in Totnau by making their way across the central Alpine chain via the Gotthard, Furka, Grimsel and Brunig passes (although admittedly following the road).

Around this time, what is more, Wilhelm Paulcke and three friends climbed the Oberalpstock on snowshoes, carrying their skis, on which they came down. But this was only a half-way measure, and ski mountaineering should really be dated from Paulcke's traverse of the Oberland in January 1897.

With four companions from the Schwarzwald ski club he left the Grimsel at 3.15am (which must in itself have been a daunting experience) and in the evening reached the hut on the Oberaar. They had heavy rucksacks with them and three of the party tried climbing on snowshoes, dragging their kit behind them on skis – by no means a successful ploy, since the overweighted boards toppled over on the first steep traverse, to the amusement of Paulcke who had already discovered that skis were preferable to snowshoes even going uphill.

Mist prevented them from climbing the Finsteraarhorn as planned and

Mountains form snow-bound national barriers and have been fought over since history began. Ski troops have therefore become a sad necessity, and of course the Swedes and the Norwegians had ski troops very early on. At least in peacetime they enjoy their training

Left Soldiers of the Norwegian army in the early years of the century taking a brief rest during training

Top right A provision column of the Swiss army on skis

Bottom right A Siberian sentry

instead they had an easy run down to Galmifirn, passing over the Grünhornlücke to reach the Concordia hut just as dusk was falling. Bad weather again spoilt their attempt on the Jungfrau, but after another freezing night in an unheated hut they crossed the Aletsch Glacier – only just avoiding a number of crevasses – and had an even dicier traverse from the Oberaletsch chalet to the Belalp Hotel. Since it was deserted they broke in and celebrated their

achievement drinking what (once down in the Rhône valley) they learnt was the proprietor's stock of vinegar.

The following winter Paulcke set his sights on Monte Rosa, in company with Dr Robert Helbling, a noted Swiss mountaineer, who had never, as it happens, skied before. Yet, unbelievably, after two days' tuition Paulcke embarked with him on one of the toughest ski tours in the Alps. On top of this, Helbling was taken ill about two thirds of the way up. Nevertheless he skied down behind Paulcke who, in his words, 'was off like an arrow, crouched forward to take the best line avoiding any crevasses, disappearing into a cloud of snow, dusting himself, and dashing off again with a joyful shout of encouragement'.

The wonder of it is that skiers more qualified for the nursery slopes should have had so few qualms about tackling the toughest ascents in the Alps. Perhaps it was because they were all experienced mountaineers to whom the lightweight Norwegian skis were, in a way, so much novel and enjoyable equipment. In any case, many of them seem hardly to have deviated from direct traverses, kick-turning or stepping round when necessary, and simply sitting down when in trouble.

Be this as it may, the golden age of ski mountaineering had begun – which Arnold Lunn puts as having been between 1898 and 1926, when the last of the 'Viertausender' Alpine peaks, Ecrins and Meije, were conquered on skis.

Most of the successful 'firsts' were notched up by Germans, who took to the new sport with immense enthusiasm. Oscar Schuster was the first up Monte Rosa; Hugo Mylius claimed Mont Blanc, and Dr Henry Hoek (an Anglo-Dutchman domiciled, like Paulcke, in Karlsruhe) blazed the trail on skis up the Wetterhorn and the Finsteraarhorn. But the Swiss were also active with many initial ascents to their credit. Paul Montadon of Thun explored much of the Bernese Oberland; Professor Roget of Geneva (who took up skiing at the age of nearly fifty) made the earliest successful crossing of the classic glacier route between Chamonix and Zermatt with Marcel Kurz, who himself achieved an impressive record of 'firsts', while Carl Egger went as far afield as Mount Elbruz in the Caucasus.

In Austria, thanks to the efforts of Colonel Bilgeri, it was above all in the army that Alpine skills were developed. As early as 1901 he had begun to train the men under his command in high mountain skiing, and later he wrote a 150 page thesis on Alpine warfare. (This was in due course captured by the Italians, who promptly put his teaching to good use with their own Alpine troops. But they did at least acknowledge the source.) Sadly, it was the Austrian skiers under Bilgeri's command who, during World War I, suffered the greatest Alpine catastrophe in history. In December 1916, snow fell continuously for a fortnight, provoking a series of avalanches that reportedly killed three thousand men in the Higher Alpine stations, including 253 who were overwhelmed in their barracks on the Marmolata.

The Italians were keener on racing than mountaineering, and indeed their military competitors won races at Eaux Bonnes and Cauterets (in the Pyrenees) in 1910; but during the war their military training centres turned out thousands of skiers who explored the most isolated valleys and often reached surprising altitudes – such as the shoulder of the Zumstein (4,540 metres). After the war the Federazione Italiana dello Sci was founded in Milan under the leadership of Conte Aldo Bonacossa, who (in the opinion of Arnold Lunn) was probably the only ski-runner who had really skied the whole of the Alps from end to end, that is to say from the Alpes Maritimes to the Abruzzi.

The French, in contrast, were late on the scene. True, some students at Grenoble founded a club called 'Les Intrépides' that explored Haute Savoie, but on the whole few French ski-runners were interested in ski mountaineering in the early days, any more than their contemporaries in North America, although Norwegians like Herman Johannsen set up the Maple Leaf Trail in the Laurentians, 'a 90 mile high route up to heaven for the purist touring skier' (to quote *Ski Magazine*).

Equally curious is the fact that the English, who pioneered mountaineering in the Alps, were among the last to tour them on skis. The prestigious Alpine Club held itself aloof from skiing and the early English skiers were not really climbers. Arnold Lunn, a notable exception to the rule, relates that the idea of the Alpine Ski Club was conceived (with the usual undergraduate fervour for lost causes, one imagines) in Owen O'Malley's rooms at Magdalen College, Oxford. Yet in due course this little group was to produce the first real ski guide to the Swiss Alps and a comprehensive study of snowcraft for skiers, who up to that point had relied on such homely yardsticks as Professor Roget's test for avalanches – which was to ask oneself whether cows were likely to feel

By 1923 competitions were becoming more frequent and Alpine training was a regular part of army life in some countries. Biathlon is today an Olympic event although very much a military exercise, combining cross-country skiing with rifle shooting. Originally classed as Military Patrol competitions, team events such as this one at

Grindelwald were not infrequent

comfortable when standing on the slope in summer. If so, he felt safe in saying, the slope was not dangerous.

Mountaineers of the old school sniffed patronizingly at such stuff. They were inclined to feel the same about the whole business of winter sports as Ruskin had felt about them:

> The Alps themselves, which your own poets used to love so reverently, you look upon as soaped poles in a bear-garden which you set yourselves to climb and slide down again with shrieks of delight.

Above Members of the Norden Ski Club, Ishpeming, Michigan, photographed in 1887, the year the club was founded. All the early members were immigrants from Trondheim in Norway

Right The famous Christiania Ski Club was founded in 1877. In 1883, when this photograph of a group of club members was taken, the club organized a Ski Association for the Promotion of Skiing which arranged the Huseby hill competitions and later moved them to Holmenkollen

Growing Pains

But then, of course, the Edwardians were great at looking down their noses. Just as mountaineers sniffed haughtily at the very idea of 'winter sports', so the top-hatted skaters looked on 'skeesters' (and tobogganers too, come to think of it) in much the same light as an Indian Army colonel's lady viewed the *box-wallahs* in Bombay. Even in 1903 skiers at St Moritz were still referred to contemptuously as 'plank-hoppers', and despite the efforts of W. Rickmers to popularize what it called 'this new method of snow-shoeing', the *Alpine Post* reflected that 'considering the exceptional facilities St Moritz can offer it is just a little strange that skiing does not occupy a more prominent position than can be remarked at the present time'.

In 1904, when this poster advertized a ski race in Glarus, the home town of Christopher Iselin, ski racing, while it had a long history in Norway, was a very new feature of Alpine life. Alpine skiing, as a separate entity from Nordic skiing, was yet to be developed and it was still a long time before the Alpine downhill and slalom events were accepted

And yet in January of that year there were sufficient English skiers at Davos to form a club – as Englishmen will when two or three (in this case seven) are gathered together. The Davos English Ski Club, founded on 6 January 1903, is thus the senior British club, antedating both the Swiss Davos Ski Club and the Ski Club of Great Britain itself by a matter of weeks.

Not that these were by any means the first, to be sure. The Christiania Ski Club in Oslo, along with Stockholm's Skidlöpareklubb and the Kiandra Ski Club of Australia were something like a quarter of a century old already; the first Swiss club had been founded at Glarus some ten years previously, and the Norden Ski Club of Ishpeming, Michigan – the oldest in the United States, with a continuous history to the present day – dates from 1887.

But for all this it was the British at Davos, and later at Adelboden, Mürren and Wengen, who laid down the ground rules for competitive Alpine skiing and gave the fledgling sport its initial boost in the Alps.

In the British Ski Year Book (vol ii, page 99) Colonel Swynfen Jervis describes how he attended a 'crowded general meeting of seven members' on New Year's Eve 1903, at which he suggested that a skiing test should be evolved along the lines of the Third Class skating test, then much in vogue. To qualify for the badge, he suggested jokingly, the candidate should be able to stand still on the level for two minutes without losing balance more than once, to turn round without taking off a ski, to ski down the nursery slopes for 100 yards with only three falls, and to come down a steep slope erect once in six attempts. But, he admits sadly, 'The President and Secretary were nasty, advanced people who looked with contempt on anyone who fell down when he wasn't moving', and the first British test eventually consisted of:

1) The descent of a fairly difficult hill without the aid of a pole
2) The execution, without stopping, of four complete turns on a steep slope
3) The ascent and descent of the Strela Pass from the Schatzalp Sanatorium (about 1,500 feet or 500 metres each way)

III. Ski-Rennen
in GLARUS 23/24. Januar 1904.

And indeed, in a slightly revised form – the ascent, for instance, had to be completed without sealskins within a time limit first of 80 and later 65 mins, and the descent, with no restrictions on the use of a stick, in 20 and subsequently 12 mins – this has remained the basis of the Ski Club of Great Britain's Third Class test ever since.

Meanwhile, as these historical deliberations were going on in the Grisons, at the other end of Switzerland a Methodist missionary named Henry Lunn was organizing the first winter sports package tours. 'In those days there was still some social stigma attached to the "personally conducted" party' explains his son, Arnold Lunn, 'and my father, who had never been to a public school, decided to reserve certain Swiss hotels in winter for the exclusive use of those who had.' By starting the Public Schools Alpine Sports Club he enabled his clients to go winter-sporting under the auspices of a club rather than of a travel agent. This euphemism worked like a charm and soon parties of young gentlemen, with their complement of sisters and parents, were romping decorously during the Christmas holidays first at Adelboden, and then at places such as Mürren, Wengen, Montana, Villars, Lenzerheide and Klosters – all of which owe their British connection to Lunn's inspiration. Even if he never actually ventured out into the snow himself, it was Sir Henry Lunn who became the high prophet of skiing to the English upper classes (who were not without influence in those days) just as later his son Arnold was to become the dominant force in British skiing for more than sixty years and be knighted for his services to the sport. 'There was a spirit of goodwill which animated all, a real friendliness which is

Left Skiing was for many years considered rather a strange activity when there was plenty of sport to be had in skating or tobogganing, and partly, no doubt, in self-defence local ski clubs were set up, such as this one posing for a picture in 1904

Bottom The Lunns were perhaps the most important family in the history of British skiing: from left to right, Henry Lunn senior; Peter Northcote Lunn, the racer; Arnold Lunn, who was to exert such immense influence over the development of Alpine skiing and ski-racing; and Sir Henry Lunn, who started the first package tours to the Alps under the respectable guise of the Public Schools Alpine Club

oftener found in a house-party than in a company of tourists', wrote a correspondent in the *Alpine Post*. (But in the same issue the Grand Hotel Kurhaus at Adelboden advertised itself as the only first class hotel that didn't take 'travelling parties'.)

As part of this burgeoning activity, the first British ski race and one of the first ever held in Switzerland (after those in Glarus and Bern the previous year) took place at Adelboden in January 1903. Youth must be served, to be sure, and the 'Public Schools Alpine Sports Club Challenge Cup' was put up for the best combined result of a ski race, a skating competition and a toboggan contest. The Kurverein, sceptical of public school skiing standards, simply placed a flag at each corner of a field and let the competitors loose. A certain E. D. Compton achieved immortality by getting round first. The following year, W. R. Rickmers, Zdarsky's disciple who had moved over from the unfruitful atmosphere of St Moritz, took the young English skiers under his wing, taught them S-turns, and set a course involving some 500 feet of climbing, 1,000 feet of downhill and some level running for good measure. There were sixteen entries and Arnold Lunn chalked up his first racing success at the age of fifteen.

A few years later, after the cup had been won outright (between 1908 and 1910) by Norman Hind, it was decided to award separate trophies for skiing, skating, and tobogganing. The Earl of Lytton presented the skating cup, and Lord Roberts of Kandahar, then vice-president of the Public Schools Alpine Sports Club, gave his name to the skiing trophy. On 6 January 1911 ten competitors left Montana for the Wildstrubel hut where they spent the night. The following morning they raced across the Plaine Morte glacier and then 5,000 feet down to the finishing point below Montana. Standards were improving by now, and Cecil Hopkinson ploughed through the natural snow (no pistes, of course) to win in an elapsed time of 61 mins. The following season the Roberts of Kandahar Challenge Cup Race was moved to Mürren, where for the last three years in succession before World War I it was won by John Mercer.

For all this, competitions were few and far between, and since pistes were unknown skiing tended to be limited to touring until well into the twenties. Quite early on Zdarsky tried unsuccessfully to interest the Norwegians in a downhill race, and organized instead a *Torlauf* on the Muckelkogel that involved passing through some forty gates at convenient distances – a giant slalom, if you like. At the same time the Akademischer Ski Club of Munich held some downhill races at Sudefeld in Bavaria. In 1909 some Germans and Frenchmen turned up at Holmenkollen for the langlauf and jumping championships, rather sportingly really, since they had as much chance as a snowball in Sahara against the Norwegians, who captured every prize in this most prestigious of all Nordic skiing meetings until in 1928 M. Lappalainen of

Finland won the 50km. langlauf.

In 1914, too, an inter-collegiate ski meeting was held between McGill, Dartmouth, Montreal and Shawbridge universities at St Saveur, Quebec, and at Villars the British Army, Navy and Air Force Cup was won by Lieut. Aubrey Newbold RN. Yet, sporadic though they may have been, these events were all part of the slow and argumentative gestation of the Alpine, as opposed to Nordic concept of skiing.

For the Scandinavians, skiing meant above all a means of getting around in the snow – a chance to enjoy the beauties of the countryside in winter. It was a sport more akin to fishing or hunting than steeple-chasing or flat racing. Even today a Norwegian gets back from work, puts on his skis and 'goes for a walk' (which may be anything up to fifty kilometres). In langlauf, a descent comes as a welcome pause to rest for a moment and regain one's breath. It is taken as easily as possible, without any attempt to make turns and schusses. But on the steeper slopes of the Alps it was a different matter. The terrain itself required abrupt turns and offered the exhilaration of fast schusses and S-turns. The essential dichotomy between the two techniques becomes clear.

Zdarsky had got over the difficulty by inventing the stem. Rickmers, his pupil, taught the snow-plough method to the early English skiers at Davos and Adelboden, who soon discarded both the Lilienfeld system and the use of a single stick for braking. Vivian Caulfeild above all expressed the new Anglo-Saxon approach to downhill running in print. His book *How to Ski* came as a revelation; it was the first attempt to explain the dynamics of skiing turns such as the telemark and the christiania. But essentially his message was one of speed: one came down the slopes as fast as one could.

Not everyone agreed by any means (in particular the Scandinavians regarded it all as a gimmick) and for a long time the young world of skiing was rent with impassioned polemics. Arguments raged about bindings, sticks, tests, and who should be admitted into the clubs. At one moment there were no less than four schismatic organizations all squabbling to represent the still minute body of British national skiing. In due course the British Ski Association, the National Ski Union and the Federation of British Ski Clubs all merged into the Ski Club of Great Britain which had been founded, agreeably enough, at a dinner in the Café Royal in London on 6 May 1903.

But this was obviously not the oxygen on which skiing could thrive. What counted most was to run on natural snow, shaped by sun, wind and frost, and to breathe the thin, crisp air of the Alps. Here, after all, was the true magic of the sport.

Prince Chichibu of Japan was described by Arnold Lunn in 1926 as a true mountain lover. The second son of the Emperor of Japan, he was born in 1902 and at the age of eighteen he developed a passion for skiing. His first big tour was among the glaciers of the Bernese Oberland in 1926, where this photograph was taken

Downhill Only

Top left Jacob Tullin-Thams, a Norwegian, won the jumping competition in the Winter Olympics at Chamonix in 1924. Jumping was one of only four skiing events at this first winter games and it was not until 1964 that ski jumping was itself split into two separate competitions – small hill (70 metres) and big hill (90 metres)

Bottom left Another great Norwegian skier, Thorlief Haug, swept up all the remaining golds in the Chamonix skiing events, winning the 18kms cross-country, the 50kms, and the Nordic Combined

Right On 6–7 January 1921 the first British Championships to be decided on a combination of downhill and slalom races took place at Scheidegg. Here are the fifteen competitors (men and women) setting off together in what was known as a geschmozzle start. Leonard Dobbs (fourth from the camera) won comfortably, and Olga Major, the first British lady champion, wears a white blouse and is sixth from the far end

In 1923, a couple of years before the FIS World Championships were officially started, jumping still played a major part in ski championships in Grindelwald. Number 64 in this competition was Accola Rene

For the British to change the regulations for ski competitions was, in a way, as unthinkable as it would have been for the Norwegians to alter the rules of cricket. And yet this was precisely what now began to happen.

The first British championship, held at Wengen in January 1921, comprised not only a downhill race but also a test involving a series of linked telemarks, stems and jump-turns as well as four stop-christianias each way. It was won by Leonard Dobbs, then up at Cambridge, who (spurred on by the indefatigable Arnold Lunn) challenged Thor Klaveness of Balliol College, Oxford to a 'varsity' race the following year.

While Cambridge had the reigning British champion, Oxford could find two Norwegians, Klaveness and Stang, both of whom were good jumpers and langlaufers but had little experience of downhill turning in soft snow. The Norwegians (who felt that they could never show their faces again in Oslo if they put up a poor performance) insisted that the course should include some level racing, whereas their Cambridge counterparts wanted as much downhill running as possible. In the end a compromise was reached, but just as the race started from the ridge above Scheidegg a light drizzle began to fall, turning the snow into slush, and the Norwegians, schussing even the steepest slopes, romped easily home to win the first varsity race by a comfortable margin. Two days later Klaveness, again in heavy snow, won the Roberts of Kandahar from the summit of the Schiltgrat above Mürren. In neither race, as it turned out, were there any long sections which an experienced jumper could not take straight, although the Norwegians were obviously unhappy on the steep, wooded parts where they could not run continuously without downhill turning. Clearly what was needed was something that would test the runner's skill more fully than straightforward downhill racing did, and Arnold Lunn began to adorn the nursery slopes above Mürren with trickily positioned flags.

Slalom had been tried before, of course, but as Lunn was quick to point out, his own interpretation of the game was quite new. For one thing, it was not to be a stylistic exercise requiring specified turns at a given flag. The new slalom was to be a race, pure and simple, with speed as the determining factor. For another, the course would no longer be defined by single flags placed at convenient spots around which the competitor turned, but by pairs of flags forming 'gates' expertly positioned to test the skill and turning technique of the runner through both long and fast as well as short and abrupt turns. On top of this, the slope would be steep.

Slalom *à l'anglaise* was tried out in 1923 and became an integral part of the British ski-running championship at Gstaad in January 1924. This was overshadowed, to be sure, by the first Parsenn Derby run concurrently at Davos (which was won by Peter Gruber of Switzerland) and above all by the first Winter Olympic Games that were held from 24 January to 4 February 1924 at

Chamonix and in which (in accordance with the international practice of the period) only the traditional Nordic events were involved. Thorleif Haug of Norway won the 18km. and 50km. langlauf as well as the Nordic Combination (decided on the combined result of langlauf and jumping) and his compatriot, Jacob T.-Thams, won the jumping. The Games ended, significantly, with the formation of skiing's first international body, the Fédération Internationale de Ski (FIS).

Yet even as Colonel Holmquist of Sweden was being elected president of this august body with Major Oestgaard of Norway as deputy, an equally significant development was taking place in the Bernese Oberland. In room 4 of the Palace Hotel at Mürren, a group of Englishmen were deciding to form a club devoted purely to racing.

Their first problem was what to call it. Tigers, silver foxes, polar bears and even seals were among the suggestions offered. Finally they agreed that the club should be named after the oldest downhill race, the Roberts of Kandahar, with a simple K as its badge. (If people didn't know what it meant, well, that was just tough cheese.) And so it happened that a remote town in Afghanistan, as unconnected with skiing as anywhere in the globe, became synonymous with the most prestigious name on the slopes.

Admittedly at this period ski racing was still a rarefied pursuit, confined to a select little group, like racquets or real tennis, and even among its few adherents the technical chat hardly got beyond whether one's hickory skis were flat or ribbed. But the British were flexing their muscles. In 1925 the Kandahar issued a challenge to Mürren's rival across the valley, where a team to represent Wengen was raised by what amounted to a press-gang around the bars. Ken Foster relates that the Kandahar team, covered with K emblems, suggested that the contest should consist of a slalom and a straight race.

> To this the Wengen team agreed, concealing the fact that most of them had not the slightest idea of what a slalom might be. They learnt all about it in the course of the morning, at the expense of a defeat of 20 points to 5.

During the lunch interval he felt that something should be done to boost morale in the face of such a glittering display of K badges, so seizing some paper napkins he sketched on them a figure skiing 'in a rather constipated position on top of the initials D.H.O. – an abbreviation for Downhill Only'. (Whether the H was put in for euphony or through inability to spell has never been revealed.) At any rate the Wengen team wore them pinned on their hats and did better in the straight races. Foster concedes that

> The idea of serious racing was an entirely novel one in Wengen at that time,

The preparation of the landing area for skiers is most important; even today skiers stamp down the snow on the steep landing slope as they did in Grindelwald in February 1923, for soft snow could catch a ski as it hit the ground and thereby trip up the jumper

as ski races had been regarded as being merely another attraction organised by the Kurverein, like ice gymkhanas. But when the team looked back on their day they found – greatly to their surprise – that they had actually enjoyed racing.

The DHO was formally founded that evening (largely, one suspects, to avenge the defeat) and despite an amiably amateur attitude soon managed to trounce its more aggressive neighbour across the valley. As a club devoted primarily to racing, the Kandahar held competitions at least twice a week during the season and gradually whipped up an enthusiastic following, encouraging young skiers to race rather than tour on the theory that the only way to become a good skier was to race systematically throughout the season. And certainly there was an almost apostolic fervour among the otherwise light-hearted crowd that congregated nightly in the yellow and grey bar of the Palace Hotel at Mürren. Arnold Lunn relates, for instance, how the first president of the Kandahar, L. L. B. Angus, was taken to hospital after a bad backwards fall the week before the Alpine Ski Challenge Cup. Nevertheless on the evening before the race he announced his intention of participating. A succession of doctors, surgeons and friends did their best to dissuade him, but a few minutes before the slalom started Angus emerged surreptitiously from the Allmendhübel railway and slid down to the starting point. 'As referee I exercised my rights and told him he was too late to enter' narrates Lunn. 'He told me to go to a place where the snow is particularly scarce. He was in great pain, but he nerved himself for two supreme efforts, ran two faultless courses and won the Cup against a first class field.'

Inevitably, some of this zest and dash spread to the Swiss themselves. The Ladies' Ski Club, founded in 1923 was the first of its kind and was followed up by the SDS – Swiss Ladies' Ski Club. The LSC and the K produced some of the best girl skiers in the world – Audrey Sale-Barker, Doreen Elliott, Jeannette Kessler – the last-named being arguably the best all-rounder in the world. Largely through the efforts of Walter Amstutz, who grew up in Mürren and raced with the British, the Schweizerische Akademische Ski Club was founded in the autumn of 1924 to raise the standard of skiing among students at Swiss universities through *Abfahrt*, or downhill racing, the basis of which, in the words of A. H. D'Egville, was

> Speed, straight running, thorough control of all turns in contrast to the specialisation of the christiania, an elastic and low running position, and complete mastery of all legitimate uses of the stick.

Perhaps the Kandahar approach differed from what was taught elsewhere more in its methods than its theory. Bilgeri, for instance, and the Arlberg school taught control and steadiness, discouraging beginners from fast straight running until they had achieved complete control. The Kandahar exponents, in contrast, believed that fear was the greatest obstacle, and that the novice should be taught right from the outset to get used to the sensation of speed. Once one could stem, they felt, the quickest way to gain confidence was to point the skis downwards and let oneself go, discovering in the process that even the most hair-raising tosses can be survived. A somewhat drastic approach, to be sure (like the theory that to teach a kid to swim one should throw him in at the deep end of the pool) but one that nevertheless proved its validity by turning out some of the best skiers of the twenties.

Andrew Irvine, who died on Everest with Mallory in 1924, was one of the original members of the club who won a beginners' race and passed the second class test within a month of putting on skis. Christopher Mackintosh, an athlete who played rugger for Scotland and became the finest downhill racer of his time; Bill Bracken, the stylist who invented 'tail-wagging' long before *wedeln* was heard of; Peter Lunn, who raced in seven World Championships; James

Right The first Oxford and Cambridge ski race took place on 2 January 1922 at Wengen. The idea originated with Leonard Dobbs, the British ski champion, who captained Cambridge and confidently expected them to win. However the Oxford team included Tor Klaveness as captain and another Norwegian, Stang. The Oxford team insisted on some level and uphill stretches being included in the race. On the day a slight drizzle meant that even the steep downhill slopes, on which the Cambridge racers would have had an advantage, could be taken straight, so Oxford won

Far right Walter Amstutz competing in the Anglo-Swiss University races at Wengen. He came second in the 1927 slalom in spite of damaging an ankle in training. A great anglophile, he became enthusiastic about skiing and founded the Swiss Universities Ski Club (SAS) in 1924. The following year his friend, Arnold Lunn, founded the British Universities Ski Club and the Anglo-Swiss race became an annual event

Bottom The 1929 British team who did so well at Zakopane in Poland: Harold Mitchell, James Riddell, Audrey Sale-Barker, Bill Bracken (who came second), Doreen Elliott and Patsy Richardson. The girls surprised everyone by taking part in the downhill and coming thirteenth and fourteenth

Riddell and Jimmy Palmer-Tomkinson, were among those who cut their racing teeth, so to speak, on the slopes at Mürren. And indeed, with its panache and sportsmanship, the Kandahar, challenging the world with a take-it-or-leave-it detachment, had that burnished elegance so characteristic of the upper classes as a whole in the lingering Indian summer of British achievement.

In 1925 the first race between a British team and the newly established Swiss Universities Ski Club was run from the top of the Tschuggen. It was won by Walter Amstutz in an elapsed time of just over ten minutes, with Viscount Knebworth sixty-five seconds behind him and a minute later Christopher Mackintosh who, unbelievably enough, finished third after having fallen into a stream, crashed into a tree, and disappeared twenty feet over a bank into another river. Yet if the honours in this initial encounter went to the Swiss, the British had their revenge the following year when Leonard Dobbs won the downhill race on the Lauberhorn and Christopher Mackintosh headed the combined slalom list at Mürren. Since the British team was made up exclusively of university runners, it seemed logical to meet the SAS on equal terms, and the British Universities Ski Club (BUSC) was founded in December 1926. Although limited by definition to members of Oxford and Cambridge, it was understood that a small number of non-university skiers could be accepted provided that they had 'distinguished themselves in first class races', which prompted John Joannides, after examining the 1927 slalom course to remark that he must thank his father for *not* sending him to a university. Otherwise, he added with a grimace, he might have had to risk his neck down it. As it was, both teams lost their top performers through mishaps of one sort or another and the SAS won by a comfortable margin.

Meanwhile the SAS had spread the net wider by organizing a series of international university meetings, first at St Moritz and then at Mürren, with a programme that included downhill, slalom and jumping events and awards for the best individual performances as well as team results. Yet although nine Germans and two Austrians joined the Swiss and British competitors, what was becoming known as the 'Kandahar revolution' still made no great waves outside university circles. In 1926 the Ski Club of Great Britain sent out a memorandum to other national authorities suggesting that downhill racing and slalom should be recognized for international competition, but not a single association replied to it. It seemed easier to get the mountain to Mohammed than convert the Nordic-minded traditionalists to the British idea of competitive skiing.

And yet, prompted by the Swiss, German and Austrian students, the feeling nevertheless grew stronger that langlauf and jumping were not the ultimate arbiters of skiing ability. The Swiss, in fact, began experimenting with what they called 'Alpine Races', in which the start was considerably higher than the finish,

The Roberts of Kandahar, the senior international downhill ski race, was first held in 1911 at Crans-Montana, where Lord Roberts, the famous general, presented a cup to the winner. This photograph of the 1927 race in Mürren shows a variety of downhill styles in deep snow. The race should have taken place on 28 December but had to be postponed for two days because of high winds. Mackintosh (seen in third place above) took over the lead and won in 3mins 47secs. Joannides (second above) came second in 4mins 22.8secs

and the course involved both a steep climb and a tough descent – from Scheidegg, for instance, down to Grindelwald, followed by a reascent to Scheidegg and a 2,500 foot (760 metre) descent to Wengen.

But this was still only a half-hearted compromise between the ideals of the Norwegians and the competitive dash of the British. In some ways the divergence between the two styles of skiing, and particularly the equipment they required, seemed almost irreconcilable: the telemark, for instance, needed a free-moving heel, whereas increased racing speeds necessitated bindings that fixed the heel firmly to the ski for turns, and this in itself involved a safety factor (which at first meant simply a strap that jerked the ski off the boot in the case of a forward fall).

The tedious and often acrimonious struggle to get downhill skiing accepted as a discipline in its own right took several years. Finally an international downhill race was held in the championships at Zakopane in 1929, and the following year the FIS included a downhill in their championship programme. Arnold Lunn met Hannes Schneider, who then ran a ski school at St Anton, in 1927 and Schneider's enthusiasm gave great impetus to the start of the Arlberg-Kandahar race. Even so, it was not until 1933, after the Arlberg-Kandahar had been run for a full five years, that the Austrians organized their own first downhill-slalom championship. By then, largely through the persistence of Arnold Lunn and Walter Amstutz, the still adolescent sport had at last taken a decisive stride forward. Henceforth skiing was to be defined by sheer speed and all the paraphernalia of slalom flags, head-to-head racing, handicaps and graded ski classes.

What finally settled the issue was the unarguable success of the Arlberg-Kandahar, still today one of the most prestigious events on the calendar. Arnold Lunn relates how one day in St Anton he bought a small cup in the village and with the help of Walter Bernays (a naturalized American) set up a slalom run on the nursery slopes for the small boys of the village. The novelty appealed so much to them that the next step was a trophy presented by the Kandahar Club for a competition in the Arlberg, to be decided on the combined results of a downhill and a slalom and to be known as the Arlberg-Kandahar. Before long it had attracted all the stars and became the top meeting of the season. Lunn believes that the British sponsorship contributed to its charisma. Competitors got a fair deal and national rivalries went by the board, so that Austrians could be heard cheering 'Matterhorn' Furrer of Switzerland or Emile Allais of France as warmly as their own Hannes Schneider. But quite apart from this, it was a great party, he remembers, somewhat nostalgically and with more than a touch of partisan spirit:

Some of the A-K prize-givings acquired a legendary fame. And in those

Skating had been a fashionable sport for a century and more and by 1923 Grindelwald offered an excellent rink beside the Bear Grand Hotel. This hotel was also famous because Gerald Fox had stayed there and it was he who had introduced skis to the village in 1891, reputedly putting them on in his bedroom and clattering down the stairs in them

> early days when the Scandinavians still dominated skiing, the A-K was the symbol of a great movement of liberation from exclusive Scandinavian control . . . Like the Gothic chivalry before the gates of Jerusalem, the brotherhood of Downhill racers in the golden age were one great family; divided as families are often by internal rivalries, but united in their passionate enthusiasm for the Kandahar revolution . . . At St Anton we raced against each other not to demonstrate the virtues of a particular nation, or political system or ski school, but to prove that Downhill racing was the greatest fun on earth . . . The A-K was at once the blue ribbon of downhill racing, and the friendliest of all skiing reunions.

This warm and splashy rebellion that the British started up on the slopes of Mürren, confident that the Gods were on their side, finally achieved its object. And no one can doubt that, by breaking through the old limitations, they had given a momentous new dimension to whipping through the snow. Schuss, christie, fall down, get up, wipe the snow off, and bash on again. This was what skiing was all about. And why, at last, after so long, plank-hopping had finally come of age.

Above The first toboggan run at St Moritz, in 1875, twelve years before the St Moritz Tobogganing Club was founded. The famous Cresta Run was not built until 1884

Speed on Runners

Right Tobogganing was Canada's major winter sport when this picture was drawn in 1870. It was a popular pastime for all the family, and a somewhat hazardous one to judge from this scene

For indeed, even if they were subsequently outclassed, the British had at least blazed the trail. Peter Kasper, long time director of the St Moritz Kurverein, and currently Swiss member of the Olympic committee, makes no bones about it.

> Winter sports were created by the English. They founded the whole thing. A century ago, when the same British families came here year after year for the winter, they started by going for walks; then they began skating. The Scots introduced curling, and the more competitive-minded raced each other on luges. We're really grateful to them for what they did. For us, the British will always remain as a sort of symbol.

Cheering words, to be sure, for the islanders at a time when union-jacks are conspicuous by their absence at most international events in the snow. And yet in one domain the British have always held their own. Not only did they elevate the humdrum pastime of sledging into a high art form and one of the supreme encounters with nature at its most dangerously iciest, but they have continued to be pre-eminent in what remains one of the last of the truly amateur sports. And, in fact, nine decades after its foundation, the Cresta is still a British club.

Tobogganing was not invented by the British, of course. The Badminton Library gives credit for this (amiably quoting a German source) to the polar bear who, when faced with a snow-covered slope, just sat down on himself and slid. And, if you like, his fellows who coasted down the snowy hillsides of Newfoundland. But so far as humans are concerned, the word 'toboggan' seems to have originated among the Indian tribes of North America who transported their food and belongings from camp to camp on small sledges. The Coughnawaga Indians in the neighbourhood of Ontario tobogganed for fun, it is said; and certainly Canada can claim to have turned sledging into a sport. Long before such things were thought of in Europe the Montreal Toboggan Club had built a run starting from a monumentally high platform with steep wooden chutes that were first covered in snow and then sprinkled with water to form a smooth icy surface. The Tuque Bleue slide on the south-west corner of Mount Royal even incorporated a wickedly angled horseshoe turn at the finish after a straight dash down some 600 feet (180 metres). And the even grander slide subsequently put up by the Essex County Toboggan Club at Orange, New Jersey was over 1,000 feet (300 metres) long with an alarming series of switchbacking drops and a heap of hay at the bottom into which the riders plunged at full lick (providing amusement for onlookers in the club-house at the foot of the run who watched their friends go 'egg-hunting', as they called it, at a terminal speed, if reports can be believed, of over seventy mph). Since the course was covered in something like nine seconds flat, it may very well have been so.

Left One of the organizers of the early races between the Swiss and the tourists was John Addington Symonds, an English writer who had a chalet at Davos

Right A local family, on the left, is matched against English visitors in one of these not-too-serious toboggan races down a steep Swiss road in the late 1880s

This dicey performance, lit up at night by coloured lamps, was carried out on 'Indian' sledges made from two pieces of ash board fastened together with thongs of deer hide. The boards were turned up in front and secured by a cross-piece at the end. Up to eight feet long and eighteen inches wide, these devices could carry four people in relative comfort if dubious security.

Just about a hundred years ago the craze caught on in Switzerland. The mountain folk in the Grisons and the Bernese Oberland had used their *Schlittli* or wooden luges to get around in the snow for as long as anyone could remember. But it was the English who first thought of racing on them.

John Addington Symonds, who had a chalet at Davos, seems to have organized the first luge races between the visitors and the locals. These took place down a narrow path from the main post road to the Hotel Belvedere. Ormond Hake, an early enthusiast, recalls that there was a small aspen tree at the bottom into which everyone crashed.

> The height of our ambition was to get up enough speed to reach a certain telegraph post which stood where the Victoria Hotel now stands. We guided entirely with our heels, the more timorous amongst us even planting the whole flat of their feet upon the ground as they descended.

From this they graduated to 'tailing' parties:

Left Tobogganing at St Moritz, Switzerland, in the 1890s, with tobogganers riding in prone head-first style as opposed to the seated luge position

Bottom left An early bobsleigh

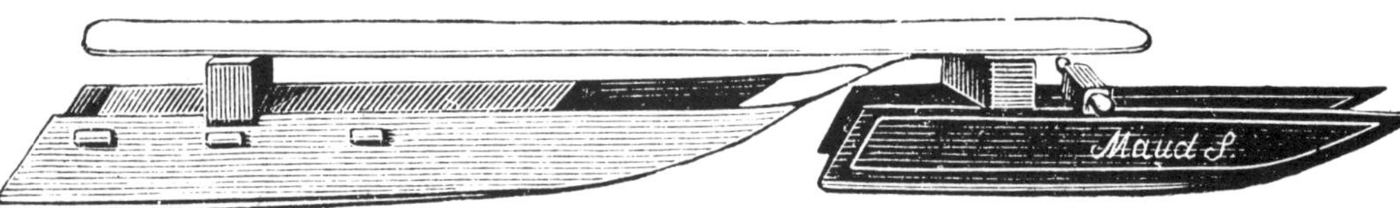

Right A party of tourists on a bobsleigh on the road from St Moritz to Celerina in 1893, four years before the foundation of the St Moritz Bobsleigh Club

> We scraped together as many *Schlittlis* as we required, tied them all in a line behind a two-horse hay-sledge, and drove to Wolfgang in solemn procession, each seated on his or her *coaster*. We then loosened our machines and made our way down to Klosters, tobogganing where the road promised fair going.

All good straightforward fun, to be sure, especially when the horses trotted round a corner, snaking the long line of connected luges sideways into the snow unless prompt avoiding action was taken. But this adolescent pastime was soon snapped into a sharper focus as people built luges to their own specification with longer runners and weighted to give better downwards thrust. A technique was developed of steering with iron pointed sticks held in each hand, and wherever a steep enough path could be found, these early tobogganers could be seen hurtling precariously down it.

The next step, inevitably, was a full scale race, which was held down a two-mile stretch of the Davos to Klosters road. Twenty-one stalwarts lined up on 12 February 1883, and the field of Dutch, Germans, Swiss and British (plus Dominions) was led at the finish by Peter Minsch, a Swiss from Klosters, and the Australian G. Robertson, who had come over from St Moritz.

Over in the neighbouring Engadine, in fact, some exuberant souls had already thought of connecting two American-style toboggans together with a twelve-foot plank, and had scared the daylights out of everyone by hurtling down the road from St Moritz to Celerina, to the disgust of the local traffic who indignantly barred the way. Though nobody was actually killed by such blood-thirsty performances, it was very nearly the end of the sport almost before it had started.

Fortunately wisdom prevailed, and with the help of Peter Badrutt, Major W. H. Bulpett constructed a three-quarter mile long course down the valley to the village of Cresta (just above Celerina) in 1884. It was a snow run with ice patches and rudimentary banks, and the first 'Grand National' with twenty competitors – ten from Davos and ten from St Moritz – took place on it early in 1885. All rode sitting on ordinary luges, and C. Austin from Davos emerged as the winner.

Gradually the run was improved and standardized, with ingeniously constructed corners and plunges (even then designated by names such as Shuttlecock and Church Leap) until in the end it became a solid sheet of ice from start to finish. Indeed, although varying marginally from year to year, the run at the turn of the century was hardly any different from the ice tube of today. Starting high up at St Moritz, it snakes down through ten very definite corners (known to riders as 'banks') designated First, Second, Thoma (after Colonel Thoma-Badrutt, one of the greatest Swiss riders, who was responsible for building the run for many years), The Rise, Battledore, Shuttlecock, Stream, Bulpett's, Scylla and Charybis. The length from the Top to Finish is 1,320 yds (1,207 m) with an average gradient of 1 in 7·7 rising at its steepest to 1 in 2·8.

Whereas the best time in 1887 was put up by twelve-year-old Bertie Dwyer (who sat so lightly on his *Schlittli* that he was reported by spectators to have been airborne for a good twelve yards at one point before finishing the run in 1 min. 58·6 secs), the advantages of coming down head-first on the American type of clipper-sled equipped with steel sprung runners were discovered soon enough. The American toboggan was not dissimilar to the present machines, though its nose was pointed; today's skeleton was introduced in 1892 by Bulpett and got its snub-nosed configuration and sliding seat in 1903, by which time the record from Top stood at 59·6 secs. By 1930 this had only been reduced by just over a second, and now, seventy years later, it stands at 54·21 secs, put up

Right A Swiss bobsled, dating from around 1905. The first Swiss toboggans had been designed in the 1880s by Christian Mathis

Bottom By the 1920s tobogganing and bobsleighing had long been two very separate and highly organized sports, but the ordinary tourist could still enjoy being drawn through Swiss villages on a simple *Schittli*

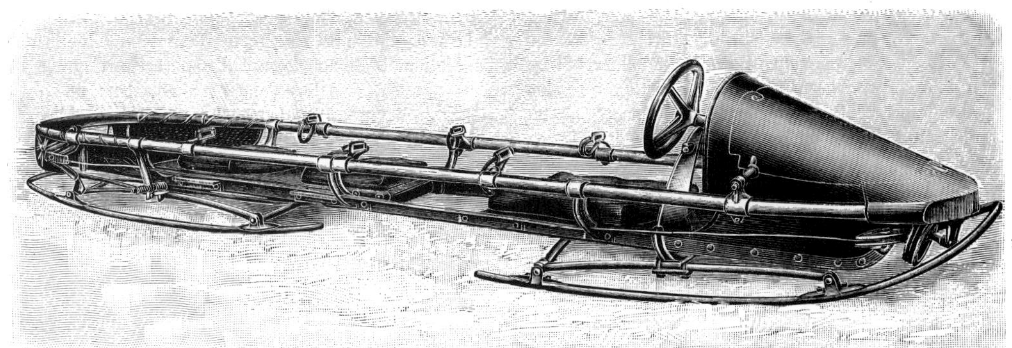

by P. Marou in 1971 (43·45 secs from Junction).

Belly-hopping downhill at nearly eighty mph with one's chin an inch from the ground before breakfast on an icy morning may not be everyone's idea of fun, but right from its earliest days the Cresta acquired a special mystique, perhaps through the sheer nerve and split-second reactions that it entailed. Very quickly, in fact, the St Moritz Tobogganing Club, which was founded in the winter of 1887, managed to elevate the simple game of sledging into what Lord Brabazon could homerically describe as the 'king of winter sports'. Yet despite the danger, and a long list of mesmeric performances, a full twenty years went by without serious accidents, until in 1907 Captain H. S. Pernell VC died from injuries after a fall and the Belgian Comte de Bylandt was killed when he hit a log that was blocking the way.

Nor (as the supporters of women's lib. will be delighted to know) were the legendary riders all men such as J. A. Bott and Colonel Thoma-Badrutt, whose duelling for the Grand National and the Ashbourne Cup lasted for ten years, or for that matter C. P. Bacon of Boston and Lieut. V. Gibbs who were the first to ride Battledore fully forward. There was a special Ladies' Grand National which Miss Webble won seven times, clocking 61 secs in 1911 against the fastest men's time that year of 59·6 secs – no mean achievement, when it is remembered that the long skirts then worn made starting difficult. Lady Ribblesdale was a

Above A four-man bob, the 'Felix', rounding the famous Horseshoe bend on the Celerina run in 1925

Right Another four-man bobsled, of the 1940s, photographed in Switzerland. It has no cowling and is virtually comprised of two smaller sleds fixed together

formidable contender, too, and in more modern times Mrs Bagulay earned her place against the best masculine opposition to get into the Curzon Eight in 1919, beating her husband for the coveted colours by one tenth of a second. But the battering sustained on the icy surface (both novice and expert alike emerge black and blue around the ribs) was considered dangerous for a woman's physique, and for medical reasons women were no longer allowed on the Cresta from 1923 onwards.

Essentially the story of the Cresta has been that of continuous attempts to shave milliseconds off the previous times, and the Club's yearbook pays tribute to such names as Captain Webb-Bowen, the first rider to beat sixty seconds from Top; Lord Brabazon of Tara with his spring toboggans and his highly individual style; Captain J. S. Coates, five times winner of the Grand National; N. Marsden, one of the earliest stylists; J. R. Heaton, who won the 1928 Winter Olympics event, and the American W. Fiske, holder of both records until 1939. Since World War II the best performances down the zig-zagging iceway have been put up by Nino Bibbia of St Moritz, the present holder of the record from Junction; Colin Mitchell, the first rider to beat Billy Fiske's record from Junction and 1959 winner of the Curzon Cup in the fastest aggregate time ever recorded, and the incomparable Doug Conner, now holder of the record from Top.

Nino Bibbia of Italy, one of the all time greats of the Cresta Run. Bibbia won both the Grand National and the Curzon Cup no fewer than eight times. In 1948, when the Winter Olympics were held at St Moritz for the second time (the first occasion was in 1928) and skeleton tobogganing was on the programme, Bibbia won the gold medal. His last Grand National win was in 1973

All these were individual performers, for the Cresta is essentially a solitary encounter with the wickedly glistening ice, and face first at that. As such it is a one-off phenomenon, unique in the world. No similar run challenges its lofty pre-eminence on the roof of the Alps, although its name, which stems from the tiny village at the crest of the valley below St Moritz, has been adopted by everyone from boutiques to cars. (I confess, as a constructor, that I toyed with it for one of our own models around 1955, but Vauxhall's got in first.)

But Wilson Smith's idea of tying two toboggans together prompted Christian Mathis (who owned the horses and sleighs in the village, and whose grandchildren now run the garages) to devise a sledge that could carry several people at a time. Although he simply fixed iron runners to a wooden plank, making the rear ones rigid and the front ones moveable, the basic principle has applied to bobs ever since. Corners could be negotiated by steering the front runners, provided that the centrifugal force did not overturn the bobsleigh, which in its turn meant that the faster it went, the more the passengers had to throw their weight inwards.

The essential difference between the Cresta and the Bob (apart from the fact that Cresta riders get up early in the morning, when the ice is coldest, whereas bobbers turn out in the afternoon) is that one is an individual performance and the other a team effort. At first the bobs were run as part of the St Moritz Tobogganing Club, but as equipment and techniques became progressively more divergent the St Moritz Bobsleigh Club was founded in its own right on 21 December 1897. Two of its founder members were women, and significantly the first competition regulations stipulated that a three-seater bob must include at least one woman rider, and four seaters and over at least two.

A fortnight later, on 5 January 1898, the new club's first race took place down 1,400yds of the road from St Moritz to Celerina, and was won by Giles St Aubyn's team on a bob called 'Alligator'. Other favourite points of encounter were the Bernina Pass from Montebello down to Moteratsch and Albula from Preda to Bergün (nostalgically revived in January 1975 on the snowed-up pass). Banks were built at the corners of the road not for security's sake but to enable the turns to be taken at greater speed, until in the end the locals wouldn't put up with it any longer, and the authorities prohibited riding on the public highways. The bobbers then had to devise a run of their own. For a while they compromised by coursing down the edge of the Celerina road, until in 1903, thanks to the help of the Badrutt family, a proper bob-run was built not far from the Cresta itself. Snaking through fourteen bends in the grounds of the Kulm Hotel for about a mile, with a 400ft drop down the hill to Celerina and including three vertically banked corners (known as Wall, Sunny and Horseshoe), it has hardly changed since the run was opened on 22 December 1903. In fact W. W. Barton's description in the *Alpine Post* of the opening run down could almost pass muster today:

> Wheugh! How we sped along gathering pace each moment . . . The minute particles of frozen snow thrown up by the Alligator's runners and the keen air being the only resistance we were sensible of. A shout from our steersman, a pull on the levers by my side and a cloud of snow was ploughed up by the Alligator's back teeth. Off, and again we tore unchecked until the mighty First corner called for another touch of the brake. Down we rushed to the Horseshoe when short and sharp came the command and up flew the snow as our speed was reduced. Round we swung and were hardly free from the bank when Clarence Martin shouted 'No more brake wanted.' Like a live thing our trusty bob bounded forward positively vibrating with pleasure at the idea. Into the big cutting and under the railway bridge we raced; then with a roar as we cleared the hardened snow we dashed down the iced dip with such velocity that our impetus carried us up the steep rise at the finish and over thirty yards of loose snow.

In due course it became the model for other major runs at Cortina, Cervinia, Garmisch, Alpe d'Huez, Innsbruck and Lake Placid. For unlike the Cresta, which has only been on the Olympic programme twice, in 1928 and 1948 when the Games were held at St Moritz (and the American Jennison Heaton and Bibbia of St Moritz were the respective gold medallists) bobbing soon became an international sport hotly contested by Germans, Austrians, Italians, Swiss, Americans and British alike. As early as 1908 the Crown Prince of Germany became honorary president of the club (and a skilful driver into the bargain) and the game began spreading not only to Davos and Engelberg but beyond the boundaries of Switzerland to Germany, Poland, Rumania and even as far afield as the United States and Argentina.

Perhaps it was the team aspect that gave it such a widespread appeal. For quite apart from the driver whose job is to steer, the man at the back, known as brake, has an almost equal responsibility. By digging one or other of two iron spikes into the ice, he can check the bob or help guide it around a corner.

Between driver and brakesman there must be a perfect co-ordination, just as the other members of the crew must lean in unison, since the slightest wrong movement can mean an agricultural session over the side. There must be perfect team action, too, at the start – which involves a complicated procedure as the bob is manhandled into position and rocked to and fro to ensure that the runners are clear for a lightning getaway. The crew scramble on, leaving the brakesman to push and get the bob moving as fast as he possibly can before jumping aboard himself. Timing is therefore all important: as much as a couple of seconds can be gained by a really snappy start. But if the brakesman falls flat on his face, the others will find themselves uncomfortably anchorless.

In the early days there were often as many as six in the crew, but since the International Bobsleigh Federation was founded in 1923 and bobbing became included in the Winter Olympics, the contest has been standardized for four-men bobs and (since 1931) two-men 'boblets'. A glance at the results in the appendix will show that whereas before World War II the honours were evenly distributed, since 1947 the Swiss and the Italians have virtually swept the board with their boblets, although frequently seen off in the four-men championships by the Americans, Canadians and Germans. And in 1964 Britain's only Gold Medal in the Olympics at Igls was won by Tony Nash and his boblet brakesman, Robin Dixon, thereby ending an eight-year Italian monopoly of the world title.

This only went to prove, let it be said, that bobsleighers prize sportsmanship above medals. Eugenio Monti and Sergio Siorpaes were the defending world champions and the British pair were their strongest challengers. Yet when Nash's axle cracked on the first of the four runs, Monti loaned him the part off his own bob for the second descent.

Perhaps, come to think of it, the quest for speed on runners is just about the last truly amateur of the competitive sports. Nor, though it started as a kid's game, is it solely for muscular teenagers. Lord Brabazon went down the Cresta when he was seventy. Paul Gallico, the novelist, first tried it when he was sixty.

Togged out like a spaceman, he found himself belly down on the sliding seat of a steel skeleton with nothing in front but a six foot slot of glaring ice, switchbacking down the gully in vertically banked curves.

'Rake', they told him, 'Rake all the way down and hang on for all you're worth.'

The all-clear bell sounded. The wooden barrier was raised. Someone gave him a push, and within a few yards the ice walls on either side began to flash past.

I dug in my toes and raked hard. It didn't seem to make any difference.

Ahead of me loomed a high curving wall of ice. I slammed into the side of it,

British two-man bob gold medallists Anthony Nash and Robin Dixon on their way to victory during the 1964

Olympics at Innsbruck in 1964

Overleaf A two-man luge toboggan in Switzerland. The weight is limited to 53lbs (24kg) maximum. Spikes are fitted to the soles of the riders' boots to assist pushing off, and there are metal rakes on the toe-caps to help braking and steering with the feet. Luge, as opposed to skeleton, tobogganing is now a regular Olympic event

Heliomalt

Above The speed-thrills are evident in this picture of snow-mobiling, a modern sport on motorized skis practised mainly on the frozen wastes of Canada

with a sickening wrench, only to dip into what seemed a bottomless crevasse of gleaming ice; at the sight of this fearful pit, I don't mind admitting that I was close to panic.

With every acceleration the sled became more impossible to control. It bounced and buckled, punching the crossbar into his stomach. He banged violently into the sidewalls, clouting his hands, elbows and shoulders.

Faster, faster, faster. Ahead a highway bridge shot up.

Just as it seemed that I must split my skull against the bridge support, the curve shot me through the tunnel . . . my world was a nightmare of glittering blue-white ice, tearing wind, pounding and battering steel. My strength was failing. At any moment I would lose my frenzied grip . . .

Suddenly I felt a sharp blow on the right side of my ribs, followed by an almost intolerable pressure. Then I was rising heavenwards (this was Finishing Bank, an upwards curve designed to slow the skeleton to a halt) . . . and then I was lying immobile on the sled in soft snow, numb fingers still convulsively clutching the steel bars.

It was over. He had done it. But did he then go tottering to the bar for much-needed solace after such an alarming experience? Not on your life. He went straight up again for another ride, hoping to clip seconds off his time.

That's how the game gets you. And why today there are more people clamouring to go down the Cresta than ever before.

Right The moment of disaster for Jim Higgins and Ronnie Walters of the United States as they skid over the top of the ice wall during the two-man event at the Olympics at Igls in 1964. Fortunately neither man was seriously hurt. The 1964 Olympics was the first time luge tobogganing was accepted as an event

Bottom right Hans Rinn and Norbert Hahn of East Germany speed through the Olympic luge chute at Igls in 1976 to win the gold. Luge tobogganists shift their weight right back to increase speed – which can exceed 70mph

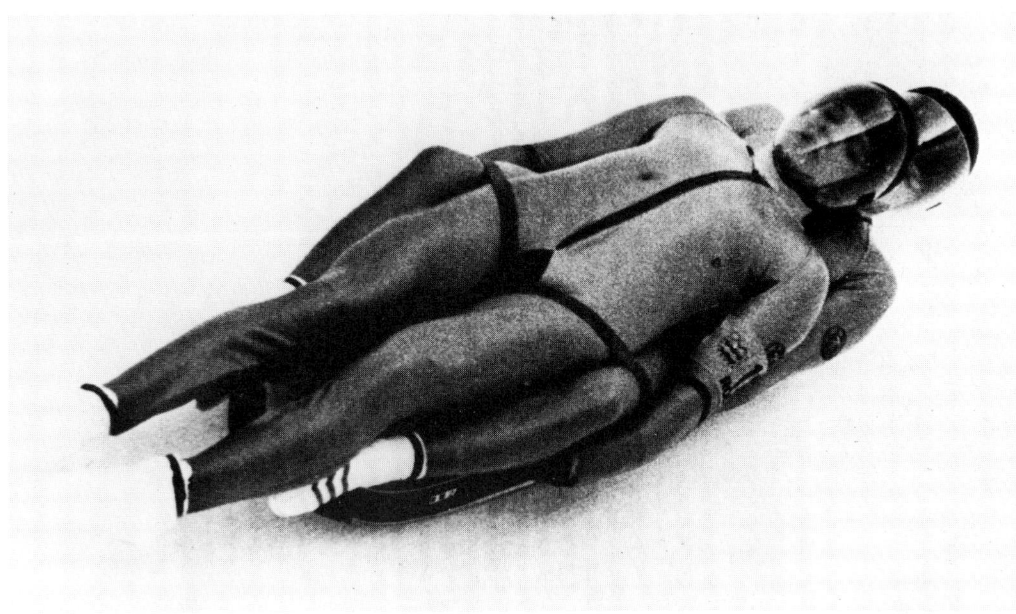

Above Few skiing centres boasted any uphill transport until the 1930s, but Rigi in Switzerland was one of the early ones – these travellers were using it in 1870. Mountain trains could also be found at Zermatt up to Gornergrat, the Parsenn railway at Davos, and the Jungfraujochbahn from Wengen and Grindelwald up to Scheidegg and beyond. But these all preceded other uphill transport for skiers by several decades

Right In 1932 the Winter Olympics went to Lake Placid in New York State for the first time. The US team won a total of six gold medals, four for speed skating and two in the bob-sled events. The Norwegians, of course, dominated the skiing events

Ski Fever Grows

In the United States, too, skiing had gradually been catching on since the early days at the turn of the century when Melvil and Annie Godfrey Dewey had founded Lake Placid as an exclusive club, keeping it open in the winter with a programme that included, as they put it, 'the sport of skiing, only recently imported from the Scandinavian countries'. But although they had the foresight to bring forty pairs of skis from Norway (along with heavy poles to be used as 'rudders') and Lake Placid soon became recognized as the leading winter sports resort in the USA, vacationers in that agreeable spot continued to spend their time skating and tobogganing or even ice-sailing on the lake in preference to slithering around the scenery on boards.

Fortunately there were enthusiasts elsewhere. The earliest US cross-country championships were held at Ashland, Wisconsin in 1907, and two years later Fred Harris of Dartmouth College, after a short spell watching what the Canadian skiers were up to at Montreal, suggested in the student newspaper that a 'ski and snow-shoe club' should be formed on the campus. Once established, the Dartmouth Outing Club not only explored the neighbouring hills, but began holding an annual winter carnival that varied langlauf with boisterous schusses down the steep Taft run, and groomed a college team that was soon challenging the Canadians. Indeed in the first inter-collegiate meet that was held at St Saveur, Quebec in 1913, Dartmouth beat McGill, and over the years produced an impressive list of stars such as Charles Proctor, Johnnie Litchfield, Percy Rideout, A. L. Washburn, and Ted Hunter along with the Bradleys, the Durrances and the Chivers. The Williams College Outing Club was founded in 1915, and the famous Sno Birds came into being after World War I at Lake Placid with, among other things, a fairly spectacular jump. Following the lead given by the English at Mürren, Dartmouth held a slalom in 1923, and the first Kandahar-style downhill race was staged at Mount Moosilauke in New Hampshire in 1926 (which put them ahead of most of the Europeans, to be sure). By this time the Canadian Pacific Railroad was already laying on special 'snow trains' to take skiers up to the Laurentians, and a year or two later Sig Buchmayr and Kurt Thalhammer opened the first fully-fledged ski school in the USA on Sugar Hill at Franconia, charging a dollar an hour for tuition.

For all this, facilities were few and far between, and you had to be dedicated to catch ski fever in those chairliftless days. Even in Switzerland, the slopes were still relatively uncrowded. When, during the course of a school outing to Villars, I first put on skis in 1930 at the age of eight (an experience, I seem to remember, that ended in tears), the skiing fraternity in their khaki breeches and baggy blue trousers were very much a minority compared with their elegant counterparts on the rinks. Which was hardly surprising, since each five-second schuss down the hill behind the village meant an exhausting ten minutes' crabwise clamber

Kleine Scheidegg achieved early recognition because it was served by one of the first cog railways from both Wengen and Grindelwald. In 1934 it was obviously a popular area with scope for all standards, and these skiers were adopting the parallel turn — Austrian Toni Seelos' method

back up again, and the whole exasperating business of guiding edgeless slats with dubious bindings through unmanicured snow lacked the fun, to say the least, of skimming blissfully over polished ice to the tune of the latest foxtrot.

Around the corner, and under the tree
The gallant major made love to me
He kissed me once, he kissed me twice
It wasn't quite the thing to do, but gosh! it was so nice.

So went the refrain to my first tentative outside edges. Later, relaxed in a deck chair with a cup of hot chocolate making a satisfying round hole in the ice, one could watch the pretty girl over there showing off a pirouette, while an old eccentric sailed by with a look of the profoundest contempt on his face, children staggered about in helpless paroxysms, and an elderly lady in tweeds clung excitedly to the instructor's arm. It was all most agreeable and, in contrast, for most uninitiated and valley-bound sceptics, skiing was a pastime neither for muddied oafs nor flannelled fools, but for the plain insane.

Perhaps. And yet what with one thing and another, the winter sports craze was gathering steam, especially among the English who, once they had savoured a first taste of *Glühwein* in Switzerland or *Gemütlichkeit* in Austria, returned year after year to their favourite locale, until the idea of Christmas away from Klosters or Kitzbühel became as unthinkable as skipping the

Left Drag lifts, or T-bars, are now very common and are suitable for nursery slopes and the open areas at the top of the mountain. They are most companionable, though awkward when a tall man and a small child travel together

Enclosure at Ascot. And, sooner or later, nearly all of them took up skiing.

Understandably, the earliest places to make headway were those with some form of uphill transport, such as Davos with its Parsenn railway; Zermatt, where a ratchet train called 'Grannie' took an hour and a half to labour up to Gornergrat; Wengen with the Jungfraujochbahn; or Adelboden, where a bus conveyed one up to the Hahnenmoos. All of which, of course, had been conceived with summer visitors in view. And then, suddenly, the one single development that was to put skiing on the map took place when a young Swiss engineer called Gerhard Müller, with the help of a rope and some motorcycle parts, invented the first drag-lift, which was installed on a slope above Davos.

Right Cable cars have their terrifying aspects, as the cars are pulled over caverns hundreds of feet down. But they rise fast, like this one

Propelled mechanically uphill, it was now possible to do a run every ten minutes or so, whereas previously, with much mortification of the flesh, a twenty minute downhill run had involved a morning's climb on sealskins.

This simple but brilliant idea revolutionized the sport. By the end of the thirties, many of the major resorts, such as Megève and St Anton, had invested not only in 'meat-hooks' on the nursery slopes but in cable cars for more ambitious skiers. By the end of 1938, in fact, Megève even had a hotel designed specially for skiers called *La Résidence du Sporting* (where a character later to be known as Lord Haw-Haw was very much in evidence, and Madame Schiaparelli drifted round in wonderful evening dresses, though not yet stretch-pants).

Over at Gstaad, one of the few Swiss resorts that the British didn't start, skiers were conveyed up Hornberg by a device called a *Funi*, actually a sleigh pulled by cables up a steep snow track, which – since the seats followed the angle of the hill – gave passengers such a funny feeling that they wanted to jump off.

Across the Atlantic, where the 1932 Olympics were held for the first time at Lake Placid (and the host country's enthusiasm, in truth, was mostly concentrated on speed skating and bobbing, which brought the Americans no less than six gold medals), the first rope-tow appeared that year at Shawbridge, in the Laurentians, and was followed a couple of seasons later by a similar device at Woodstock, Vermont, powered, it appears, by a Model T Ford. Primitive though this may have been, Woodstock soon found itself the centre of a minor skiing boom.

> Countless skiers remember it as the site of their first competitive lumps [commented *Ski Magazine*]. Bunny Bertram [the former Dartmouth ski team captain who had set it up] used to amuse himself and others by running the rope at a fast clip – around 25 miles per hour – which would shorten the agonizing time it took to get to the top. It also had the side effect of spewing unwary skiers of low avoidupois off into orbit at the top of the hill.

The news soon spread and other places followed suit. At Jackson Hole, once the last frontier of the old West, where pioneer skiers had cut boards out of red fir and fastened them permanently to leather boots with canvas tops, the tractor-driven rope-tow turned Snow King into Wyoming's first ski resort. Stevens Pass near Seattle went a stage further, putting six in a series, each faster than the one below, which must have needed good nerves, to say the least. 'Rope-tows were to skiing what Henry Ford's Model T was to the nation a couple of decades earlier; they provided a cheap, fairly reliable method of uphill transportation,' says *Ski*. And soon they were chugging happily from coast to coast.

In the Laurentians, where enthusiasts skied down the mountain trails that wound through the woods, Bill Pauly from Germany set up a ski school in the St Jovite area, and began teaching a technique nicknamed the 'Berlin squat', in which the skier descended the hill in a low, careful crouch with his skis far apart. In the winter of 1933 some of his pupils, calling themselves the 'Redbirds' went to Mürren where to everyone's surprise their leader, George Jost, won the coveted Arlberg-Kandahar race. Arnold Lunn, in fact, was so impressed by the Canadians' performance that he straightaway suggested a return match in Canada. By all accounts the Quebec-Kandahar, which took place at Mount Tremblant a month later, was hardly for the faint-hearted. The twenty

Emile Allais after his victory in the downhill at the FIS Championship at Chamonix in 1937. Allais also won the slalom and the Alpine combined, marking the French entry into first class skiing with a grand slam

contestants started together and simply schuss-boomed to the bottom. One of them ended upside down in a tree, and George Jost romped home again in 15 mins 10 secs. Since that time the Quebec-Kandahar has been run every winter and has been won by such superstars as Tommy Corcoran, Guy Périllat, Peter Duncan and Rod Hebron. Moreover in 1949 Ernie McCulloch, now school director at Mount Tremblant, defeated the entire French Olympic team in this traditional event.

But trans-atlantic successes were still something of a rarity in those baggy-pants days. For some time after the FIS had formally recognized downhill racing in 1930, the British continued to dominate the slopes. That winter, which Lunn defines as the *annus mirabilis* for British skiing, Colin Wyatt and Barry Caulfield won the Anglo-Swiss university race; Bill Bracken took the combined cup on the Lauberhorn; and although Christian Rubi of Switzerland got home first in the downhill event, he was only just ahead of the British pack. On top of this, the DHO club beat the Swiss at Wengen, while at Mürren the English ladies triumphed over their Swiss opponents. Elsewhere it was much the same story, although before long the Swiss skiers began to redress the balance with such formidable contenders as Walter Prager of Davos, Otto 'Matterhorn' Furrer of Zermatt, David Zogg of Arosa and Rudi Rominger of St Moritz. The Austrians, too, soon began to show their paces. Toni Seelos, who became the unchallenged master of the slalom in the mid-thirties (sometimes winning by a margin of ten seconds or more), took the World Championship both in 1933 and 1935, while Bruno Leubner and Friedl Pfeiffer walked off with the Arlberg-Kandahar in 1928 and 1936. The French took a while longer to get into their stride. Emile Allais, for instance, came behind every member of the British team in the 1934 World Championship, but subsequently won the Arlberg-Kandahar, in 1937, and pocketed the World Championship both in 1937 and 1938 despite the fact that his protégé, James Couttet of Megève, had created a sensation when only sixteen by walking off with the downhill event. The Germans, likewise, made their presence felt from 1934 onwards. Christel Cranz, arguably the greatest woman racer of all time, who lived at Interlaken (where her father had a textile works) and learnt to ski at Grindelwald with Erna Steuri (herself the best Swiss lady skier), won the World Championship every year between 1934 and 1939 except in 1936 when, to compensate, she and Franz Pfnür ran away with both gold medals in the Olympics at Garmisch-Partenkirchen. And once the Norwegians had taken to the idea of Alpine skiing as opposed to langlauf, Birger Ruud and Laila Schou-Nilsen (the sixteen-year-old prodigy who subsequently became Norway's tennis champion as well) notched a double Norwegian victory in the Olympic Downhill.

As the thirties wore on the odds against the British lengthened, if you like, for every Alpine and Scandinavian valley could produce as many crack performers

Birger Ruud, already known as 'King of the Ski Jumpers' went to Germany to work in 1935 and took part successfully in several downhill races. He caused a sensation in the Garmisch Olympics of 1936 by winning first the men's downhill race and then the special ski jump

as the snowless British Isles. Nevertheless, the British universities team continued to beat their opposite numbers right up until the war. Progressively, though, the sport was becoming commercialized as downhill racing evolved into a yardstick for measuring the virtues of the various national schools, and, by definition, the resorts in which they operated. In the process some of the easy-going sportsmanship of the early days disappeared from competitions where success, sponsored by government subsidies, was of crucial importance to the ski school and the tourist industry as a whole.

The emergence of these schools was in some ways the most significant development in the era before World War II. The English idea, as propagated by the Kandahar at Mürren, had been simply to aim the skis downwards after a quick prayer and hope for the best. Hannes Schneider, at St Anton, believed in a more scientific approach. Drawing on the experience of Zdarsky and his old rival, Bilgeri, he gradually evolved what became known as the Arlberg method. 'Hannes insisted that it was a method, and not a technique', explains Rudi Matt, who at sixty-six still heads the ski school that made the Arlberg famous.

> What he aimed at was to equip people to ski in all weathers, and to cope with light changes, snow changes and slope changes. So he took them in groups according to their standard. He believed in using two sticks instead of a single long pole, and what he taught over sixty years ago is what we teach now – the snow plough, traversing, turning into the hill, and stem-christies.

Rudi, who was born the same year that Hannes Schneider founded the St Anton school, has been with it for over half a century. He was World Slalom Champion in 1936. Techniques differed then, and rotating and the shoulder swing, along with upward unweighting and *vorlage*, were coming into fashion. Nonetheless it was the knees that did the work. 'Ski-lauf ist knee-lauf' he says with a smile, looking out of the great plate-glass window of his office in the new school block. 'Equipment has improved so much over the years, particularly bindings. All the same, it's the skier that counts, not the boots.' He attributes the success of St Anton to its teaching. In the Christmas period of 1924 there had been just eighteen visitors. Now there are 200 instructors alone, and 25,000 spectators watched the Arlberg-Kandahar races on Kapell in 1973. Thanks to good instruction, huge numbers of medium-strength skiers cheerfully negotiate the moguls on the standard run down from Galzig (once the site of the old Arlberg-Kandahar races); and although many of the pistes are knee-slamming enough, the accident ratio has been reduced from three per mil to three-tenths per mil, which says a good deal for the cautious Arlberg methods of teaching.

Meanwhile, over at the other end of the Alps, the French began from around

1936 to develop a technique directly inspired from racing, and especially from the Austrian Toni Seelos' stylish parallel christianias, that became known as 'appel-rotation'. Gone was the stem-christie: with skis tight together and knees slightly bent, the shoulders were swung in the opposite direction to the turn that was being made, and the skis were then brought round by a simultaneous horse-kick type action of the heels (known as the ruade). One of the most elegant but difficult of all turns, it was taught in seven stages according to a method elaborated by Emile Allais (and later James Couttet) and has only lately been superceded by the new jet-style, which is notably faster through moguls and curves.

The Swiss, too, were playing with a parallel movement based on counter-rotation – that is, turning the shoulders in the opposite direction to the legs and skis. This asymmetrical position, championed by the so-called St Moritz school, certainly helped Rudi Rominger to become the top slalom racer of the day.

These varying techniques were brought to the USA by first a trickle, then a stream of prominent skiers who were obliged to leave Germany and Nazi-occupied Austria. Otto Schniebs went to Dartmouth, where he imparted the Austro-Bavarian creed, along with the philosophy that 'skiing is a way of life'. Hannes Schneider, exiled from St Anton, took the Arlberg disciplines to North Conway, New Hampshire. Luggi Foeger went to Yosemite; Otto Lang to Mount Rainier; Friedl Pfeiffer to Sun Valley, and Sepp Ruschp to Stowe.

> At first we in the United States stabbed wildly at the sport, tasting the fun, the exuberance, the beauty [writes Robert Scharff]. We had learned to get to the slopes by way of the riotous snow trains and to get to the top by way of sundry lethal contraptions, but we were still bashing and crashing our way downhill, more horizontal than vertical 90 per cent of the time.

But once exposed to the dedicated teaching methods of these expatriate Europeans, American skiing made impressive strides – as the ski troops in the Tenth Mountain Division were later to demonstrate in World War II, during the Italian campaign.

What with one thing and another, indeed, the cheerful haphazard days of sealskins and haversacks were now over and done with. Major lift installations were being built, pistes were being groomed, stretch-pants were about to appear, and the Cinderella of winter sports was all set to explode into one of the biggest money-spinners of all time.

Above By the early sixties 'drive-in' skiing was very much a feature of the North American winter sports scene. Members of the Ottawa Ski Club, for instance, could drive to any one of a half-dozen hills like this, park their cars, and start skiing

Right America's new resorts soon began to breed some high calibre skiers. Bud Werner of Colorado was tragically killed by an avalanche while filming near St Moritz in 1964. Here he is competing in the men's downhill during Olympic trials at Squaw Valley in 1959

The Post-War Scene

10

Left Mussolini saw the value of tourism to a country suffering from unemployment and encouraged Giovanni Agnelli, head of Fiat, to build a ski resort at Sestriere on a high pass between Turin and Briançon. The architecture, with its round-tower hotels, was very advanced in its day and the Principe di Piemonte Hotel, set like the Sleeping Beauty's palace slightly away from the village, became the smart place for Italians to congregate. Skiing, however, was never ignored, and a fine network of slopes covered the great bowl of mountains round Sestriere. Being near to Turin, the village has developed to cope with the great crowds which drive up during weekends. Large car parks and plenty of lifts near the centre help to avoid bottlenecks

After the war, it all looked the same. The train curved through snow-laden pines; the hotel porters were lined up at the station; the welcome was warmer than ever; the beds had their familiar duvets; and one's skis, after six years of neglect, were still safely stored in the *Ski-Raum*. But, although no one quite realized it at the time, a revolution was beginning. All that lovely white powder was turning into gold, and the winter sports pattern was about to change out of all recognition.

For, having started like Zermatt and Chamonix as climbing centres, or like Davos as a *Kurort* for tuberculosis, or like St Moritz as a fashionable summer watering place, the established resorts had happily, if haphazardly, grown into winter sports centres, each with its definable atmosphere and its faithful habitués who returned season after season. (Some families had been coming for four generations to the same hotel at Grindelwald, to quote one example.) In each place the routine was almost hallowed by tradition. At St Moritz, for instance, the winter season started on 18 December, and lasted until 28 February when, as if by divine ordination, those in the know packed their bags and (if they wanted to go on skiing) moved over to Zermatt, where instead of having breakfast in bed at eleven they joyfully battled for a place on 'Grannie' at half past eight. To be seen in St Moritz in March was unthinkable – and anyway Elsie would be expecting them at the Mont Cervin bar.

Right Davos today. The modern town extends for nearly three miles through Davos Platz and Davos Dorf and includes everything to keep the winter sports enthusiast happy. Above it lies the Weissfluhjoch Research Centre, where weather, and in particular avalanches, are studied to ensure the safety of skiers everywhere

Be it Adelboden at Christmas or Kitzbühel in February, the ritual was very much the same. You stayed *full pension* (or American plan) in a hotel and headed out each morning for the funicular complete with packed lunch (which, however grand the establishment, was always the same: ham sandwich, rolls, boiled egg, chocolate biscuits and an orange). Before the war, with twenty-five Swiss francs to the pound and five to the dollar, life was relatively inexpensive, and even in 1948 I can remember staying at the Palace at St Moritz for the equivalent of two pounds a day. But as prices began to rise and currency became restricted (for the English, at least) the incentive to lodge more economically grew. In après-ski fashion one usually did the rounds, and by no means all of those who made the scene in the flossy hotels were actually staying in them.

It was the Germans, come to think of it, who first hit on the idea of commuting in from the neighbouring villages – which was logical enough for anyone who had driven up by car. For a while the smart money slept cosily in some posting inn down the valley and spent its waking hours on the slopes and in the *Stüblis* like everyone else. But then, as the old post hotels were modernized and prices crept up wherever one went while pistes and cable-cars became more jam-packed than ever, the game was reversed. Instead of commuting in from outlying spots, knowledgeable folk returned to the classic resorts, but radiated outwards towards less crowded terrains for their skiing.

At St Moritz, for instance, skiing life was first centred round the Dorf and the slopes of Corviglia, but gradually people moved out to Campfer, Sils-Maria, Celerina, and even down the valley as far as La Punt and Zuoz, returning to elbow their way onto the creaky old Corviglia-bahn and Stavros Niarchos' new cable car up to Piz Nair. But once this had become too much of a good thing (especially during the week-end invasion from Zürich and Milan) dedicated downhillers made a daily migration to Diavolezza or Lagalp on the Bernina, or over the Julier to the untapped pastures of Bivio and Savognin. (Nowadays, of course, the whole of the Engadine is so well integrated that the carefully-groomed slopes above Corviglia with their non-stop network of hoists are once again as good a bet as any.)

But this was only a part of the story. The most significant development since World War II, to be sure, has been the pre-planned 'instant' community designed from scratch instead of being tacked onto existing villages or mountain resorts. The theory behind these *ex nihilo* supermarket ski paradises was to seek out a suitable chunk of mountainside and, starting with a completely empty canvas, to paint in resorts on a functional basis rather than trying to make the best of a difficult job with existing but inappropriate buildings. In Europe the prototype for these rationalized packages was Sestriere, dreamt up during the Mussolini era by Giovanni Agnelli of Fiat in the hope of bootstrapping the endemically poor mountain region west of Turin by means of tourism. Rather at the same time the indefatigable Lunn had his eye on Méribel in the French Savoie as an ideal spot to create a winter sports industry from square one.

Méribel had to wait until after the war, but in the USA Sun Valley suddenly sprouted as if by magic around 1936 in an isolated Idaho sheep pasture. In an effort, it seems, to boost the turnover of his Union Pacific Railway, W. Averell Harriman had commissioned an Austrian expert, Count Felix Schaffgotsch, to find a suitable site for a purpose-built winter sports centre. After sniffing round most of the West he finally hit on a little valley just north of Ketchum, once a mining boom-town, but which by 1936 was almost deserted. Once Schaffgotsch had skied the sun-drenched, treeless slopes against the splendid backdrop of Mount Baldy, he reported to Harriman that 'it contains more delightful features than any other place I have seen in the US, Switzerland or Austria for a winter sports centre'. Union Pacific wrote the cheques, and a few months and a few million dollars later Sun Valley emerged as America's first pre-packaged, custom-built resort, complete with an Austrian-staffed ski-school and a chair lift designed by a banana loading expert who used the same principles for transporting humans as for bunches of bananas.

In due course 'The Valley' spawned some of America's best-known racers, like Gretchen Frazer, Shirley McDonald, Grace Lindley, Barney McLean and

Ernie McCullough, but in many ways it was a generation too early. The skiing fraternity was still too limited in those pre-war days to justify the vision of Harriman, Agnelli and Lunn, and in Europe at least remained anchored to the creature comforts of Grand hotels and the spiritual satisfaction of virgin trails.

Strictly speaking, Courchevel, up in the snowy wastes of Savoie not far from Méribel, was also triggered off before the explosion of mass affluence and international addiction to snow sport had got under way. And in fact when it started in December 1947 there were just two lifts, two hotels, two instructors, and a bare twenty visitors. But since then it has proliferated into a ski megalopolis with 17,000 beds and access to 187 miles of pistes which are served by 100 ski-lifts and a corps of 150 *pisteurs* to groom almost a hundred square miles of slopes – the largest spread of runs available anywhere on a single lift ticket, indeed, with the possible exception of the Arlberg and the Engadine. Comprising four separately structured villages linked by pistes, roads, and lifts, that are designated by their altitude in metres, starting with Courchevel 1300 (which used to be the hamlet of La Praz) along with Courchevel 1550 (originally Morion) and moving up to Courchevel 1650 and 1850, this astonishing quartet was built straight from the drawing board and will ultimately form part of an even larger galaxy of computorized resorts dotted through three valleys. Funds to launch such a grandiose concept were supplied by the local Savoie authorities, the central French government, and a private consortium of investors headed by the Rothschilds (who along with their banks and their vineyards already owned a good slice of Megève).

Although building was regulated from the start by tough zoning and construction rules, the master plan provided for vast condominium blocks of flats, many of which can be rented by the week, and glittering caravanseries which include the celebrated Hotel des Célibataires for singles only. Boutiques now abound, and the sybaritic après-ski agenda includes everything from dining in gastronomic splendour at Ya-Ca off a cavalcade of courses to a transvestite show at *Comme ils disent*. From 11pm to 4am a dozen discothèques are in full swing. It is at once a planner's dream and a conservationist's nightmare. You either love it or you hate it. There's no half way.

Courchevel set a pattern that has been reproduced all over France at, for instance, Les Arcs, La Plagne, Pra Loup or Avoriaz, and in other parts of Europe such as Anzère in Switzerland and Almdorf in Austria. Vail, Keystone, Copper and Jackson Hole are the American equivalents. In the sixty mile long valley at Jackson, where French trappers named one range of mountains the Grand Tetons (which, being interpreted, means 'big breasts') and the other the 'Gros Ventre', a Californian advertising man recently founded a 25 million dollar resort called Teton village, complete with lodges, motels, hostels, shops, restaurants, condominiums and swimming pools. A cable car takes you up two

Sun Valley, Idaho, in the fifties, with the buses which shuttled skiers back and forth from village to slopes. Sun Valley was favoured by filmstars and the wealthy and was one of the very first villages to be purpose-built for skiers

and a half miles to the Rendez-Vous peak in twelve minutes flat, and there at your ski-tips, from an altitude of 10,450 feet, or slightly higher than either Piz Nair or Gornergrat, is a vertical run back of 4,000 feet, which is no skin off your nose, to be sure.

Whether these places triggered off the skiing explosion or the other way round is as debatable as the hen and the egg. But as the fifties merged into the sixties, skiing had become so much part of the pattern of winter life that isolated wayside hotels equipped, Norwegian-style, with all necessary amenities, began catering for passers-by who stopped off for a quick day's sport. In America the instant-skiing idea was developed even further. Complete resorts, as standardized as supermarkets, sprang up in the neighbourhood of New York, Chicago and Denver for the week-end skier. Centred round a huge parking lot, each had a vast, self-service 'eatery', ski-rental shops, first aid posts, and a network of parallel lifts to runs sprayed with artificial snow when nature failed to oblige. The only thing they lacked was hotel accommodation. And ambience, if you like.

All of which is a far cry from the Alpine valleys where wooden farm buildings still huddle across the road from the smart hotels and barns house cattle at the foot of the funicular. And although few of the urban skiers who become temporary residents each winter may give it a thought, the skiing explosion has brought fundamental changes to the ancient rhythms of agricultural life in those villages in Savoie, Tyrol or the Bernese Oberland that have suddenly been transmogrified into resorts.

It has meant prosperity, to be sure. The farmers have sold off plots of land for building at inflated prices, and encash fat rentals from the ski lifts for crossing their fields. Winter is no longer a dead season with little to do but feed the hens and cut wood. The young have no time for such chores any more. They are now ski instructors, lift operators, or are driving snow-cats. The girls work in tea shops and boutiques. A whole new life-style has opened up on their doorsteps. Huddling over their *Veltliner* and *Stumpen* in a smoke-filled *Stube*, the older generation seem almost strangers in their own village. And yet, come the melting of the snow, the farms must be manned once again. Can the traditional life survive? And, if village life disintegrates, will the distinctive flavour of each place be lost in a standardized pattern of banks and pizzarias?

'What we really lack is those old Alpine chalets,' sighed an American resort operator in the midst of his concrete jungle. 'We'd make a fortune if we had some weather-beaten stones.' Aesthetes may cringe at Sun Valley's neo-Tyrolean architecture, but at least it has character and, after forty years or so, has come to terms with the environment, which is more than can be said for a good many of the new places. Even at Grindelwald the village elders, peering out of Paul Steuri's cosy, low-raftered Beau-Rivage at the brassy new buildings that are springing up all along the main street, can only shake their heads and wonder. Progress and prosperity have their compensations, but raise human problems, too.

Fortunately their children have no such doubts as they wedeln down the slopes with their well-heeled pupils and wind out the night rocking in the local discos. The day brings profit and the night brings fun. Who could ask for more?

Which brings us, incidentally, to the après-ski scene.

Above 'The fair sex, when engaged in that fascinating but rather tomboyish sport of Skiing wear daringly short skirts, so as to leave themselves freedom of movement. Small hats are advised, as the larger ones are apt to get disarranged by the wind . . .' So the ladies of 1906 just managed to preserve their grace and decorum

Above Dinner at the Canadian snowshoe club in the 1890s, when Norwegian type skiing was still relatively unknown in Canada and snowshoeing and tobogganing were the most popular winter sports

Après-Ski

What's worth telling you can't possibly say, and what you can say isn't worth telling.

Anikò Badrutt

As wife of the owner of the Palace Hotel at St Moritz, she should know. After all, that's where the action reaches its rarified peak. And yet, ever since winter sports started, après-ski has been an essential part of the fun. For some people, perhaps, the main reason for going.

Extra-mural activities took up much of our Victorian forbears' time at St Moritz too, as it happens. After a skating picnic on the Silser See or a tailing party to Celerina, it was customary to repair to the 'Scotch Tea Rooms' in the centre of the village, where crumpets, scones, and tea-cakes, as well as American biscuits, were served. A bath followed as one changed for dinner (black tie or uniform and long dresses were mandatory in every self-respecting establishment) before foregathering around seven in the foyer for a brandy and soda or sherry, the ladies in armchairs and the men perched attentively on the arms or on the tables. At seven-thirty came the *table d'hôte* with anything up to 350 guests seated at long tables in carefully graduated pecking order according to rank and seniority of stay.

Be it the Grand at Les Avants, the Bear at Grindelwald, the Kursaal at Maloja, the Belvedere at Davos or the Kulm at St Moritz, each British-patronized hotel had its own self-appointed House Committee that organized entertainments, and it is not difficult to visualize the miasma of intrigue and well-bred ornery that must have surrounded these social events. A correspondent from Davos complained in a letter to the *St Moritz Post* in October 1887 of the gossip that went on, but added nevertheless: 'Here, as elsewhere we laugh, chat, dance, flirt, play cards, skate and skeleton'. And indeed more, often, than just that. The Davos Literary Society held weekly lectures at which Henry Read discoursed on 'The influence of Art in everyday life', John Addington Symonds gave a scholarly dissertation on 'Lyrics from Elizabethan Song Books', The Reverend Harford Battersby explained how the Irish had brought the Gospel to the Swiss, and M. J. Michael enlightened his audience with 'Some facts about the Inside and Outside of Insects'. The 1,070 guests listed by the Davos Kurverein in December of that year were entertained by *tableaux vivants* at the Belvedere Hotel, while their counterparts at St Moritz could participate in guest concerts or sing glees and carols at the Kulm.

Unlikely as it may seem, moreover, at a time when Wimbledon was still known chiefly for its croquet, tennis tournaments were held in mid-winter on the asphalt courts of both the Belvedere at Davos and the Kulm at St Moritz. Mixed doubles seem to have been the principal event, and tobogganers returning for midday refreshments were frequently assailed with the cry

Top The former glories die and where can you now hear the strains of music played by a live band (not pop) being wafted across as you eat your picnic?

Bottom left The late Victorian age gave people time – time to spend the winter in the Alps, providing the money was there, and time for a ten course meal as a natural way of life. Such meals today would ensure that the pistes were clear of all but the most dedicated skiers, while the majority slept off the surfeit

Bottom right Amongst those avant garde ladies who, by 1924, were happy enough to cast aside their voluminous skirts and sport the latest in knee breeches was Mrs J. N. Tollenaar

Menu

du 9. Avril 1896.

Oeufs de vanneau.

Saumon, sauce viennoise.

Jambon garni.

Dinde farcie.

Tête de veau en tortue.

Canetons rôtis.
Bécasses aux croûtons.

Crême au chocolat.

Fromage.

Fruits.

Dessert.

Top The Palace Hotel at St Moritz – a perfect setting for the high court of winter sports with its two towers and general fairy castle appearance

Bottom Formal evening dress demanded a veritable trunkload of clothes for the winter sports traveller and a fancy dress ski race would have posed few problems. Grindelwald skiers, as these were, even had a train so there was no question of walking up in this unusual garb

'Anyone for *patters*?'

Yet the highlights of the social programme were the weekly dances in the various hotels, and decorous affairs they were too. Along with the *Mount Charles* skates bought from Thornhill's in New Bond Street, a shady hat for walking and a dark serge dress, cut rather short on account of the snow, ladies were enjoined to bring evening dresses, ball dresses, and by no means to forget their fancy dresses either. Splendidly garbed as a Lady at the Court of Louis XIV, or as Joan of Arc, the Virgin Queen, a Turkish princess or a Venetian *houri*, the general's wife would lead off the proceedings with a swish and a swirl, and later preside graciously at a prize-giving for the most original get-ups. Young officers appeared as harlequins or bedouins, or simply opted out in their regimental dress uniform (unaware, perhaps, that they looked just as remarkable). But, dance card in hand whatever the guise, everyone whirled his appointed partner through Highland reels and stripped-the-willow boisterously until eleven, or, if the steam held up, until nearly midnight. On less festive evenings there would be party games and whist drives, *bezique* and backgammon, and amateur dramatics for good measure. No one could complain that there was nothing to do.

Much of this frantically organized activity lingered on in Alpine resorts until edged out by short dresses, double-breasted dinner jackets, and the Charleston. And, as skiing caught on, one cellar after another was converted into a night spot with an accordian, a pianist, or a three-man band. In due course many of the international stretch-pant brigade, making their first appearance at cocktail time, found the soft lighting in the bar a good deal more congenial than the robuster glare of sun on snow. Not so long ago Alfred Hitchcock could be seen in his favourite corner of the Palace remarking with a trace of pride that he had been coming to St Moritz off and on for thirty-five years and hadn't played any winter sports yet. 'Furthermore, I don't intend to,' he added, with faint defiance.

He was right in his way, of course. A lot of fun was to be had without ever getting any snow on the boots, and quite as much energy could be devoted to social athletics as to outdoor sports. The women of St Moritz were legendary, after all. Girls in wonderful dresses, sparkling with diamonds, their furs as crisp as the mountain air outside, shimmered cheek to cheek round the dance floor with men whose profiles were as well publicized as their names. Royalty and café society (the precursors of our Beautiful People) filled the tables of the Grill.

Small wonder, therefore, that those who thrived on competition should have invented the off-slope sport of celebrity spotting. The only equipment needed for this beguiling pastime was a score card, keen eyes, and a concentration on the passing crowd.

Scoring was ten points if you recognized a celebrity, twenty points if he greeted you first, and fifty points if he bought you a drink. It could be played in almost any of the well-known haunts. A profitable circuit around St Moritz was Hanselmann's at tea-time (rum-grogs, the Cresta crowd, and Baronesses by the window), moving on to the Carousel Bar at Suvretta House (apéritifs, a sprinkling of dinner jackets, the international set), and ending up at the Chesa Veglia (late night dancing, Italians with titles, Americans struggling with *Bündnerfleisch*). With such big names of the fifties as Greta Garbo, Joan Collins, Yul Brynner, Joan Fontaine, Lili Palmer, the Duke of Kent and Mrs Eleanor Roosevelt all reputedly taking the air in the same *Stube*, it is hardly surprising that some energetic folk scored as many as a thousand points in a hard evening's game. (In the process, of course, they collected bar chits that, laid end to end, would stretch from the Palace to Piz Nair.)

Probably the most fabulous caravanserie above snow level (and certainly the only hotel to hang a Rafael in the bridge room) the Palace gave a Leitmotiv to the après-ski scene, and schooled many a fledgling millionaire and accredited starlet in the intricacies of the high-flying spree. Ruling monarchs, industrial tycoons from the Ruhr, threadbare European nobility, oil barons and ship-owners – all the most fabulous and many of the most tedious of the *Almanach de Gotha* and the Cholly Knickerbocker set, as well as some quite ordinary people – thronged its corridors, vying to see who could spend the most with the greatest *éclat*.

Not all of them created as much of a problem to the management, admittedly, as a visiting Oriental potentate who was in the habit, as though in his own country, of driving through the village in a sleigh and pointing at the women who attracted him.

'Send me that one at six,' he would order his equerry, 'and that one after dinner.'

It needed all the diplomacy of the Badrutts to explain that (for instance) Barbara Hutton or Rita Hayworth would not appreciate such attentions.

'I do not understand,' growled the Majesty, unimpressed, 'if they want more money, give it to them.'

Possibly on account of the pace all this engendered, some of the habitués who had previously wintered in one or other of the 'big-four' Hotels (Palace, Kulm, Carlton and Suvretta House) began moving into private chalets. Stavros Niarchos, for instance, for so long the setter of the St Moritz scene, slipped into a pink, thirty-room hideaway near the Suvretta ski lift with a private cinema and a bar giving an underwater view of the swimmers in the heated pool. Count Rossi (of Martini fame) disappeared to the crest of a pine-clad hill. Others, like Charles Oppenheim (banking and real estate), continued to keep in touch with their affairs on a private teleprinter from the Palace, or like Gunter Sachs, took a long lease on one of the tower apartments, thereby giving the lie to the

Right One of the problems of stardom is that a contract may forbid you to ski. Such was the plight of Brigitte Bardot when filming in Spain in 1968. She took a break to join her husband, Gunter Sachs, in St Moritz and even if she had to play spectator he appears well booted

Far right In the heyday of the twenties, entertainment in winter resorts was a major aspect of the holiday, but Charlie Chaplin and Douglas Fairbanks, photographed in St Moritz in 1926, seem to have reached the slopes, even if they only had one ski apiece

heedless Englishman who remarked crustily that, 'The Palace is full of people who go there to look at the people who no longer stay at the Palace'.

Much of this chic and chichi was eroded when the indoor tennis court was converted into a black and velvet discothèque called the King's Club early in the sixties, which siphoned people away from the famous old pink and eau-de-Nil bar upstairs, and although this has now been revived (with a psychodelic décor of black and white frescoes) its passing marked the end of an era. Indeed, as Hans Jorg Badrutt rather sadly admits, the *belle époque* of après-ski is over and done with.

> Before, one went into the Palace bar between six and eight and everyone was there. One met up with the girl one had seen on the slopes, and one took

it from there. Now you meet the girl on the ski-lift and miss out the drinks. It's just 'Your room or mine?' to which she's likely to reply, 'If you're going to make a problem out of it, let's forget it.' Après-ski now is all up in the rooms.

Well yes, perhaps. Unabashed though these off-slope intimacies may now be, a full day in the snow leaves most skiers with little fuel for a night on the town. So nowadays there tends to be more ski than *après*. 'Nothing is organized any more,' explained Hans Scherz at the Gstaad Palace, the only place that can afford to be snooty towards St Moritz. 'There's no participation any more. That's really the major change since the war.' Yet organized or not, his well-heeled guests tend to congregate in the hall between five and seven for *patisserie*, backgammon and chat, while the night owls move downstairs to the GreenGo discothèque where breathing space is at a premium but by manipulation of some glass doors the indoor pool becomes part of the night club. With bikini-clad nymphlets and music piped in (to say nothing of the snowscape dramatically floodlit through the pool windows) it is an eyeful and an earful for the most dedicated dissipate – especially on gala nights when palm trees are imported from Hawaii and wild flowers flown in from Tahiti.

Gstaad's favourite slogan is that every guest is a king, but every king is only a guest. And certainly this jumbo-jet-set democracy seems to appeal to heads of state and their ilk. Juliana of Holland, Baudouin of Belgium, Bhounmipol of Thailand, Rainier, Bourguiba and Mobuto are among the habitués who like to relax in some pinewood-panelled chalet and exchange fondu parties with the Kennedys and Princess Soraya, or slip down to Saddredin Khan's night spot, the Cheserie. The simple chalet life is something that has to be seen to be believed. Yet some of those engaged on the private party circuit take time off to ski as well (or rather, should one say, go up the hill to the Eagle Club for lunch).

Fashions change, to be sure, but elegance is gospel to the caviar and crêpe set. 'The accent is once again on chic,' rejoiced Anikò Badrutt in February. 'Jeans are out; people are tired of them. Everyone is smarter this year.' Yet it certainly is a more relaxed form of smartness. Gentlemen are no longer required to wear ties in the Palace at Gstaad (though most of them do) and like a breath of fresh air informality has spread to Gunter Sachs's Dracula Club at the top of the bob run at St Moritz, where jaded spirits are revived by a bevy of bunnies shipped down from the ozone-filled island of Sylt. At Megève, where Parisians gather at Les Enfants Terribles in the Hotel du Mont Blanc, the walls of which were decorated years ago with murals by Jean Cocteau, the style has always been easy – almost 'camp', if you like. When the sun has gone down and the skis have been stacked, one's options for hoopla are as variegated as the Alps.

But whether your taste lies in drinking *Glühwein* at the Walliskanne in

Prince Karim, the Aga Khan, raced for Persia in the 1964 Winter Olympics at Innsbruck and, starting number 60 in the giant slalom. He finished 53rd, 26secs behind the winner, Frenchman François Bonlieu, over the 1,500 metre Axamer Lizum course. He came 59th in the downhill

Zermatt or simply waxing your skis at St Anton (or, over in the States, in rocking at Vail's Nu Gnu, the Boiler Room at Sun Valley, the Tram Bar at Snowbird or Danny's at Aspen) the message is the same. After a day in the snow, the night is for fun.

Left Sonja Henie in the 1930s. The present world-wide popularity of skating owes much to her early influence. Gold medallist at each of three Winter Olympics, 1928, 1932, and 1936, the glamorous Norwegian won ten consecutive World Championships, 1927–36, introduced the shorter skirt, and became one of the world's wealthiest women after starring in ten feature films and touring the world with lavish ice shows

Right Barbara Ann Scott, Canadian ice queen of the early post-World War II era. She was twice world champion, winning in 1947 and again in 1948, in which year she also won the Olympic gold medal

The Steel on the Ice

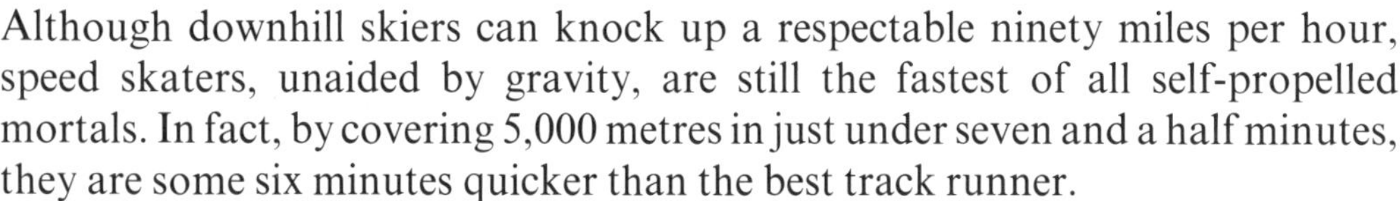

Although downhill skiers can knock up a respectable ninety miles per hour, speed skaters, unaided by gravity, are still the fastest of all self-propelled mortals. In fact, by covering 5,000 metres in just under seven and a half minutes, they are some six minutes quicker than the best track runner.

For centuries, indeed, given the right sheet of ice, they have been the fastest thing on two legs. And while the Dutch organized competitions down the frozen canals in the sixteenth century, it was the Danes who first staged what was billed as an 'artistic skating competition' 125 years ago, in which competitors, after racing backwards for a mile, were then required to negotiate a number of obstacles that had been set up on the ice.

Artistic or not, speed skating soon grew into a major sport, almost entirely dominated by the Norwegians (although Jack Shea and Irving Jaffee collected four gold medals for America at Lake Placid in the 1932 Olympics) until the Russians began to challenge their supremacy after World War II. Since racing meant anything from 500 to 10,000 metres, moreover, speed skaters had to be both sprinters and stayers to carry off the overall championship – a combination that enabled Hjalmar Andersen of Norway to win the 1,500m., the 5,000m., and the 10,000m. events in the 1952 Olympics at Oslo, and Lydia Skoblikova of Russia to collect all four gold medals at Innsbruck in 1964.

Far left Gretchen Merrill of the United States makes a spectacular stag jump while competing in the 1948 Olympics at St Moritz

Top left Peggy Fleming, of the United States, three times world figure skating champion, 1966–8, and Olympic gold medallist in 1968, seen here in action during the free skating event on her way to the Olympic gold medal. She was one of skating's most graceful performers

Bottom left The Swiss champion, Hans Gerschwiler, in practice for the Olympics of 1948. The previous year's world champion, he came second to his rival, Dick Button, in the games

Right Carol Heiss, of the United States, five times world figure skating champion, 1956–60, and Olympic gold medalist at Squaw valley in 1960

As the steel skims across the ice, to be sure, virtuosity can mean both pace and grace. The slightly sinister, batman-like shape of the speedster, bent aerodynamically forwards with hands clasped behind to conserve energy, seems to let the ice flow endlessly beneath him, whereas the artistic skater carves intricate designs around a pivotal point, or weaves, jumps and spins into a chirographed spectacle. When the Scandinavians organized the Northern Games at Stockholm in 1901, both speed and figure skating were included in the repertoire. Axel Paulsen, the first great Norwegian skater (who developed the jump that still bears his name), was expert at both, and dominated the scene. But as specialization set in over the next two decades, artistic skating began to embrace an ever increasing range of figure and free movements, fuelled to some extent by the success of a Berlin ice-ballet company that staged an operetta on ice called *Flirting at St Moritz* and whose skilful pair-skating packed the New York Hippodrome for over a year.

Bernard Ford and Diane Towler, best of a long line of British ice dancers who won the world title four times, 1966–9, seen during an exhibition in 1967

Yet for all this professional *éclat*, the higher echelons of amateur skating remained curiously hidebound; and international competitions were of little more than academic interest until suddenly, at the 1924 Olympics, a rather plump little girl burst on to the scene. She was only eleven, but her childish swagger and brilliant smile brought a new dimension to women's skating. In artistry and interpretation alike, Sonja Henie was to revolutionize the sport.

Until this point it had been constricted by the classic 'school' figures and a demurely contrived 'poetry of movement' convention that in fact was little more than variations of the standard turns, linked with simple stunts. Now, planning her programme like a ballet (which she had studied) in which jumps and spins flowed naturally from rockers and counters, Sonja Henie blended both power and art into a dazzling sequence of brilliantly executed figures. And what is more, discarding the old ankle-length dresses and wide hats, she sported unhampering mini-skirts and a heart-warming smile.

From a child wonder, this blonde little Norwegian girl became the superstar of the ice – a household name that splashed skating onto the headlines, and inspired a whole generation to follow her lead. For a decade she won every title in sight. She was World Champion for ten years running, and took three Olympic gold medals.

Yet when, with a neat sense of timing, she turned professional after her Olympic victory in 1936 to launch her extremely successful ice shows (Sonja had a good head for business, and her only great extravagance, it seems, was a fondness for telephoning friends all over the world), another young prodigy was already challenging her supremacy. Two thousand spectators had crowded round the rink at Garmisch-Partenkirchen to see whether a fifteen-year-old English girl could dethrone the legendary Sonja. She didn't, but it was touch and go. However the stage was now free for Cecilia Colledge and her equally

Left Oleg Protopopov and Ljudmila Belousova of the USSR in practice at Davos for the World Figure Skating Championships of 1966. They held on to the title which they had first won in 1965 and were to retain until 1969 when they lost to Irina Rodnina and Alexsei Ulanov, also of the Soviet Union

Right Alex Gorshkov and Ljudmila Pakhomova, of the USSR, winners of the first Olympic ice dance championship, at Innsbruck in 1976. The same year they won their sixth world title at Gothenburg

brilliant rivals, Megan Taylor and Daphne Walker, to tussle for the honours. Once again, the British school was on top.

For under the impetus of Sonja Henie, skating had caught on and covered rinks had opened at London and at places like Brighton. Competition was growing and skaters were being scientifically trained – with the emphasis on technique rather than artistry. To qualify for the coveted British silver and gold medals, it was necessary to perform with machine-like precision. In the last years before World War II, the British girls, along with London-trained Hans Gerschwiler, were virtually unbeatable. But their meticulous movements had more elegance than charm.

After the war these faultlessly groomed performances were quickly overshadowed by the exhilarating verve of the new North American school. Sonja Henie had shown what skating should be. Now Barbara Ann Scott of Canada and Gretchen Merrill of Boston, each in her own special way, gave a dazzling new look to the art of free skating. Poised and fairy-like, Barbara Ann had a delicate charm; more ethereal and dramatic, Gretchen brought a glamour to the ice that has rarely been matched. And among the men, Hans Gerschwiler's intricate steps were surpassed by the athletic gyrations of Dick Button and his 'barrier' high jumps, who for five years dominated the rinks with an ever more spectacular repertoire of leaps and spins, speed and dash, culminating it all with the first real *triple* loop jump in the 1952 Winter Olympics. Before finally turning professional, this outstanding performer won five World Championships, two Olympic crowns, and seven successive American titles.

He was succeeded by the perhaps more artistic though rather less athletic

Hayes Alan Jenkins, and subsequently the Canadian, Donald Jackson. What each of them made clear was the importance of elevation. The higher the jump, the more scope to rotate. For a while it became something of a craze, both among the men and the women. (Gretchen Merrill once leapt clean over my MG TC, its windscreen flat, on the Olympic stadium at St Moritz.) But the scene was also enlivened by the fire and daring, if you like, of Jacqueline du Bief, the French champion, as she battled against the classic competence of England's Jeanette Altwegg, who took the gold medal at Oslo in 1952 and was probably the finest school skater of the past three decades. (Mlle du Bief, in contrast, once suggested that school figures hurt a skater's performance.) Next came the delicious Tenley Albright, who sturdily executed ooh!-provoking feats, and Carol Heiss, also from the States, who at nineteen already held four world titles, having scored an unbelievable hat-trick of sixes (that is, the maximum possible score), and David Jenkins of America, the first to pull off a triple *Axel* jump.

In 1911 Lily Kronberger of Hungary had brought her own military band to the Viennese championships, and now forty years later everyone began adapting his performance to specially chosen music. Rhythmic, ballroom-style dancing was given a place in international competitions in 1952 and for the first nine years was held by British pairs until Pavel Roman and Eva Romanova of Czechoslovakia broke what had become (rather surprisingly, really) an English monopoly. It differed from pair skating, as Courtney Jones once remarked, by the fact that both feet never left the ice at the same time, whereas lifts, spins, spirals and spreads were all part of the increasing sophistication of free skating *à deux*, which could also include *shadow skating* – a difficult technique where both partners perform the same steps, jumps and spins in unison although separated from each other.

At the other end of the skating spectrum, ice-hockey – the fastest of all team games, and perhaps also the oldest, certainly on ice – has a double-pronged ancestry. Bandy, also known as shinney or shinty, no doubt began simply with

Left Charles Jewtraw of the United States winning the 500 metres sprint in the first Winter Olympic Games at Chamonix in 1924

Above Eight years later, in the first Winter Olympics at Lake Placid, Americans were once again among the winners in speed skating events. In the picture is John Shea, in training for his victories in the 500 metres and the 1,500 metres

Right Ard Schenk, of Holland, possibly the greatest ice speed skater of all time. Three times world champion, 1970–72, he became on the final occasion the first to win over four distances. He won three gold medals in the 1972 Sapporo Olympics and during his career set fourteen world records at distances ranging from 1,000 to 10,000 metres

Left The Canadians beat the Russians in the championship match at the 1924 Olympics at Chamonix

Right Emotions rise high as Russia scores the winning goal against the Czechs at the 1976 Winter Olympics. The padded gear and crash helmets contrast strongly with the almost casual clothes worn by the 1924 teams

boys knocking a 'cat' about a frozen surface with bent sticks. In the last century, played on ice like hockey but to association football rules, it seems to have been popular all over Europe. Quite independently, though, the Canadians were developing their own version of ice-hockey, using a puck that slid instead of a ball that rolled. Rules were drawn up; and the first club founded at McGill University in 1893. Introduced into England at about the same time by visiting students, and given a fillip by the Prince of Wales and the Duke of York (later Edward VII and George V) who turned out for a match on the lake at Buckingham Palace, the Canadian game soon supplanted the indigenous bandy (which is still played in Scandinavia, however). The International Ice-Hockey Federation was founded in 1908, and two years later Great Britain won the first European championships at Les Avants in Switzerland.

Nevertheless they were not in the same league as the Canadians, who won every match from the start of the World Championships in 1920 until World War II, except in 1933 when the USA triumphed and the British achieved a sensational form upset by beating them 2–1 in the 1936 Winter Games at Garmisch. Oxford University certainly fielded one of the strongest teams of all in those pre-war years (but as I remember, they were mostly Canadians in dark blue colours). So decisive, indeed, was the Canadian supremacy that in the 1924 Olympics the Toronto Nationals, sporting the red maple emblem, dismissed Czechoslovakia, Switzerland and Sweden in quick succession, scoring 110 goals without the loss of a single one themselves.

Since World War II the game has caught on all around the globe, and today more than twenty nations participate in the World Championships each year. Canadian supremacy was never seriously challenged until the Russians gave them a shock in 1956, and now these two superpowers of the ice seem to share the honours fairly evenly in the yearly tussles.

CCCP
CCCP

Left John Curry of Great Britain, whose unique style won him the Olympic figure skating title at Innsbruck in 1976. He went on to win the world crown at Gothenburg three weeks later. Adding a new dimension of balletic grace, he included triple jumps and elegant spins without disturbing the artistic continuity of his exceptional performance

Top right A fierce tussle as the USA struggles against Canada during the 1967 Ice Hockey World Championships at Vienna. The Canadians came third in the World Championships that year, the Russians winning the crown

Bottom right Speed skating at the Winter Olympics at Innsbruck in 1976 took place against a magnificent mountain backdrop. In the picture is Ewa Malewika of Poland. Sheila Young of the United States took the gold in the 500 metres event and also won the silver medal in the 1,500 metres

Left Annemarie Proell of Austria won the World Cup five times in succession before her retirement in 1976. Here she is competing at Oberstaufen in 1972. Her speciality was downhill, for which her tall strong figure and her bravery were particularly well suited

Right The great Jean-Claude Killy competing in a World Cup downhill race. He pioneered a new ski technique of sitting back on the heels and keeping the points of the skis clear from the snow

Overleaf Ski marathons still have some of the atmosphere of the thirteenth-century race over the mountains when the king of Norway's infant son was carried away from danger by his faithful troops. The competitors in this 1970 Engadine marathon swarm along in a colourful mixture of ages, sizes, and speeds

Competitive Skiing 1947-75

evian

Hardly, then, had the dust and debris of war had time to settle in Europe than the exiles returned to their haunts (rather gingerly, perhaps, because the victors were short of foreign currency, and the others were still in some disarray) and the Arlberg-Kandahar was run again at Mürren in January 1947. But competition skiing really got back into its stride with the first post-war Olympics that were held the following year at St Moritz, which had hosted the Games two decades previously. By now, the Alpine Combination had emerged as the most popular event, even if, mystifyingly enough, it only happened on paper. (Competitors' times in the Downhill and Slalom were converted into points, and the winner was the one with the best aggregate performance.) It was won by Henri Oreiller of France, although Edi Reinalter sprang a surprise by capturing a gold medal in the Slalom, while James Couttet took the silver in the same event. Hedy Schlunegger got a second gold for Switzerland in the Ladies' Downhill, and the Americans notched up their first Olympic skiing success when Gretchen Frazer won the Ladies' Slalom by half a second. 'It's just a swell dream,' she told Arnold Lunn when he congratulated her, 'Don't pinch me, or I'll wake.'

The Nordic Combination, in which a racer competes in both cross-country and jumping events, was won in 1964 by Tormod Knutsen of Norway. The long thin skis used for cross-country skiing are very light and the soft running boots are attached only at the toes

Yet dream or not, the Games showed that skiing was healthier than ever, especially as professional instructors were now allowed to compete. In 1950 the World Championships were held for the first time in the States, at Aspen, where Zeno Colo of Italy won both the Downhill and the Giant Slalom, and the Austrians dominated the ladies' department. (The Nordic events were scheduled to take place at Lake Placid, which hardly lived up to its agreeable name, by all accounts, when because of a lack of snow, the langlauf had to be switched to Romford in Maine.) And then, at long last in 1952, the Olympics were staged at the birthplace of skiing. The great Holmenkollen jump was rebuilt in their honour on the famous hill overlooking Oslo, just above the slopes of Huseby where Sondre Norheim had cleared 18 metres eighty-four years back and the earliest military competition had taken place a century before that. Between 100,000 and 150,000 people watched Arnfinn Bergmann soar to victory down the 140 foot high jump and saw the local favourites walk off as usual with all the cross-country titles (save the 50 km. race, won by Finland's Veikko Hakulinen.) But perhaps more significantly still, they were able to cheer Stein Eriksen as he brilliantly triumphed in the least Nordic of all events, the Giant Slalom, which replaced the Alpine Combination. Stein really poured it on, to the delight of all Norwegians, and from this moment the breach between the two main skiing disciplines was finally healed. For the first time, too, the Games were covered by international television. Skiing was coming of age, to be sure.

Stein Eriksen went on to repeat his triumph at Are in Sweden during the 1954 World Championships, winning everything in sight except the Downhill (which went to Christian Pravda of Austria). Following this, the Austrians came

Russia, with a tradition for rugged women, has always dominated the cross-country events. In the 10 kilometre event at Seefeld, during the 1976 Olympics, it was Raisa Smetanina who won the gold medal

conclusively back into the picture when Toni Sailer of Kitzbühel took three gold medals in the 1956 Olympics at Cortina and then proved beyond doubt at Badgastein in 1958 that he was the greatest Alpine skier of his time.

For the record, the World Ski Championships are held every two years and the Olympics every four, but in Olympic years, as it happens, the Games serve as the Championships. Apart from this, there are the classic races such as Austria's Hahnenkamm at Kitzbühel, Switzerland's Lauberhorn at Wengen, the French Grand Prix de Megève, and the venerable Arlberg-Kandahar, still the senior downhill-slalom competition which, stemming from the old Roberts of Kandahar race, has been held every year since 1928. (At first the A-K was run alternately at Mürren and St Anton, but as a protest against the Nazi Anschluss and the arrest of Hannes Schneider by the Gestapo it was held at Chamonix in 1938. Now jointly organized by Britain and the four Alpine nations, it is staged in rotation at Mürren, St Anton, Chamonix and Sestriere.) As proven events down the most challenging pistes in the Alps, these classics are a real test of the skier's mettle. And, needless to say, the events produced the men. Indeed the story of skiing since 1950 is very largely the story of its stars.

Of the four great skiers who initiated this technical age – Henri Oreiller of France, Zeno Colo of Italy, Christian Pravda of Austria and Stein Eriksen of Norway – the blond Norwegian, predictably known as 'Viking', was surely the most outstanding. A practised acrobat, he could leap from one edge of his skis to the other, which gave him an astonishing speed and precision round corners. Eleven years his junior, Toni Sailer, who was born and brought up in Kitzbühel and began skiing almost before he could walk, won his first race when he was eleven and beat Christian Pravda, one of Austria's all-time greats, in a giant slalom when he was still only fifteen. For three years Toni was the junior champion, and then in 1955 he not only set up a new downhill record at Cortina, but also won the Lauberhorn and the Combined at Megève.

During the run up to the Olympics the following year, the dark-haired young Austrian won everything in sight, including the Lauberhorn again and the Hahnenkamm above his home village. In the Games themselves he first came down the Giant Slalom 6·2 sec faster than the next man, and then won the Slalom from Japan's Chiharu Igaya by a full 4 secs. Finally in the Downhill over the two mile long Falornia course, which was so treacherously iced that all but 17 of the 75 starters came to grief, he romped home 3·5 secs ahead of Switzerland's Raymond Fellay, thereby becoming the first Alpine skier ever to win three Olympic gold medals in the same year, and by an astonishingly big margin, too.

Toni Sailer added three more world titles to his total before the FIS, laughable though it may now seem, disqualified him from competition because, in their view, he had violated amateur rules by acting in some skiing films.

Left Gustavo Thoeni of Italy has had a long string of successes in the World Cup. He has specialized in the giant slalom, an event which demands strength and endurance from the racer. He is also consistent in slalom, which demands acrobatic agility and quick reactions, and in downhill, for which speed and bravery are the chief requisites

Right Heini Hemmi was the surprise winner of the men's giant slalom in the 1976 Olympics. The small Swiss builder mastered the long steep icy second course with a tremendous burst of speed

Today, at forty, skiing's first superstar has a hotel at Kitzbühel and presides over the local ski club as well as coaching the Austrian team.

If Sailer's story was that of a copy-book success, his contemporary 'Bud' Werner (both were born in 1936) had a rough ride to the top – which, at least on results, he never quite reached. Yet no one can doubt that Bud Werner was one of the really great skiers. Through sheer guts and a win-or-crash attitude, he became the first American to hold his own against the best that Europe could produce, and an idol throughout the USA. 'There are only two places in a race,' he once remarked, 'first and last. I only want one of them.' At seventeen, he won the Downhill at Oslo – the first major men's event to be carried off by a transatlantic skier – and during twelve seasons of racing scored on plenty of other occasions. In 1958, for instance, he beat Toni Sailer himself by a stunning 5·2 secs in the Slalom at Wengen, and took the Lauberhorn Combined title. But somehow or other he all too frequently literally burned himself out of the scenery. Everything happened to Bud. The Austrians called him *der Pechvogel* ('tar-bird', or 'hard-luck kid' if you like). Only too well I remember the weekend in April 1964 when he was filming at St Moritz. A whole bunch of them, bronzed and laughing, were up at Corviglia when I emerged from the funicular. It was a fabulously warm day and everyone hitched on to the meat-hook up to Tres Fluors.

We took different runs down so I didn't see it happen. But from what I heard afterwards an avalanche broke, and Bud Werner and Barbi Henneberger, the German Olympic skier, schussed down ahead of it. Skiers of their calibre could have beaten any avalanche; but as luck would have it, they collided, and the snow mass engulfed them. *Pechvogel.* The Austrians, alas, were only too right.

5

Trouble of a different kind hit Karl Schranz, who succeeded Toni Sailer as Austria's champion and the world's top skier. In seventeen years of racing this prodigy from St Anton won just about everything going – the A-K eight times, the Lauberhorn four times, and the Hahnenkamm three times. And indeed more, much more. Early years of poverty had left him with an abrasive obsession to succeed. Sponsored by the Kneissl ski firm he notched up more victories than any skier had ever done before. Yet one thing eluded him: an Olympic gold medal. He should, perhaps, have taken top place on the podium at Grenoble in 1968 after he thought he had won, but was disqualified instead. And he certainly should never have been singled out for banishment from the Games at Sapporo in 1972 by the tetchy octogenerian head of the Olympic committee.

France, like Austria, has produced many champions – one has only to think of Guy Périllat, Charles Bozon, Michel Arpin, Gaston Perrot and Leo Lacroix, to name but a few – but only one Killy (whose name, it would seem, stems from Kelly forbears in Ireland). Brought up in Val d'Isère by parents who gave him every encouragement, Jean-Claude won a gold *chamois* medal when he was eight and was soon spotted by the French talent squad. By 1965 he was already up near the top, and in 1966 he really got into his stride with wins at Adelboden, Hahnenkamm, Megève and Chamonix, a diamond 'A-K' badge, and an overall win in the FIS championships at Portillo in Chile. But his superstar status began in 1967 when he made a grand slam of the major races, winning nine classics in a row to walk off with the first World Cup. The following year he secured three gold medals in the Olympics at Grenoble and a second World Cup. So much better was he than the others that it was almost a joke. And so, having nothing more to win, he retired at the age of twenty-four – only to stage a come-back four years later, more for the fun of it than anything else, when once again, racing against the pros, he showed that he was still the best skier in the world.

The only one he didn't totally eclipse was Nancy Greene of Canada. But then she was a woman – the most consistent woman racer in the business, even if the world and Olympic titles eluded her. In 1967 she won the World Cup by rather less than the flicker of an eyelid (or, more precisely, seven hundredths of a second) from Marielle Goitschel and, like Killy, captured it again in 1968.

And yet who could doubt that Marielle Goitschel was the most sensational woman skier since the war? Plenty of lady champions had made their mark, to be sure. Italian girls like Celina Seghi, Giuliana Minuzzo and Carla Marchelli all had moments of glory. Erika Mahringer, Dagmar Rom, Traudl Hecher and Christl Haas had mounted the podium for Austria; Andy Mead and Jean Saubert had done likewise for America. Madeleine Berthod had won a gold medal for Switzerland in 1956, and France had been well served by Lucienne Couttet-Schmitt, Thérèse Leduc and Annie Famose among others. But Marielle, so ably seconded by her sister Christine, notched up such a string of

Top The 1952 Winter Olympics were held at Oslo. The men's downhill was open at the top and very fast down a narrow cutting for the rest of the way. Zeno Colo of Italy won, beating competitors from twenty-six other countries

Bottom In the same games, a crowd of 25,000 spectators assembled to watch the men's slalom in the hope of seeing the Norwegian hero, Stein Eriksen, win. Perhaps the expectations overwhelmed him for although acknowledged as the world's greatest slalomer he only managed to take second place. Happily, however, he won the giant slalom in superb style

Overleaf Her long dark hair tucked into her helmet, Fabienne Serrat of France shows bravery and mastery of technique as she tackles the downhill at Val d'Isère in 1974. The Criterium de la Première Neige, held in the French resort each December, is the opening event of the ski-racing season. Racers come together after a summer of fitness and glacier training and the results are scanned as pointers to the rest of the season

victories in Europe, America and even Australia that for a few amazing years the women's events became almost a family affair.

These, then, were the superstars – the top performers in a pack (or a circus, if you prefer) that competed in every Olympic and classic race. But as skiing escalated during the sixties into a mass sport with a television audience of millions, which made it a potential gold mine for equipment manufacturers and consumer market advertising, it became obvious that there had to be a focal point. The big money was moving into skiing and, like football, motor racing or tennis, the individual results had to be linked and work up to a climax.

The World Cup (as distinct from the World Championships) was conceived during the summer races at Portillo in 1966. Sponsored by the Evian mineral water firm, the French paper *l'Equipe* and *Ski Magazine* of America, it was intended to define the year's champion men and women skiers by a system of points similar to the world championship for racing drivers. In certain designated races (13 in 1975) the placings in the slalom, giant slalom and downhill were attributed points (25 for first place, 20 for second, 15 for third, and so on) and the competitor with the highest total for any three events at the end of the series was awarded the World Cup.

What it boiled down to, in fact, was that whereas the Olympics and the World Championships were peak prestige awards in which racers were crowned (or went uncrowned) on the basis of a single race every couple of years, the World Cup was awarded to the best overall skiers, based on a whole season's performance.

When the first World Cup meeting was inaugurated at Berchtesgaden on 5 January 1967, the *Salzburger Nachrichten* wrote:

> What Christian Pravda, Stein Eriksen, Othmar Schneider and later Anderl Molterer and Toni Sailer dreamt of in their days was a competition based on the results of the most important winter races. Today it has happened . . .

Unquestionably in so doing it turned skiing into big business. For manufacturers like Head, Rossignol or Kneissl skis, Lange boots or Salomon bindings, it was the ideal platform for advertising campaigns aimed at the burgeoning ski markets all over the world. For resorts where the races were held the intercontinental television coverage gave unimagined opportunities to publicize their amenities. As in the case of other sports before, the media moved in so massively that the egregious gilt shadow of Madison Avenue hovered over every piste.

In the skiing climate of the late sixties, this was perhaps inevitable. But what it all too surely meant was that participants were no longer really engaged in a sport. World Cup racing was a deadly serious, beady-eyed affair with the extraordinary new billion dollar ski industry turnover as its target.

Competitors in the 'White Circus' were groomed and pampered by their sponsors regardless of cost. They were trailed by plane-loads of equipment and dozens of specialized aides. Like their counterparts in golf, tennis and motor racing, they found themselves earning six-figure incomes. Some people began to wonder whether skiing was not being dehumanized by all this. In the pre-war Olympics, after all, only one pair of skis had been allowed for both downhill and slalom, and it was stamped by the scrutineers beforehand. Now racers had computors to advise them precisely what type of equipment to use at any given moment. Peter Kasper, for one, feels that things have got out of hand when nine million Swiss francs are spent on the Alpine ski races as they were in 1974. 'The World Cup ruined everything' he will tell you flatly. With so much money being committed to a handful of top stars, he is concerned whether there will be enough left to support the broader skiing structure.

Yet as an amiable change from such hard-nosed professionalism, and a hark-back, if you like, to the old amateur days of Mürren in the twenties, there have recently sprung up a series of events such as the 'Chamois' in France and Ski NASTAR in the States, in which the average skier can show his paces. Also dreamt up some eight years ago by *Ski Magazine*, NASTAR (which is short for National Standard Race) was devised to enable any skier who wished to match his performance against the best exponents in the country of the same age-group on a handicap basis, rather like with a golf handicap, in fact. How it works is that top pros and racers from the major American ski resorts are invited to a pace-setters' race at the beginning of each winter. The winner becomes the national pace-setter with a zero handicap, and the regional pace-setters have their ratings adjusted by the percentage that they are slower than him. All other competitors receive a score based on the percentage that they, in their turn, are slower than their local pace-setter's corrected rating. This is then computorized on a national basis, and any skier who enters and gets a handicap can judge his skill against people of his own age throughout the country. Participants, indeed, range from beginners to ex-champions. In 1974 they included three-year-old Christina Locker at Bryce Mountain and eighty-seven-year-old Joe Ross, who won a silver medal for his performance at Vail. The National Championships take place at the end of the season when some eighty of the lowest-handicapped men and women are invited to somewhere like Sun Valley and unleashed against each other. Mayhem may ensure, but if nothing else it is a very good party.

Even as downhill skiing became a mass consumer sport, what is more, increasing numbers of enthusiasts began rediscovering the joys of langlauf. In Scandinavia, of course, skiing in the Nordic fashion is part of everyday life, like taking a sauna or fishing or sailing. When a Norwegian returns from work at four o'clock on a winter evening, he puts on his skis and 'goes for a walk', which

Top left William Kidd of the United States on his way to a silver medal in the Olympic slalom of 1964. Two other Americans, James Huega and Bud Werner, came third and eighth. Kidd was the first American to win an Olympic skiing medal

Middle left Karl Schranz, who won almost as many fans for his handsome face as for his skiing, competing in the Arlberg-Kandahar, which he won both in 1969 and in 1970

Bottom left Toni Sailer, the Austrian hero, after winning all three gold medals in the Winter Olympics at Cortina in 1956. The Kitzbühel boy started as favourite and won every race by a comfortable margin

Above Piero Gros of Italy speeds down the treacherous icy slopes at Axamer Lizum to win the 1976 men's Olympic slalom in a combined time of 2mins 03.29secs. Another Italian, Gustavo Thoeni, took the silver and Willy Frommelt of Liechtenstein came third

may mean anything up to ten or twenty miles through the floodlit trails of Frognersetten. Cross-country skiing is deeply rooted in the life style of Finns, Norwegians and Swedes, who still tend to regard downhill skiing (or slalom, as they always call it) as something of a Sunday afternoon pastime.

Right from the earliest days when the Nordic championships were staged on Huseby Hill, and competitors, after jumping, were required to dash up the cross-country track that led back to the top and then jump again (the winner being whoever had the best style and got round quickest), cross-country and jumping have been linked together – somewhat incongruously, since quite different skills are called for, and a good cross-country runner is not necessarily a good jumper. But it made for becoming an all-rounder, if nothing else. The first to shine at this particular combination in the early Olympics were Thorlief Haug and Johan Gröttumsbraaten and between 1924 and 1936 the Norwegians captured the Nordic Combination every time, taking first, second and third places on each occasion. Since World War II, however, other nations have moved into the game. The Russian women, in particular, began to chalk up successes from 1954 onwards, while at Sapporo in 1972 an East German won the combined, a Pole and a Japanese the jumping, and the Russians took the 30 km. cross-country as well as the three women's events.

For all this, the Scandinavians have never really lost their grip on what is, after all, a Viking pursuit. Martin Lündstrom and Nils Karlsson of Sweden dominated the Nordic events just after the war, and Veikko Hakulinen of Finland leapt into prominence in the 1952 Olympics at Oslo and again at Cortina in 1956. But for nearly a decade the man to beat over a distance of fifty kilometres was always Sixten Jernberg of Sweden.

Even remoter from downhill boogying is the Scandinavian idea of linking cross-country skiing with rifle shooting. The Biathlon, as this curious mixture of opposites is called, was first included in the winter Olympic programme at Squaw Valley in 1960.

Usually held over a twenty kilometre course, the competitor is required to fire a total of twenty rifle shots at targets on four ranges set up at roughly equal intervals along the way, unslinging his rifle, loading and falling flat on the snow in double quick time without undoing his skis. As a test of marksmanship, the distance of each range is different, varying between 100 and 250 metres, and any shot off-target incurs a two-minute penalty. To get a good grouping in bad visibility and when out of breath needs considerable control, to be sure.

Perhaps predictably, the Russians now seem to do best at this militaristic pastime, which many Alpine skiers have hardly even heard of. And, come to think of it, most of them would probably agree that to 'maintain a balance between reality and glory' (as Free-styler Bob Theobald would say), one might just as well opt for hot-dogging.

Top left A colourful start to the 4 × 10kms relay race in at Seefeld in the 1976 Winter Olympics. As usual, the serious competition lay between the various Nordic countries and the Russians. On this occasion Finland took the gold medal, Norway came second, and the USSR third

Bottom left Biathlon requires a competitor to ski across country, stopping at four ranges to fire a total of twenty rifle shots. In the individual event time is added for each missed target; in the relay the racer must run a penalty lap for missing a shot. Sometimes aim is taken standing, sometimes kneeling, and sometimes lying flat. At each range the biathlete must control his racing heart and panting lungs and steady his aim. Finns and Russians dominate this rather military event

Right It is said that from the 90 metre jump at Innsbruck you look down first on the cemetary, then on the church, and finally on the red light district – an encouragement to jump far!

Left This Swiss University Ski Club member is trying out a monoski. Both feet are attached to the platform on a single ski. No chance of snowploughing here

Right Television brings money to sport but demands spectacle. Hot-dogging provides colour, excitement, speed, and sometimes beauty of movement. The sideways backscratch demonstrated here is one of the basic jumps

The Scene Today

Left Today's boots and bindings are models of complexity. Here a test is being made on a long screw, which allows the upper part of the boot to be adjusted. The forward lean and high back help to keep a racer in the best position for speed but can also cripple the holiday skier. Happily manufacturers of ski equipment have recently been developing boots and bindings in different ways so that the two-week-a-year skier can benefit from light, simple and cheaper equipment, while the racer continues to get maximum support and control

Below and right Ski-flying is a heart-stopping spectacle. The skier takes off from the top of a cliff like a great bat. On thermals he can float for miles, pulling on the harness to control the direction of his deltawing. This must be the ultimate in air transport

It's an attitude of harmony, of living and environment. You are breaking away from the rules ... You are rebelling against skiing on the ground.
Scott Brooksbank, as quoted by *Ski*.

Top One variety of ski-flying. You attach yourself by harness to a pair of glider wings, ski fast downhill, and take to the thermals. Beginners can learn at the end of a leading rein which brings them back to earth (usually with a bump) if they float too high. The expert here is taking off from Villars to fly down to the Rhone valley

Bottom The earliest form of ski-bob – a simple snowcycle. This one is still used today at Grindelwald in the Bernese Oberland. The rider does not wear the little skis which help the sporting ski-bobber to brake and control his cycle

For those with a nostalgic turn of mind, the good old days were always best. And some sports, to be sure, had an easy, swashbuckling touch that has been lost in our computorized, egalitarian world. But up in the snowfields, it's the other way round. New equipment, well-groomed slopes, and a proliferating catalogue of runs have brought skiing to a new level of sophistication and enjoyment. Even a moderate performer can now pack in more downhill running between breakfast and tea-time than would have been possible in a week a little while back. Perhaps because of this, people are skiing better than ever before. Good tuition, improved skis and bindings that give greater control and cut down the risks have enabled expert and recreational skier alike to nip down the slopes both faster and further. All of which leads to the conclusion that the golden age of skiing was not in the past: it's right now.

For, come to think of it, when a whole new generation began taking to the pistes after World War II (many with army surplus stock skis and any clothing that came to hand) skis were still hewed out of hickory or ash. Use of laminates was the first move away from the clumsy one-piece hickories, and around the middle of the fifties experiments began with fibreglass and metal skis. To begin with there was a good deal of distortion and breakage, but in due course top skiers began to switch to the French-made Allais and the Austrian Kastle metal skis. The break-through came in 1964 when an Olympic race was won on aluminium skis with plastic bottoms and steel edges made by Head of America. Lighter and easier to maneuver, Head Standards soon became the Chevvy of the slopes (and the skis to pinch, if you didn't look out). And not long afterwards, sophisticated plastic-laminated skis, which were found to have the best characteristics of both wood and metal, began to appear in a bewildering range of psychodelic colours.

Until twenty years ago, moreover, the main aim of bindings was to lock boot and ski and to prevent any danger of the boards coming off unintentionally. Such 'bear-trap' devices accentuated the likelihood of injury as speeds increased and pistes became overcrowded. Recently, however, release bindings with precisely calibrated mechanisms that sustain vibrations and shock, yet respond to the thrust from any direction when the skier falls, have been developed, offering a high degree of protection to ankles and legs from the agonizing twist that so inevitably ends in a plaster cast.

Footwear, too, has changed out of all recognition since the days when people skied in ordinary everyday boots, and Arnold Lunn could write that part of the routine was to remove them and rub one's frozen feet in the snow to revive

circulation. Today, leather has virtually been replaced by plastic, and boots comprise a fibreglass shell with soft malleable plasticine-like material inside that adjusts itself to the wearer's feet, or a foam-injection interior moulded to the right fit. As often as not they have canted soles and a built-in forward lean, while some, catering to the new jet-turn vogue, feature calf-supporting 'spoilers' that come almost up to the knee.

Exhilarating, too, has been the change in ski clothes. For years, in Henry Ford's old dictum, you could choose any colour you liked so long as it was black. Erna Steuri, the Swiss champion in the thirties, remembers that she wanted to have a change. To help, her tailor took some white material and dyed it red, an eccentricity (she believes) that started the fashion for brightly coloured wear. Pants, moreover, were then so baggy that, after she had lost a race by fractions of a second, an Austrian came up, shaking his head, and asked: *'Mädel, warum tragst du solch weite Hosen?'* (Why do you wear such wide trousers?) The first move towards today's streamlined look were the stretch pants of the fifties, but now, following the lead of the racers and the hot-doggers, the slopes have erupted with every fluorescent hue in the colour spectrum – glistening purple and orange snake-tight racing suits, shining blue and yellow gloves, baby-blue knee pads, red and white checkered outfits that

Top left and right Hot-dogging at the European Championships at Bayerische Zell – a competitor turns a backwards somersault

Bottom left Either you like ski-bob or you hate it. Easier to control than skis, for the rider has four points of contact with the ground, it is popular with older and more timid beginners. But it can go very fast, too. Those who hate it say it can damage the spine and that a lot of uncontrolled riders mixed with skiers can be dangerous. Some resorts ban ski-bobs, others welcome them, and some even build special ski-bob pistes

might be something out of a pack of playing cards or the Siena *Palio* (you name it, it's there) – all looking stupendous against the white of the snow. No other sport, come to think of it, can offer anything like such a range of sartorial options.

Yet if the skiing scene is excitingly in tune with our nuclear age, part at least is a reaction against what anthropologists call the 'changed molecular structure of society', meaning (in this context) not only the flow of wealth to the commodity rich, but the mass explosion of the skiing population. Indeed with an estimated twenty-seven million skiers in five continents spending a global figure of something approaching five billion dollars a year, some sort of reaction was bound to appear. Sparked off in the States around 1962 by Stein Eriksen flying off the jump at Aspen with his arms stretched out and then going up and over, and by the sight of Art Furrer doing javelin turns and charlestoning down the hill, an astonishing form of free style skiing broke out among exuberant young Americans. Hot-dogging was, if you like, an offshoot of the pop and drug scene, yet whatever one may say it involved the skill and courage to turn over in the air on skis, and to do figure tricks through the moguls or on the flats. Three distinct forms of this craze soon emerged, in the shape of free style skiing, aerial acrobatics, and ballet. Some of these stunts were gymnastic gimmicks, to be sure, or just a mind-boggling way of letting off steam. When boogying down through the bumps, for instance, free stylers deliberately crossed their skis and rolled defiantly over as if they were hurling themselves through the Hawaiian surf, or flipped aerial cartwheels off a jump in a dazzling display of high-diving on skis. Unlike such body-bruising contortions, however, ballet (which was mostly inspired from figure skating) meant stringing royal christies, 360 degree turns, outriggers and cross-overs together with grace, fluidity, and a certain discipline, too. 'In free skiing you can feel it happen,' rhapsodized John Clendenin, winner of the US National Freestyle competition both in 1972 and 1974:

> It's a rushed feeling, very elating. You're right on top of it. In aerials you cross your heart and hope that everything goes smoothly. My favourite, though, is ballet. It's unique, creative. You can actually go out and do something that has never been done before.

Predictably too, while some played the new game for kicks (and later for cash) others invested these tribal rights with a sort of mystical vision, like learning Aikido from a Japanese master. And, as can happen with a far out cult that has its own dress (polychromatic racing suits) and its own special argot ('zapping into the kicker' for instance, meaning to go fast on to the jump, and 'taking it to the bridge' meaning going flat out), it eventually led to the ultimate desire to broaden the boundaries of what could be done and, like Icarus so

On the eve of the 1976 Olympic downhill one ski manufacturer decided to cash in on the publicity pouring out of Innsbruck by announcing a new 'miracle' ski. The holes in the front tip were said to let the air through and save the racer half-a-second per minute. Franz Klammer gave the new idea his approval – but did not use the skis when he won the downhill the next day

Overleaf Look up a worn piste and you will see a quilted pattern covering the steeper slopes. Moguls, taking their name from the Viennese dialect for little humps, are cut by turning skis. Recently, shorter skis have changed the shape of moguls, making them difficult to negotiate for those who prefer their skis longer than head-high

many centuries before, to fly as freely as the birds in the sky.

Ski flying had hitherto meant soaring off a jump for a hundred yards or so. But now, hitching himself to a kite-like device, an American named Mike Harker took off from Germany's highest peak and, followed by television cameras, glided for twelve minutes down towards the woods of Irewald, thereby giving European audiences their first glimpse of what became known as 'Delta', or kite skiing. Roger Staub, the veteran Swiss champion who had triumphed down the Giant Slalom in the 1960 Olympics, spelled out the dangers of winging on skis. 'If you make a mistake, you will fall like a stone,' he said in a television interview, 'Equally if you make no mistakes at all but a gust of wind crops up, you can crash just the same.' Ten days later, Staub was dead. A tiny turbulence had upended his Delta, and he plummeted helplessly down. And yet, for all the manifest hazards, no less than twenty schools now teach it in Europe, and Delta kites, plus a week's free instruction, are currently on sale in Germany at 1,993 DM a time. Indeed, when skiing at St Moritz this year, I spotted two pupils from Mike Harker's school at Schuls take off from Piz Nair and drift gracefully down to the lake below.

At the other end of the scale, of course, those who like everything about skiing except the expense, the crowds, the risk (and going downhill too, perhaps) have turned back to the oldest form of Nordic trekking. It is no longer just the Scandinavians who, dressed in light knicker breeches and knee stockings, slog rhythmically along the trails or glide contentedly through the snowscape. Nor just the old folk, for young skiers are as keen as their elders. Cross-country skiing has caught on so fast, in fact, that whereas five years ago Sport Scheck of Munich opened a langlauf course with three teachers and thirty pupils, they now have thirty teachers and over five hundred devotees under training. The French, likewise, have taken up *ski de fond* with such gusto that instructors nod knowingly and explain that if you have spent years zooming through nature, the time comes to see what you've been missing. Cross-country skiers may still be in the minority, but every February plane loads of them head for the 53 mile Vasaloppet in Sweden, the longest international marathon of the lot, and no less than ten thousand entrants, including men in their seventies and eighties (but no children, for whom it is considered too strenuous) compete each year in the Engadine race from Maloja to S-Chanf.

Probably, of course, the recondite, well-heeled skier will say that the ultimate that the sport can offer is at places in the Rockies such as Bugaboos, Monashees and Kariboos which can only be reached by helicopter and where incredible snowfields offer powder, wind crust and spring snow all on the same day. Yet for ordinary mortals there can still be little in the world to touch the delicious chill-thrill exhilaration of just zipping down a well-groomed hillside. Fashions change and you may wave your arms wildly about or bob your head or carve jet

The popularity of cross-country skiing has exploded all over the world. Those in favour say it keeps you fit, takes you away from crowded pistes into quiet woods, involves no ski-lift tickets and is unlikely to leave you with a broken leg. The Scandinavian word for trail – *liope* – can now be heard all over the Alps

turns 'sitting backwards' as if in an armchair, but when you finally christie to a stop and look back at the whole scintillating scene – the sun glistening on the snow, the blue sky above white-capped mountains, the interweaving pattern of trim brightly coloured figures turning, schussing, tumbling, and standing in groups laughing, your heart must surely soar. For, when all is aid and done, it's quite simply the greatest fun sport ever invented.

Resort Maps

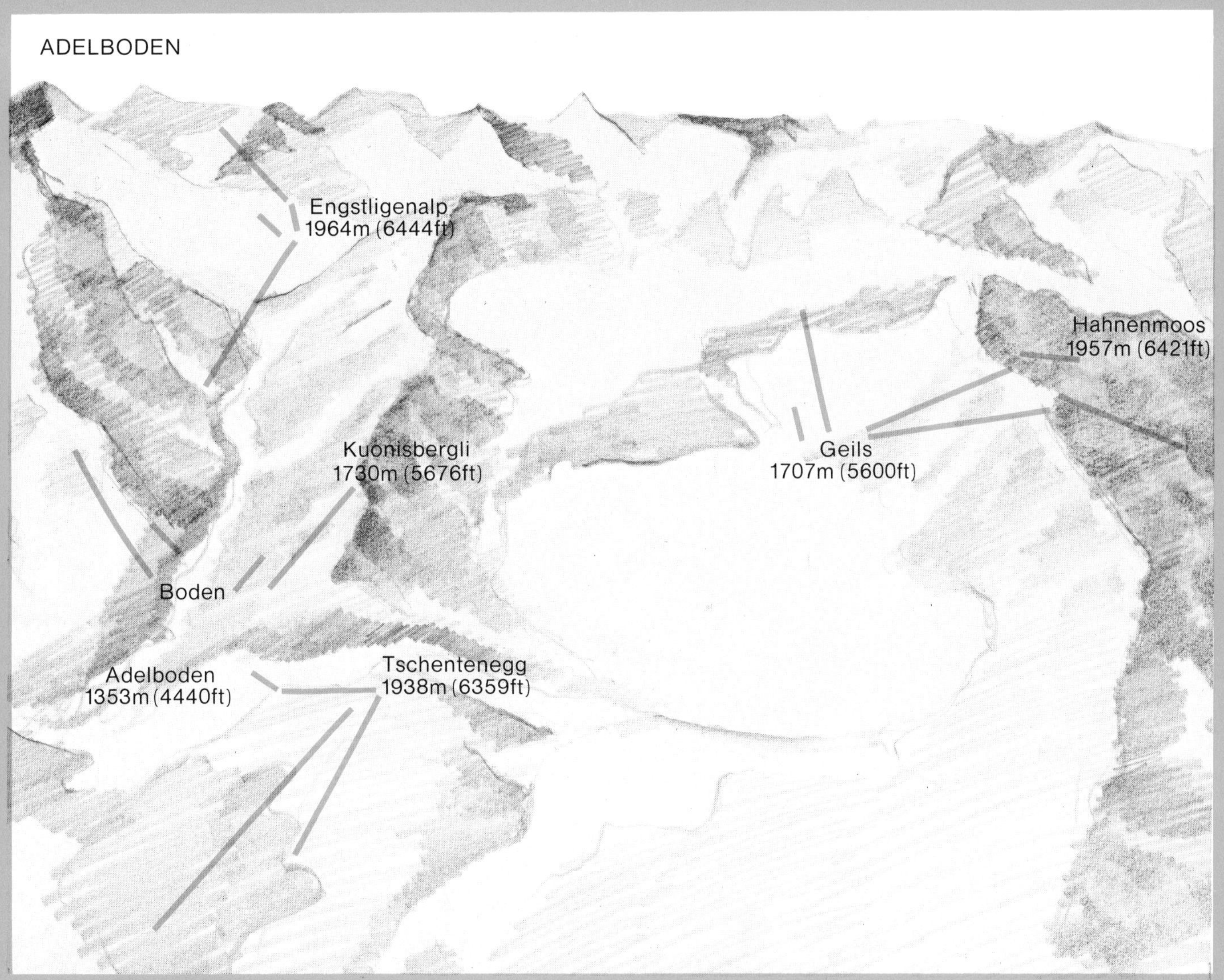

Adelboden, Switzerland
It was Dr Fred Rubi who built up the ski race reputation of Adelboden when he became *Kurdirektor*. There are excellent giant slalom courses on the Kuonisbergli and Schwandfeldspitze and it is here that World Cup giant slalom races are held each year.

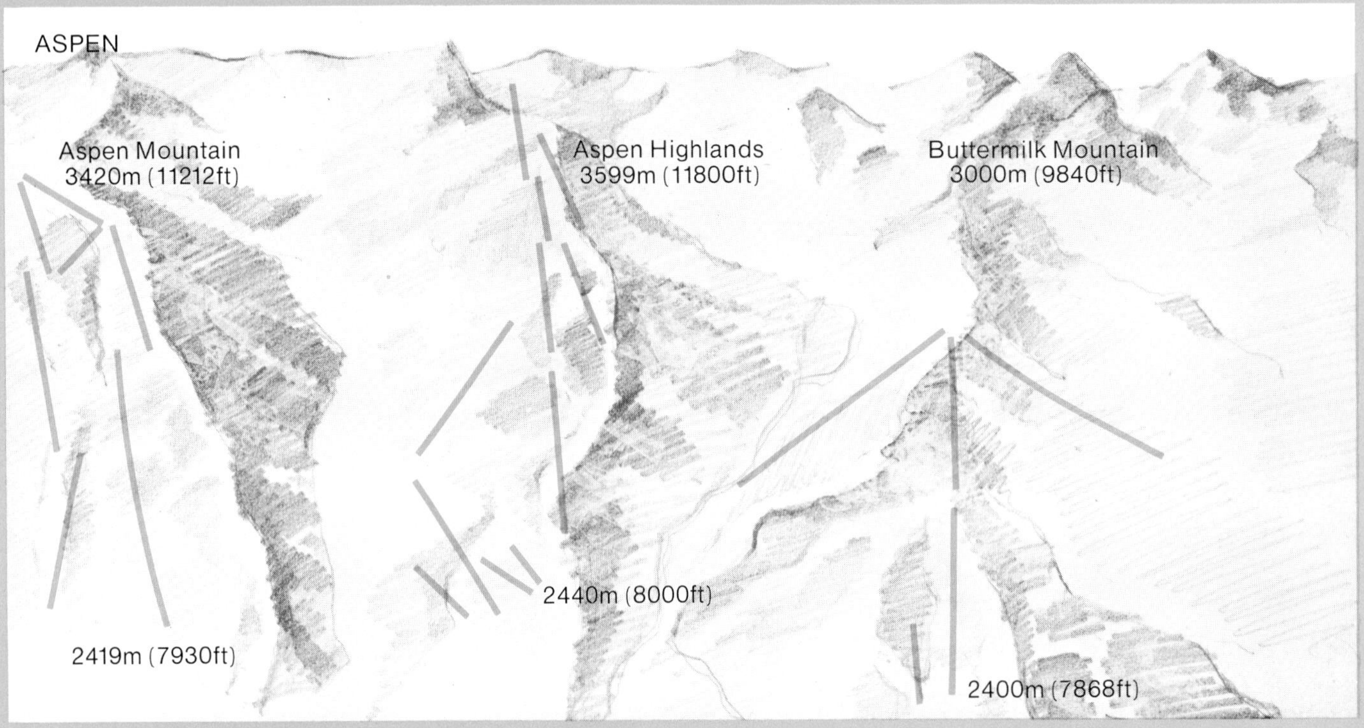

ASPEN
Aspen Mountain
3420m (11212ft)
Aspen Highlands
3599m (11800ft)
Buttermilk Mountain
3000m (9840ft)
2440m (8000ft)
2419m (7930ft)
2400m (7868ft)

BERCHTESGADEN
Jenner
1874m (6148ft)
Königssee Dorf
Berchtesgaden

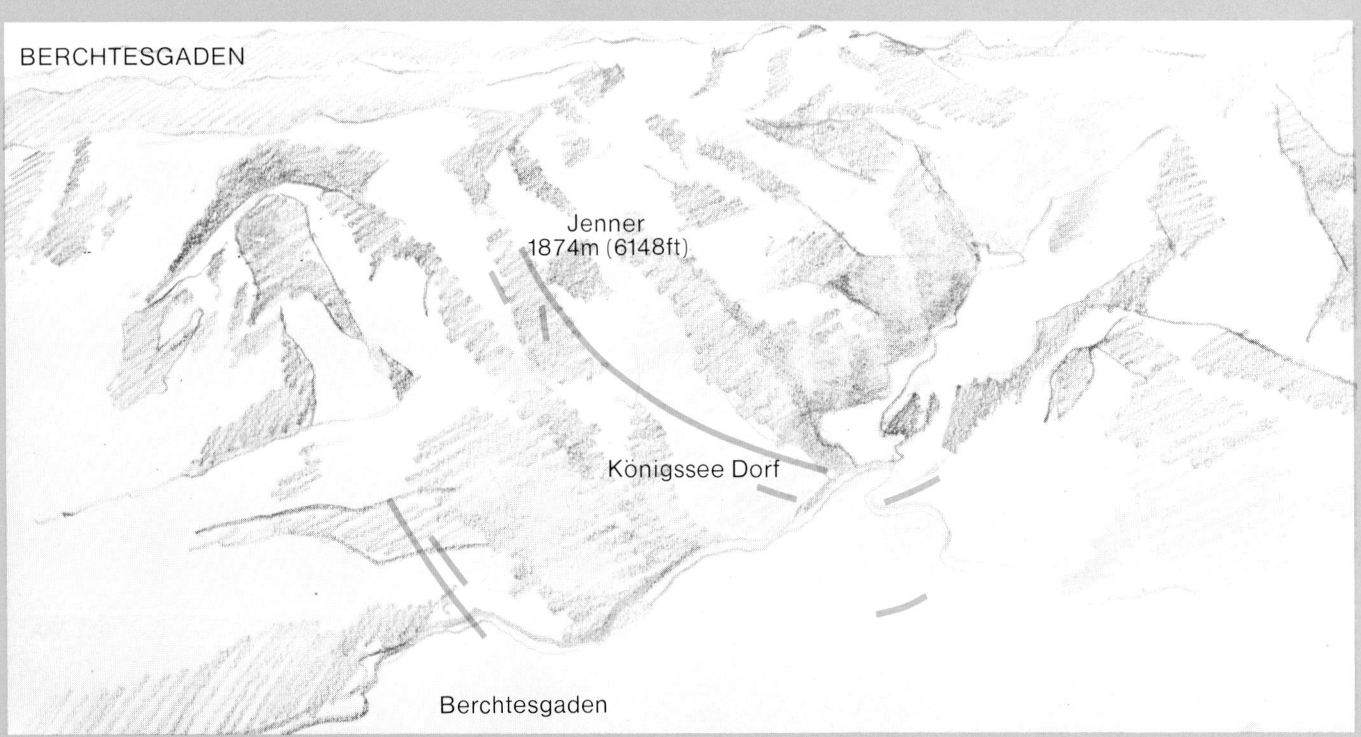

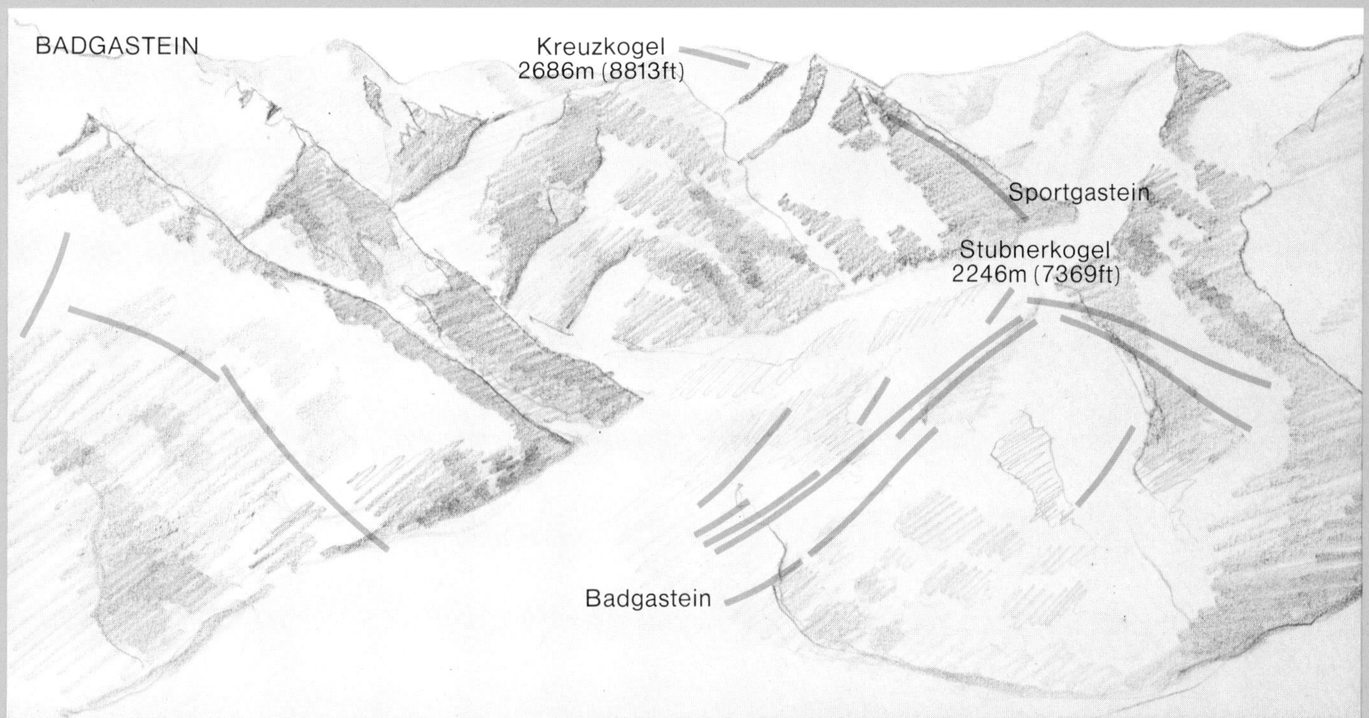

Aspen, Colorado, USA
An old silver-mining town, Aspen boasts no fewer than three main ski areas – Aspen Mountain, Aspen Highlands and Buttermilk. Snowmass, too, is only six miles down the road. The Roch Cup is held here in March and the event includes downhill and slalom for men, as well as downhill and giant slalom for women, all being World Cup events.

Berchtesgaden
Berchtesgaden is in a corner of Germany surrounded by Austria – it lies between Saalbach and Salzburg. The first World Cup Slalom was held here in 1967 and slaloms and giant slaloms are run regularly on the Jenner, the Gold Pokal being a regular World Cup event.

Badgastein, Austria
An Edwardian spa town, Badgastein has excellent slopes and the ski facilities have recently been expanded by the development of Sportgastein. Silver Jug races for women alternate with a similar race at Schruns as World Cup events.

Chamonix, France *see overleaf*
Starting as a base for climbers, Chamonix was one of the first villages to develop its steep slopes for skiing. In 1938 it became a home for the Arlberg-Kandahar (joining St Anton and Mürren). The race organization is well experienced and the Arlberg-Kandahar continues to be run there. Chamonix was host to the World Championships in 1937 and 1962. In recent years it has joined with Megève and St Gervais to offer a week of World Cup racing to both men and women.

CHAMONIX
Mont Blanc
4807m (15772ft)
Aig. du Midi
3842m (12606ft)
Les Grands Montets
3275m (10745ft)

Chamonix
1035m (3396ft)

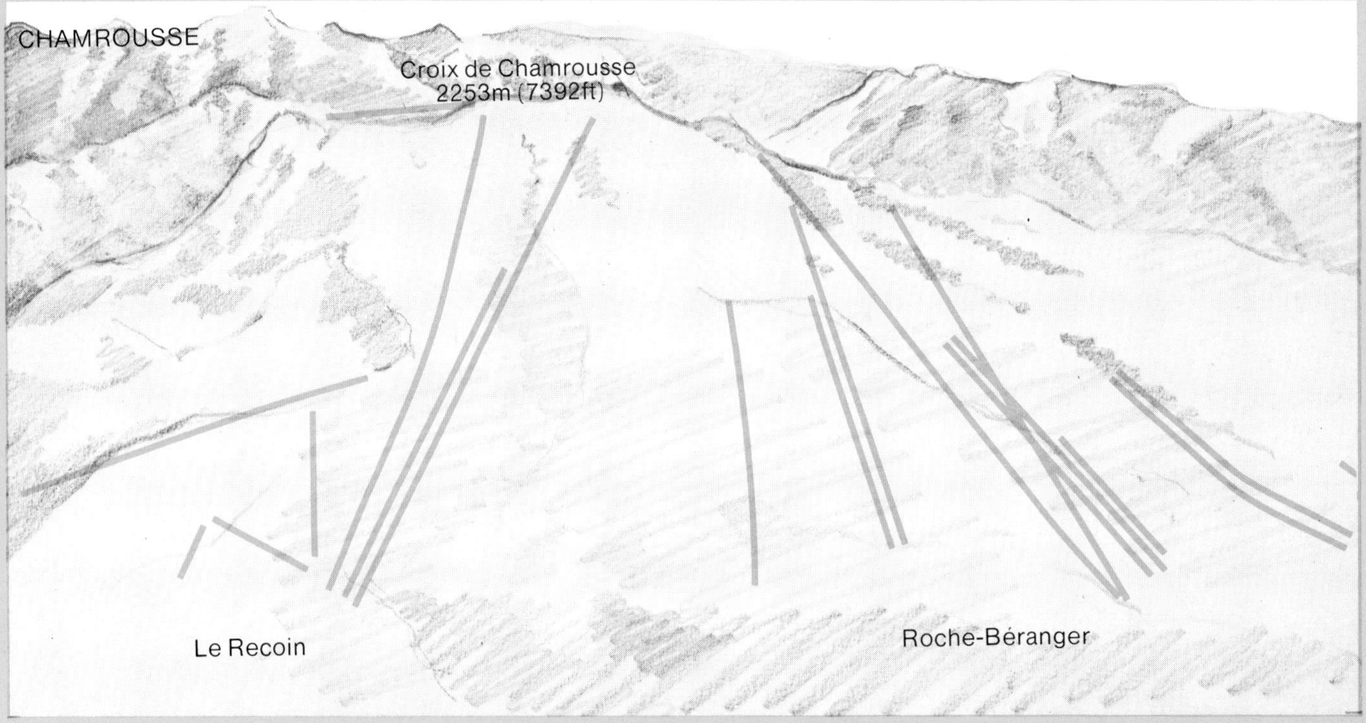
CHAMROUSSE
Croix de Chamrousse
2253m (7392ft)
Le Recoin
Roche-Béranger

CORTINA
Tofana
3243m (10640ft)
Cristallo
3216m (10552ft)
Cortina d'Ampezzo
1224m (4016ft)

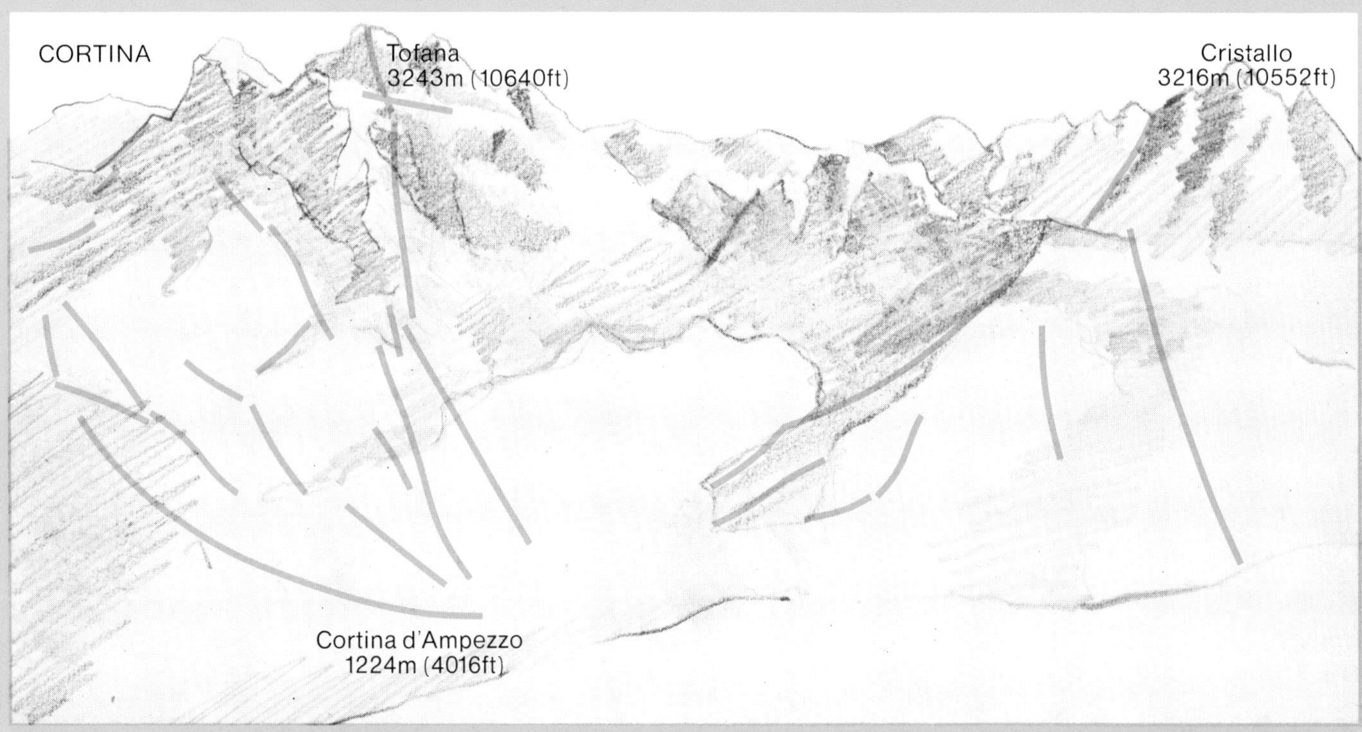

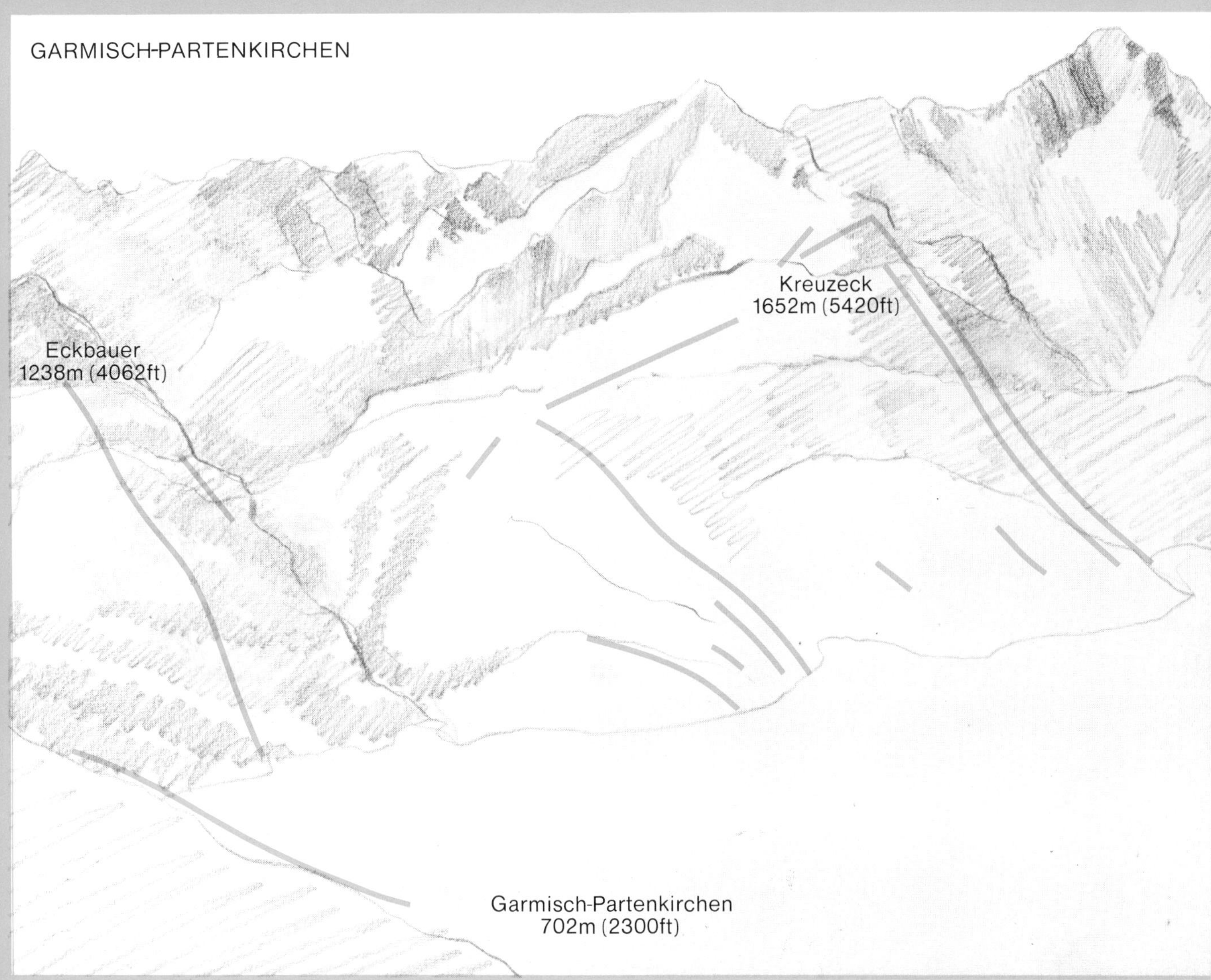

Chamrousse, France
The downhill events in the 1968 Olympic Games were held here. Chamrousse is divided into two parts – Le Recoin and Roche-Béranger. The area is also noteworthy for its good cross-country skiing, particularly on the Arselle plains and the surrounding forests.

Cortina, Italy
Cortina in the Dolomites organized the World Championships in 1932. At the Winter Olympics there in 1956 Toni Sailer took gold medals in the three skiing events and made the world realize that a local boy by winning races would bring thousands to ski on his home slopes and to imitate his style.

Garmisch-Partenkirchen, Germany
Twin valley towns surrounded by high mountains, Garmisch-Partenkirchen became an Arlberg-Kandahar centre soon after the end of the Second World War. The Olympics there in 1936 were marred by the first amateur-professional dispute – over the inclusion of ski teachers in the races. Garmisch-Partenkirchen will host the World Championships of 1978 in the Alpine events.

GROUSE MOUNTAIN
Grouse Mountain

INNSBRUCK
Patscherkofel
2247m (7372ft)
Birgitzkopfl
2098m (6884ft)
Axamer Lizum
Fulpmes
Innsbruck

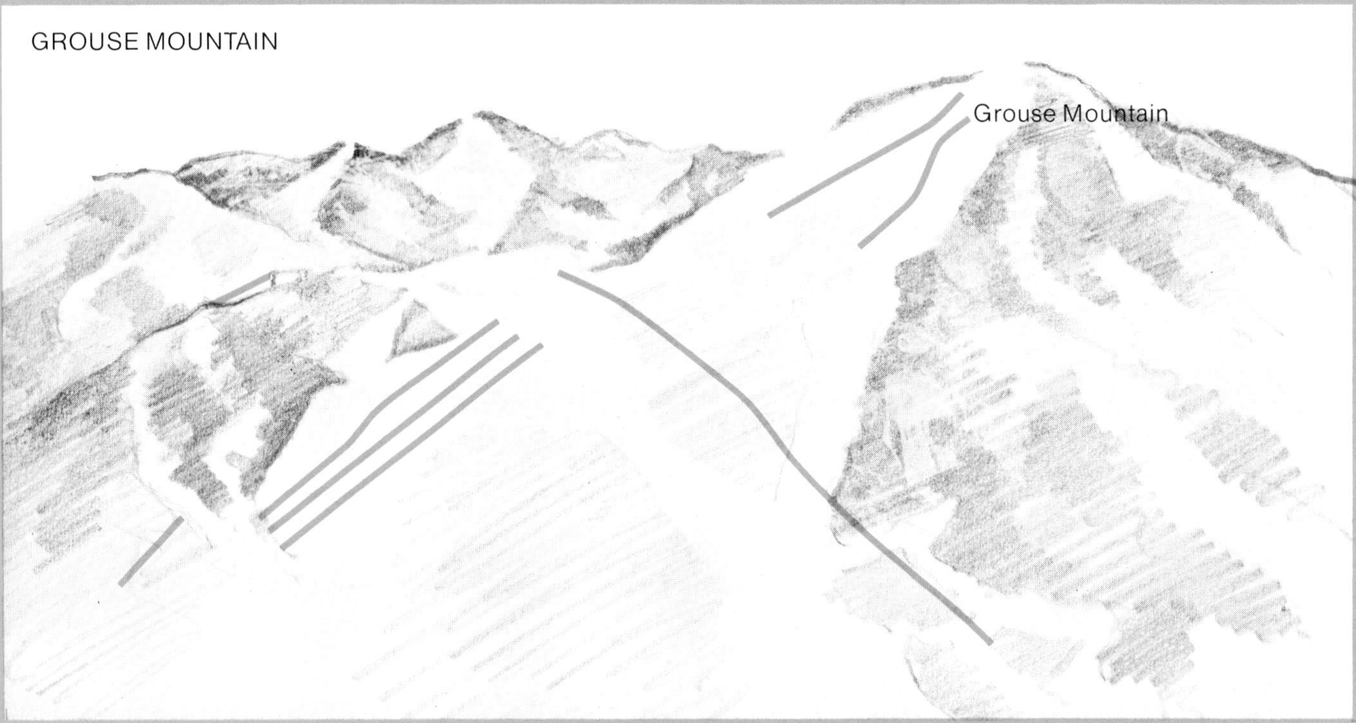

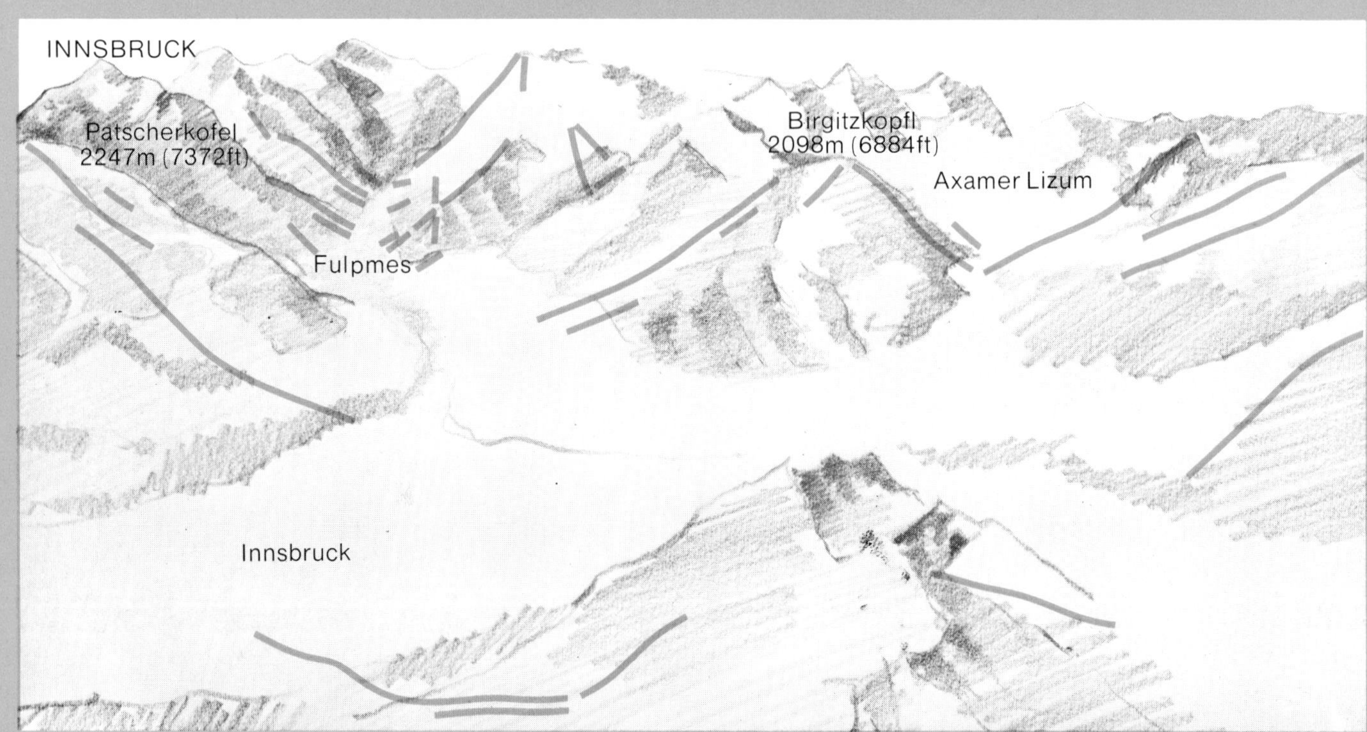

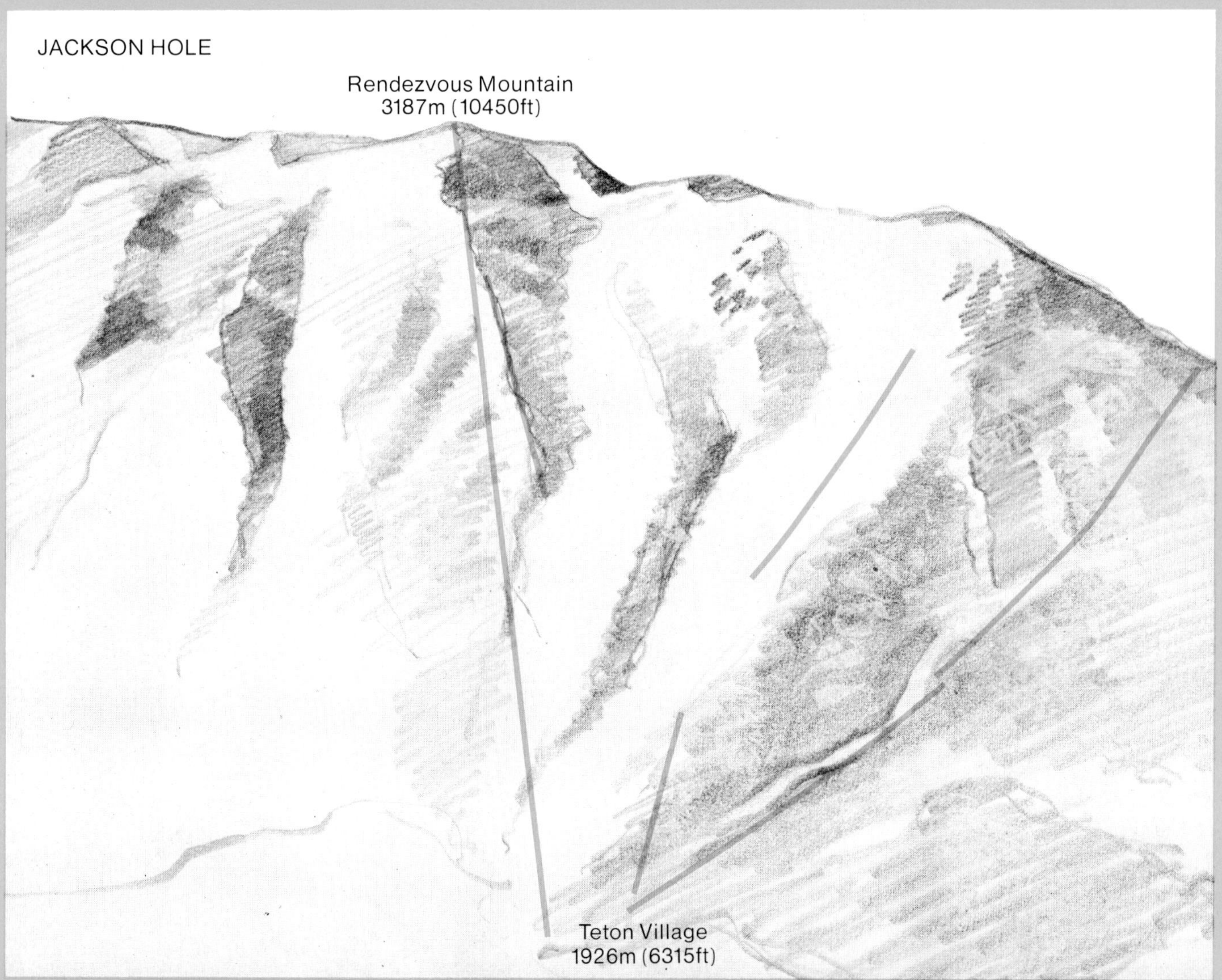

Grouse Mountain, B.C., Canada
Only fifteen minutes from the heart of Vancouver, Grouse Mountain is served by a 5,400ft (1,647m) cablecar. Like Garibaldi, also in British Columbia, it has been the venue of World Cup races.

Innsbruck, Austria
The small town is circled by winter sports resorts with good lifts rising out of the town itself. It is no wonder that Innsbruck was chosen for the Olympics in 1964 and again in 1976. In 1964 there was a shortage of snow and the army had to bring in truckloads and spread them across the pistes.

Jackson Hole, Wyoming, USA
A hole was where the trappers used to come down in winter and Jackson Village retains a great deal of the old atmosphere of the Wild West. It has great modern facilities, however, with a spectacular 2.4 mile (3.9km) aerial 'tram' and a vertical drop of 1,261m (4,135ft), giving an exciting World Cup course.

Jungfrau, Switzerland *see overleaf*
The Jungfrau region of Switzerland comprises three major resorts: Mürren, where Sir Arnold Lunn set the first modern slalom on the nursery slopes back in 1923, and where the Arlberg-Kandahar was held for many years; Wengen, home of the famous Lauberhorn race; and Grindelwald, where the Swiss girls founded the Schweizerische Damen Ski Club in 1932, and the SDS race has been the major annual event ever since.

JUNGFRAU region
Eiger
3970m (13026ft)
Oberjoch
2468m (8098ft)
Grindelwald
1034m (3393ft)
Axalp

Jungfraujoch
3454m (11333ft)
Schilthorn
2971m (9748ft)
Lauberhorn
2472m (8111ft)
Mürren
1634m (5361ft)
Wengen
1276m (4187ft)
Lauterbrunnen
796m (2612ft)
Interlaken

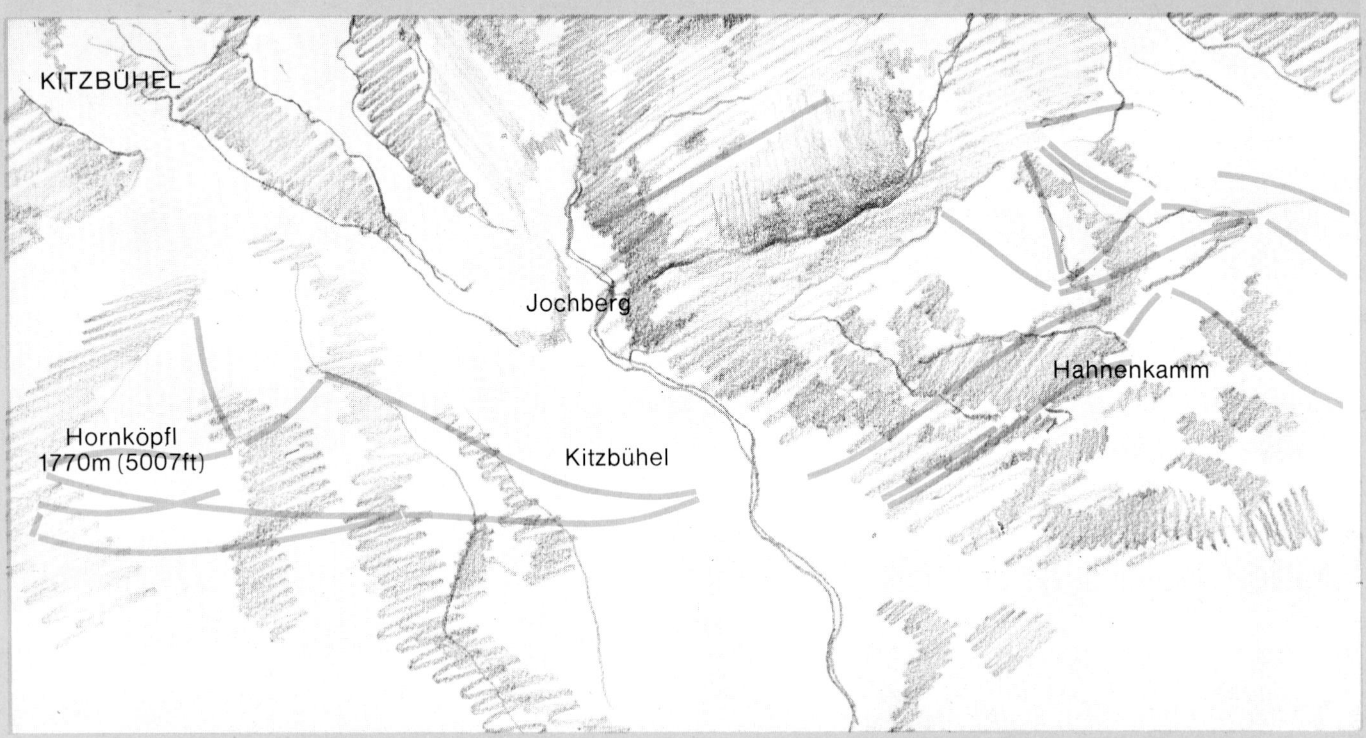

KITZBÜHEL
Jochberg
Hahnenkamm
Hornköpfl
1770m (5007ft)
Kitzbühel

KRANJSKA GORA
Vitranc
1565m (5135ft)
825m (2707ft)
Kranjska Gora

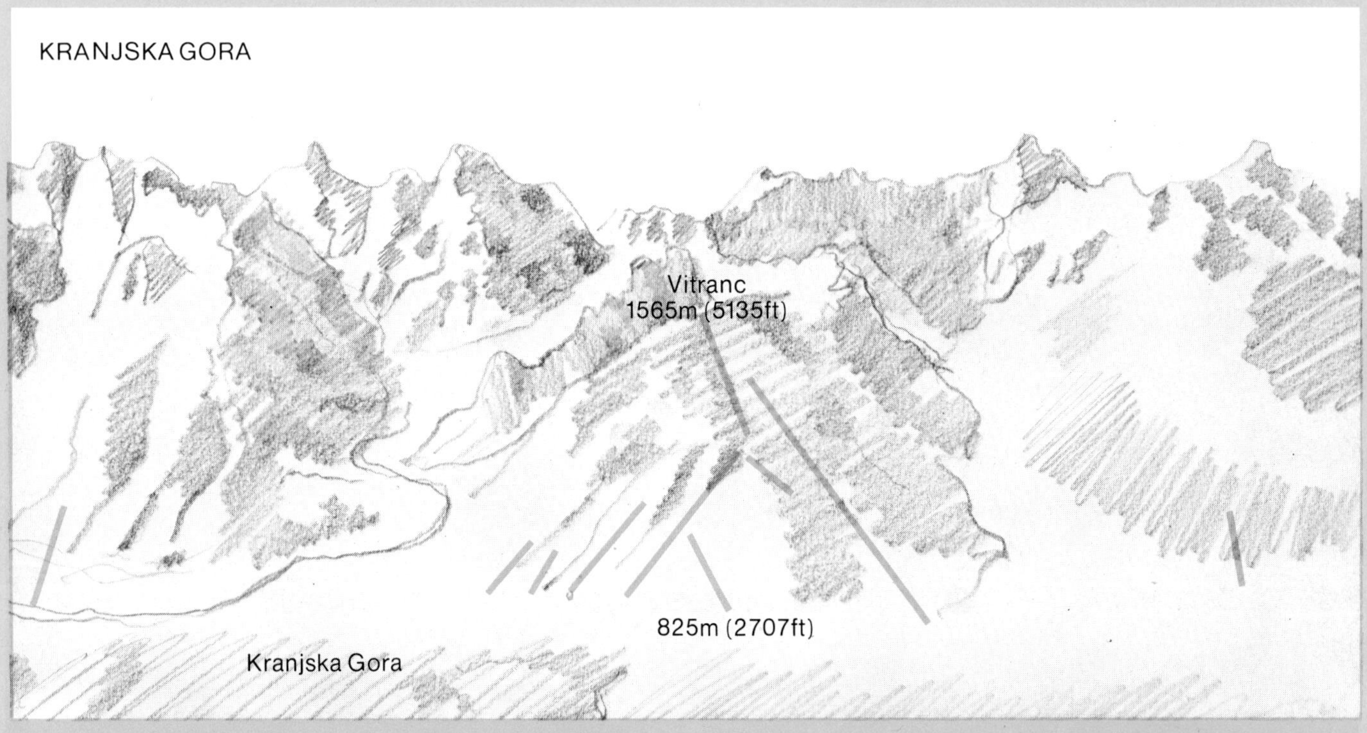

Kitzbühel, Austria
The Hahnenkamm is one of the classic men's downhill races which has been assimilated into the World Cup calendar. The course down the Streif always produces an exciting event. In 1975 Franz Klammer, in spite of a leg bruised in training and a misjudgement early in the race, stormed down to win and set a new record time.

Kranjska Gora, Yugoslavia
Up in the north-west corner of Yugoslavia, near the Austrian and Italian borders, Kranjska Gora runs World Cup or European Cup events regularly on its Vitranc mountain. Planica, just down the road, has been famous for its ski jump since before the war.

Les Gets, France
Les Gets is one of nearly a dozen resorts which go to make up the vast Portes du Soleil region on the borders of France and Switzerland, south of Lake Geneva. Among other resorts in the group Avoriaz and Morzine also hold races. Les Gets usually runs women's races.

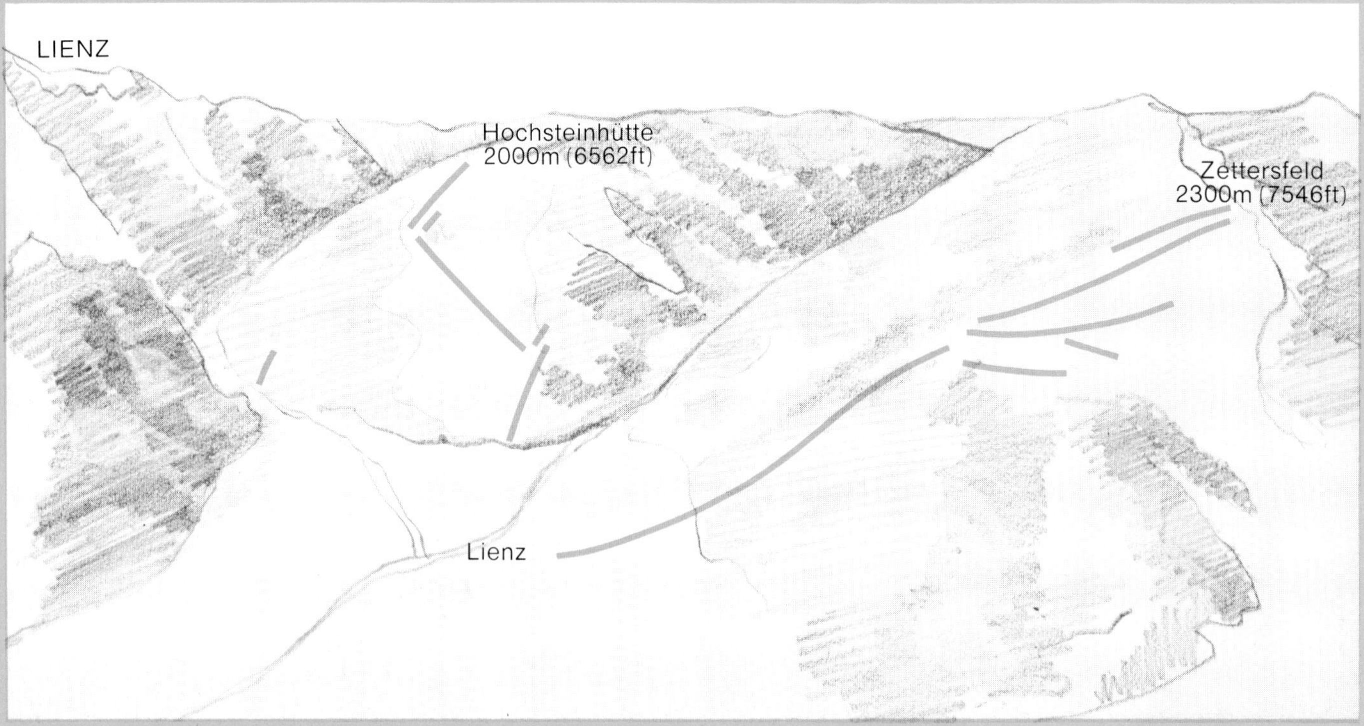

LIENZ
Hochsteinhütte
2000m (6562ft)
Zettersfeld
2300m (7546ft)
Lienz

MADONNA DI CAMPIGLIO
Passo Groste
2443m (8015ft)
Madonna di Campiglio
1550m (5086ft)
Campo Carlo Magno

Lienz, Austria
Home of the 1964 Olympic slalom champion, Josef Steigler, Lienz is the skiing centre of the East Tyrol. It has held World Cup slalom and giant slalom races for both men and women.

Madonna di Campiglio, Italy
Madonna runs the slalom and giant slalom events for the 3-Tre races, while the downhills are held in Val Gardena. The two areas are not far apart, Madonna lying just south of Bolzano.

Maribor, Yugoslavia
In Yugoslavia, not far from the Austrian border, Maribor runs the Golden Fox race for women each year, as a World Cup slalom and giant slalom. The courses are held on the Pohorje mountain.

MEGEVE

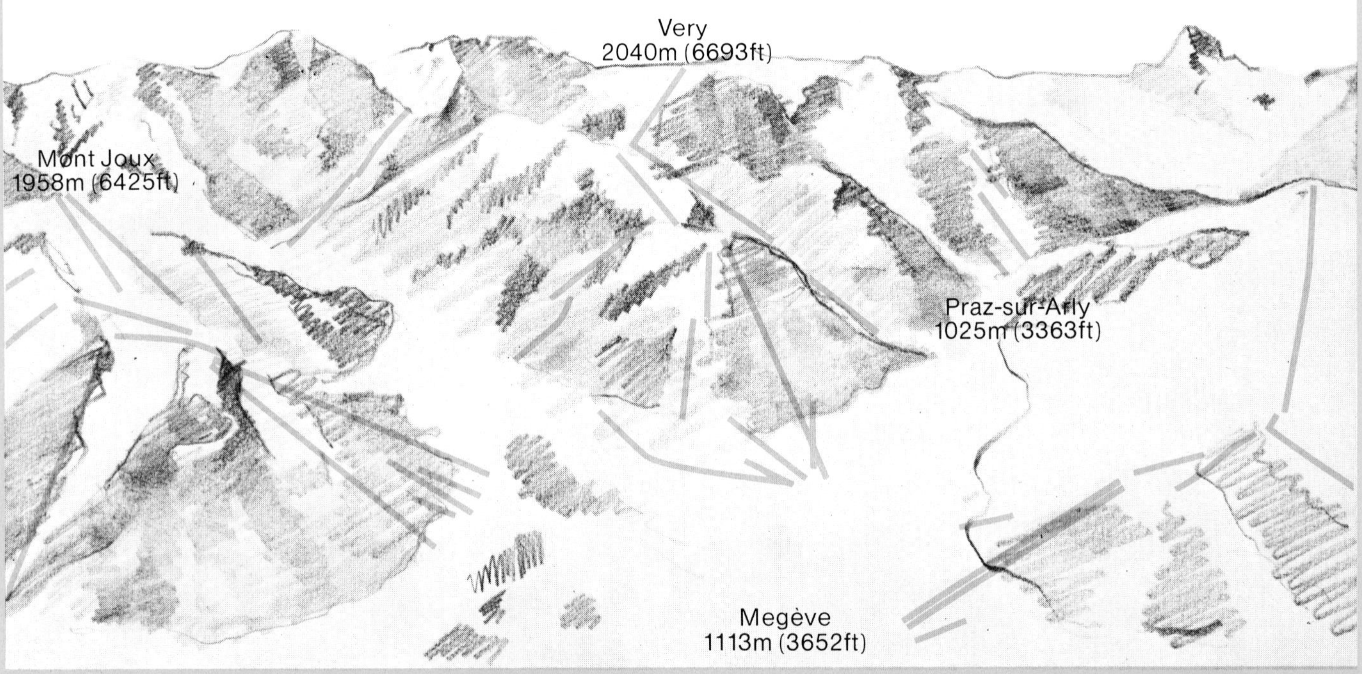

Very
2040m (6693ft)

Mont Joux
1958m (6425ft)

Praz-sur-Arly
1025m (3363ft)

Megève
1113m (3652ft)

MONTE BORDONE

Palon
2098m (6884ft)

Monte Bordone

Vanese
1300m (4265ft)

Trento

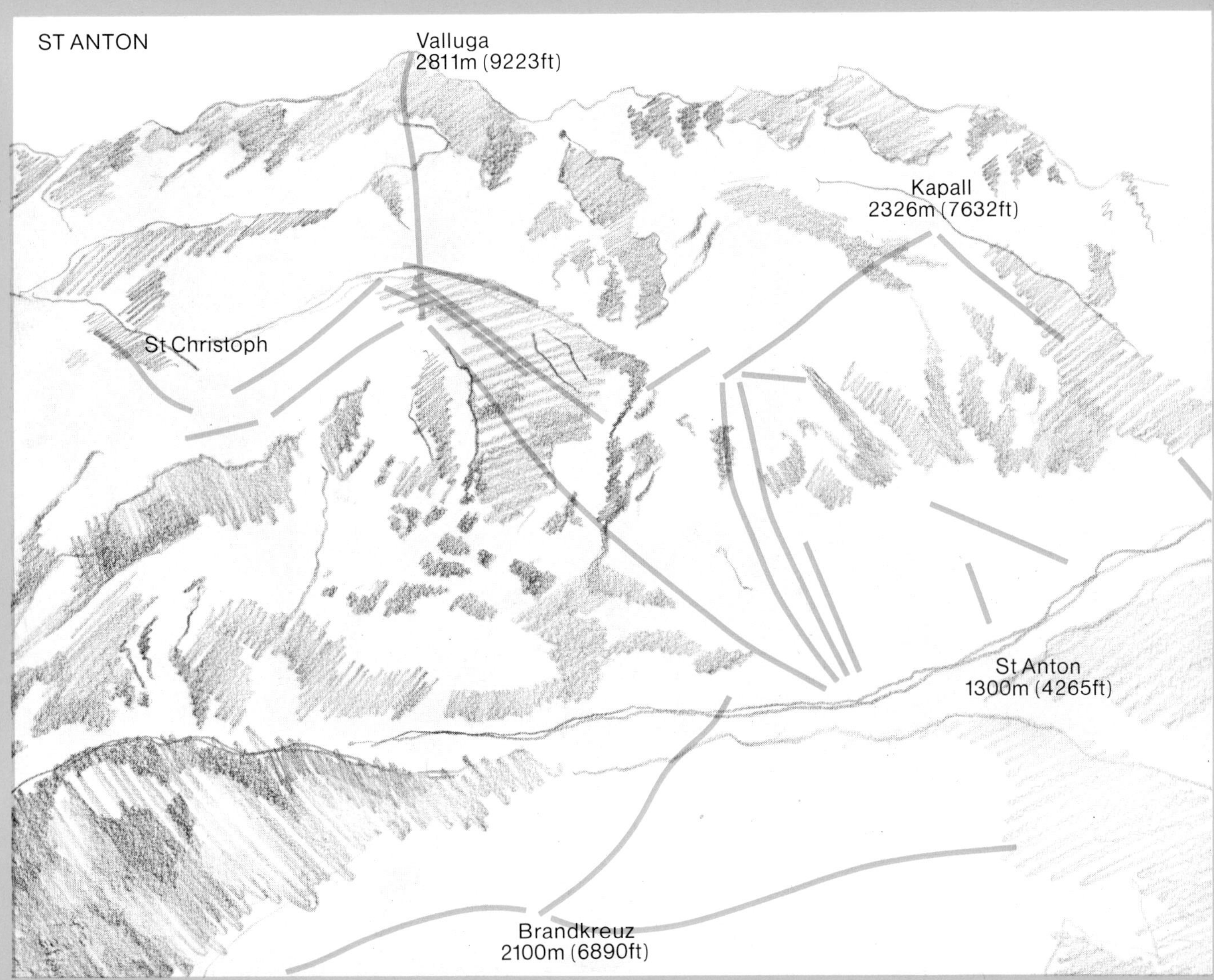

Megève, France
Megève was one of the most fashionable prewar French resorts. It now combines with nearby Chamonix and St Gervais to form the Mont Blanc racing area. The three resorts have such a variety of courses and such a fund of experienced organizers that they can run combined events for both men and women, such as the Arlberg-Kandhar.

Monte Bordone, Italy
Monte Bordone lies close to Trento, in the Italian Dolomites. It has been used for both World Cup and European Cup races.

St Anton, Austria
Hannes Schneider developed the famous Arlberg technique in this village and, with Sir Arnold Lunn, founded the Arlberg-Kandahar here in 1927. Sir Arnold refused to run the event here in 1938 after the Anschluss when Hannes Schneider had to leave for America. The A–K is still held at St Anton and the ski school is the most famous in the world.

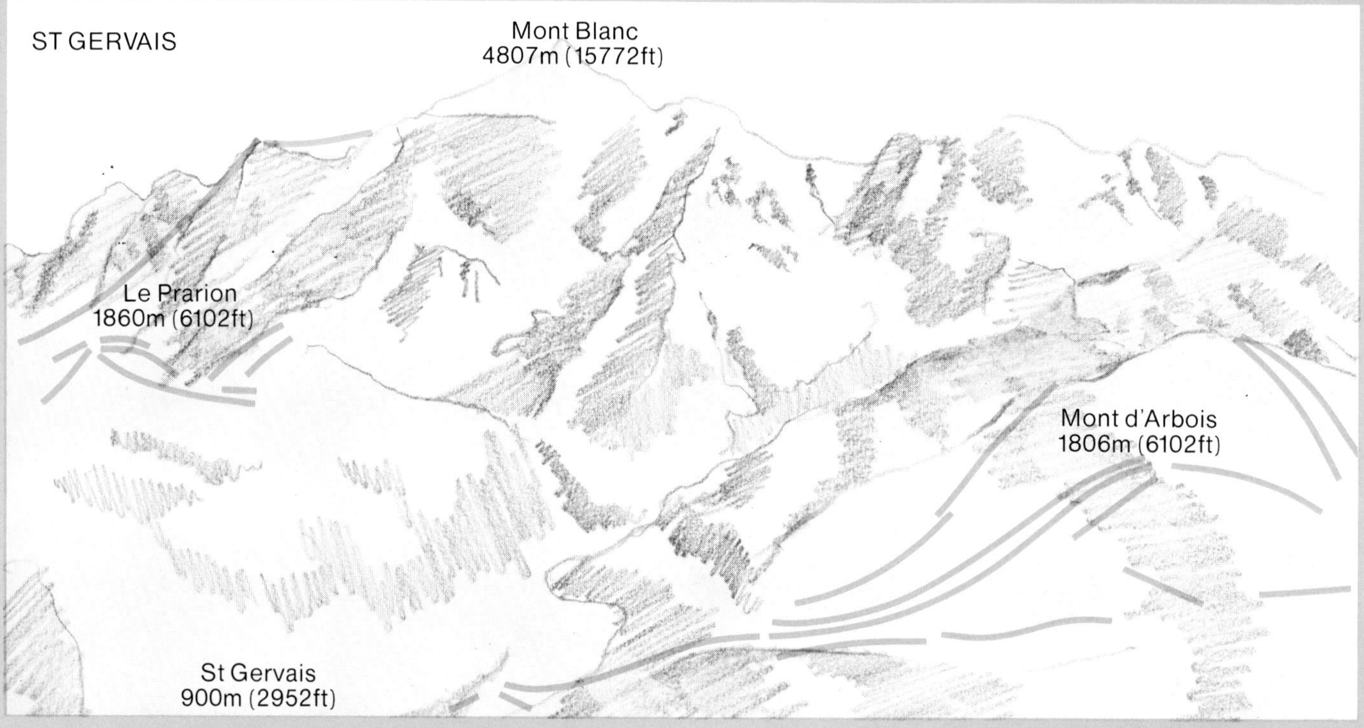

ST GERVAIS
Mont Blanc
4807m (15772ft)
Le Prarion
1860m (6102ft)
Mont d'Arbois
1806m (6102ft)
St Gervais
900m (2952ft)

SAPPORO
Mount Teine

Mount Eniwa

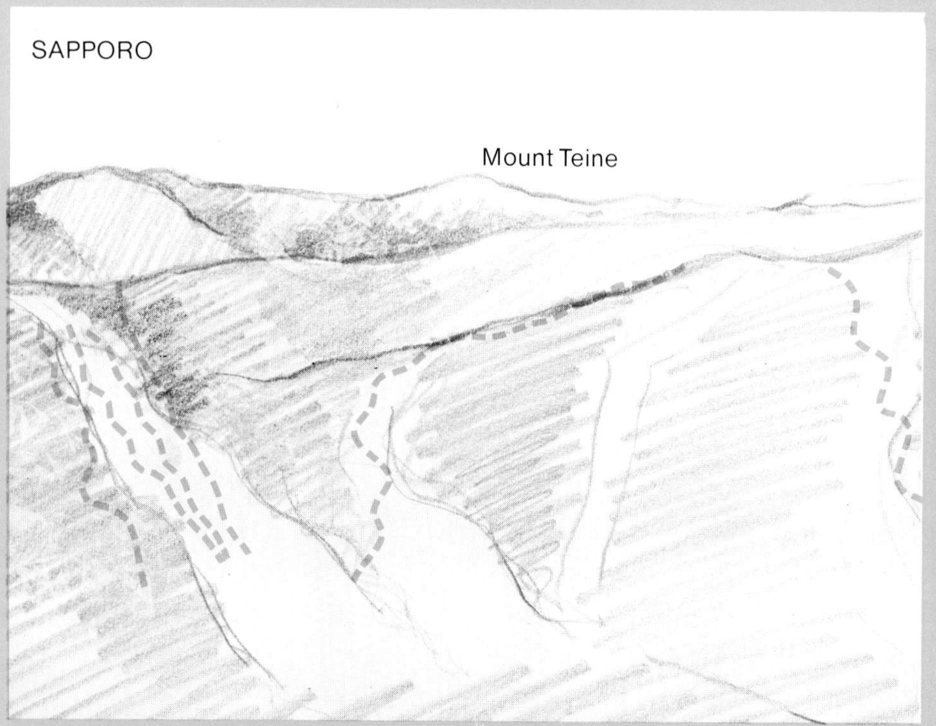

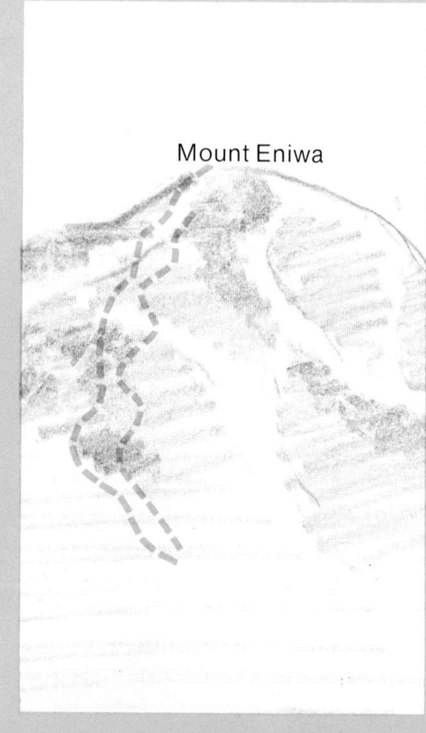

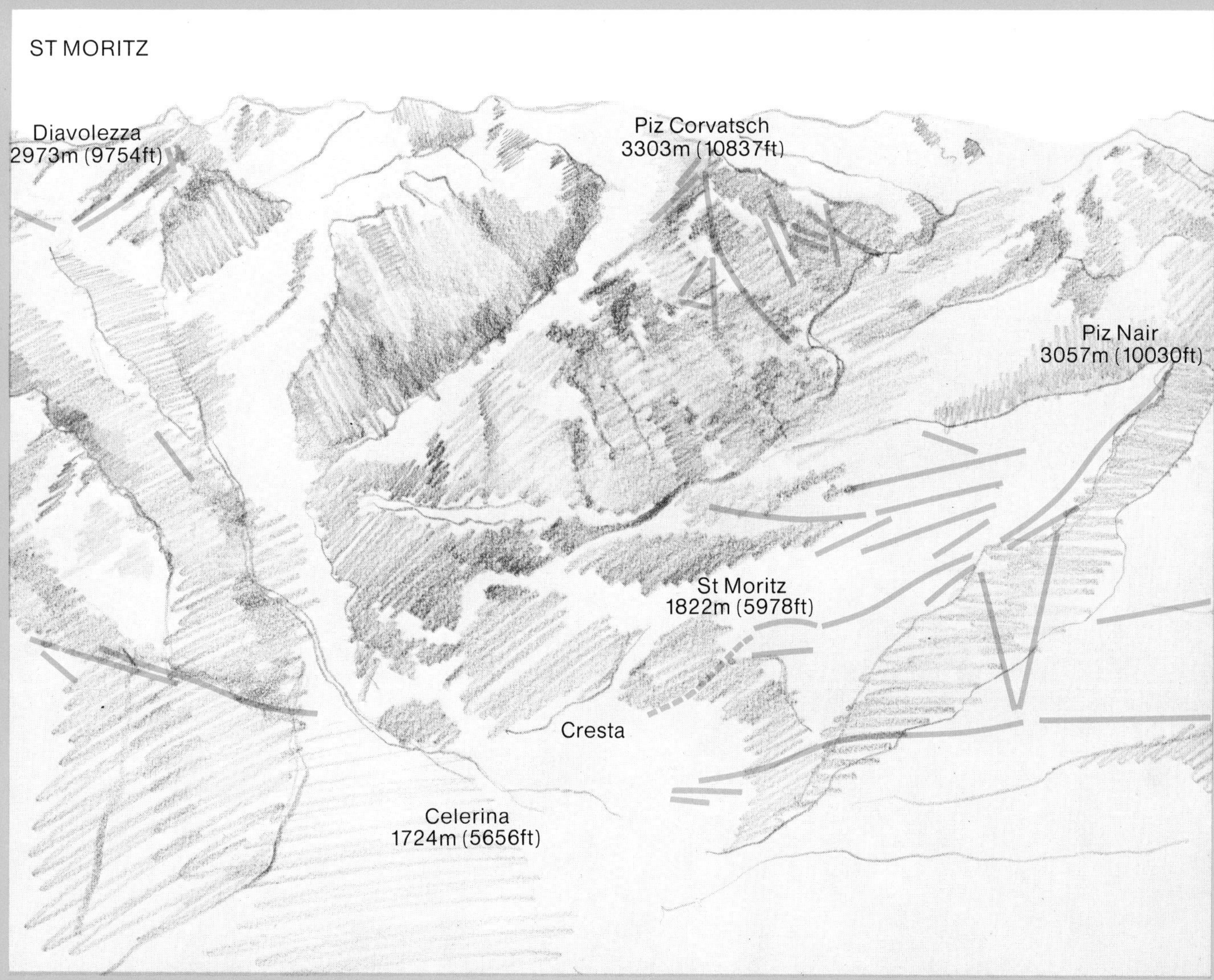

St Gervais, France
St Gervais is linked with Megève and Chamonix in the Mont Blanc ski racing area. It has been used for World Cup events – both slalom and downhill.

Sapporo, Japan
For the first time, in 1972, the Olympics moved east and Japan played host. The Swiss benefitted from a careful reconnaissance the previous winter during which they learned much about snow conditions and courses. This resulted in their team winning gold and silver medals in the men's slalom, silver and bronze in the men's giant slalom, and gold in the women's giant slalom and downhill. The courses shown are, from left to right: men's slalom; the two women's slaloms; second men's slalom; women's giant slalom; men's giant slalom; men's downhill, and women's downhill.

St Moritz, Switzerland
Cradle of winter sports, St Moritz has an impressive record of race organization including two Winter Olympics, 1928 and 1948, and the World Championships of 1974. Many of its visitors come just to watch 'the beautiful people' but the skiing areas from the town itself are excellent and those of the surrounding mountains such as Corvatsch, Sils Maria, Lagalp, and Diavolezza are unparalleled. The Engadine Ski Marathon is one of the great mass cross-country events of the year, attracting hundreds of competitors.

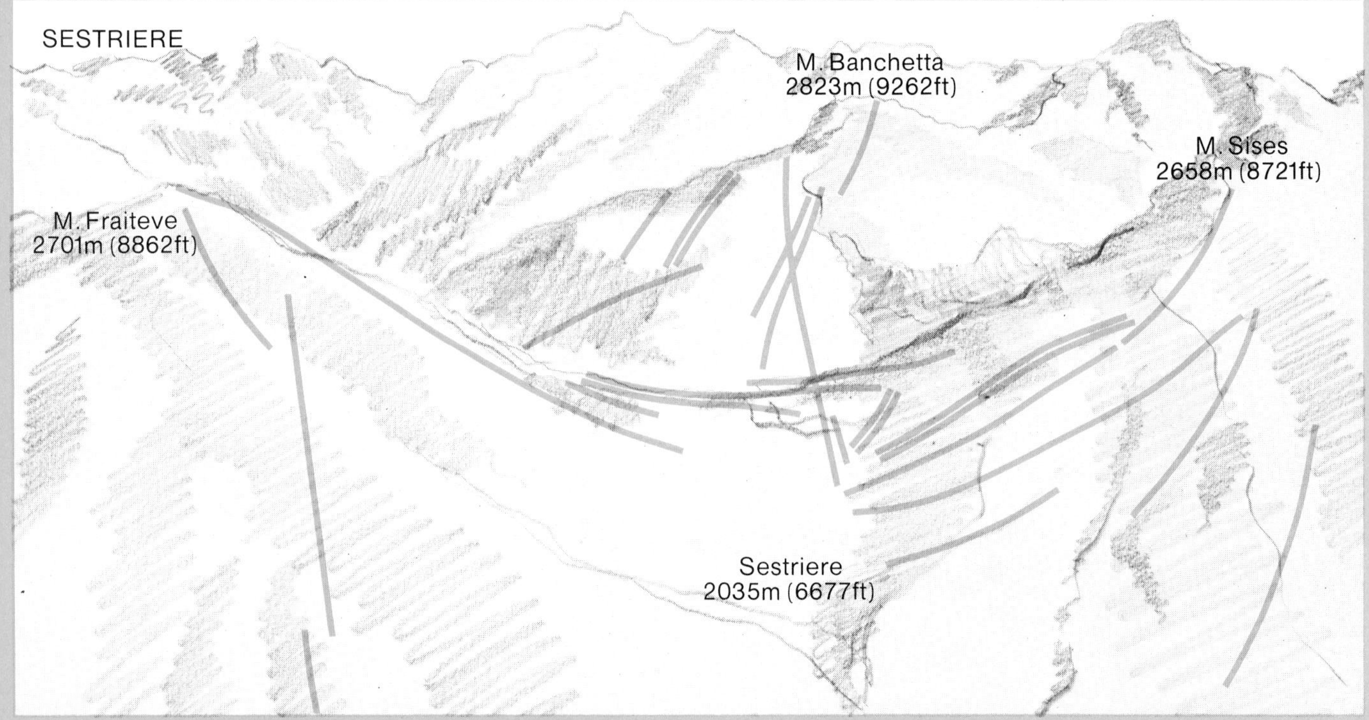

SESTRIERE

M. Banchetta
2823m (9262ft)

M. Sises
2658m (8721ft)

M. Fraiteve
2701m (8862ft)

Sestriere
2035m (6677ft)

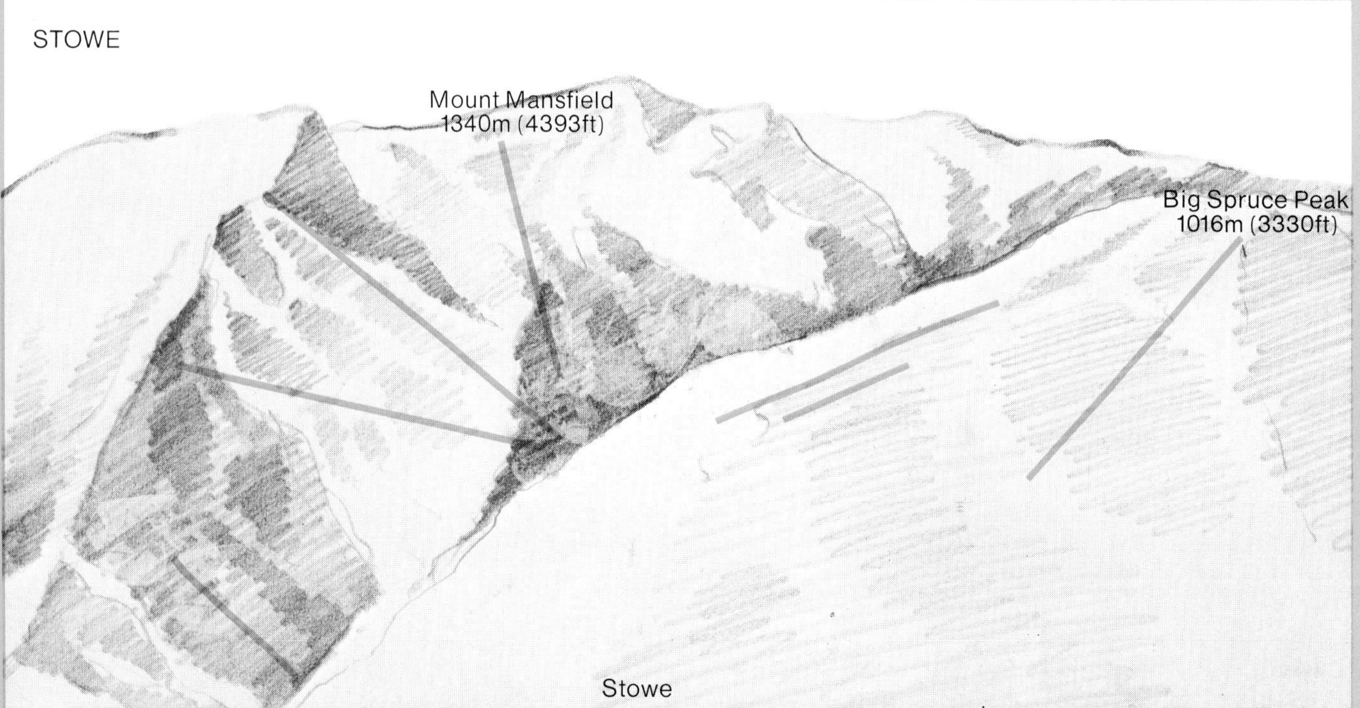

STOWE

Mount Mansfield
1340m (4393ft)

Big Spruce Peak
1016m (3330ft)

Stowe

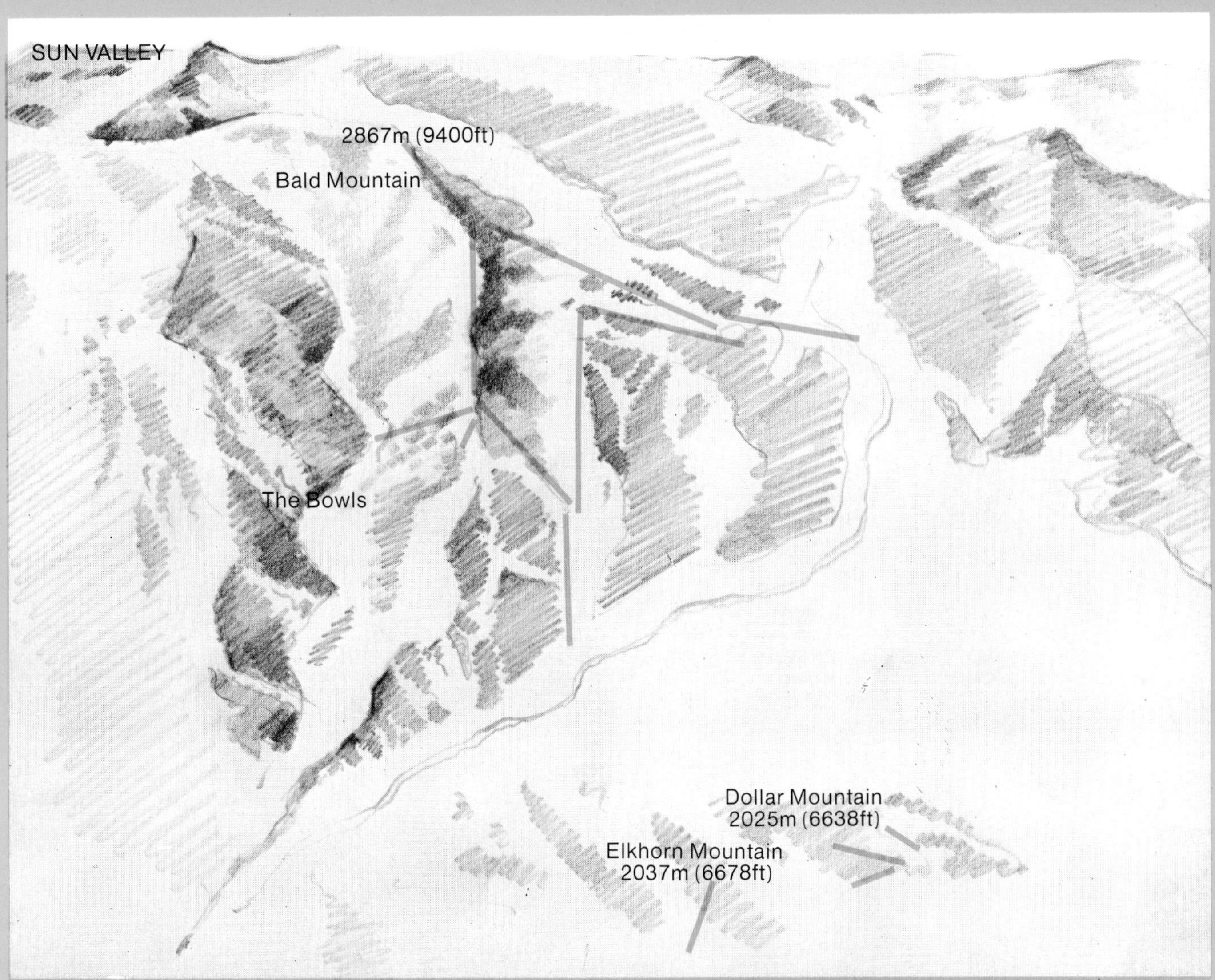

Sestriere, Italy
The Italian venue for the Arlberg-Kandahar until quite recently, Sestriere was built by Fiat under the impetus of Mussolini. Its round tower hotels still give it a special atmosphere and its slopes are snowsure, lying as it does on a high pass.

Stowe, Vermont, USA
Stowe, with its two great mountains, Mount Mansfield and Spruce Peak, is the ski capital of the eastern United States. It has been a frequent venue of United States National Championship races.

Sun Valley, Idaho, USA
The 1976 World Cup opened in this, America's oldest ski resort. A major rebuilding plan (to be completed in eight years) should result in a concentrated village with easy access to the slopes for hotel visitors.

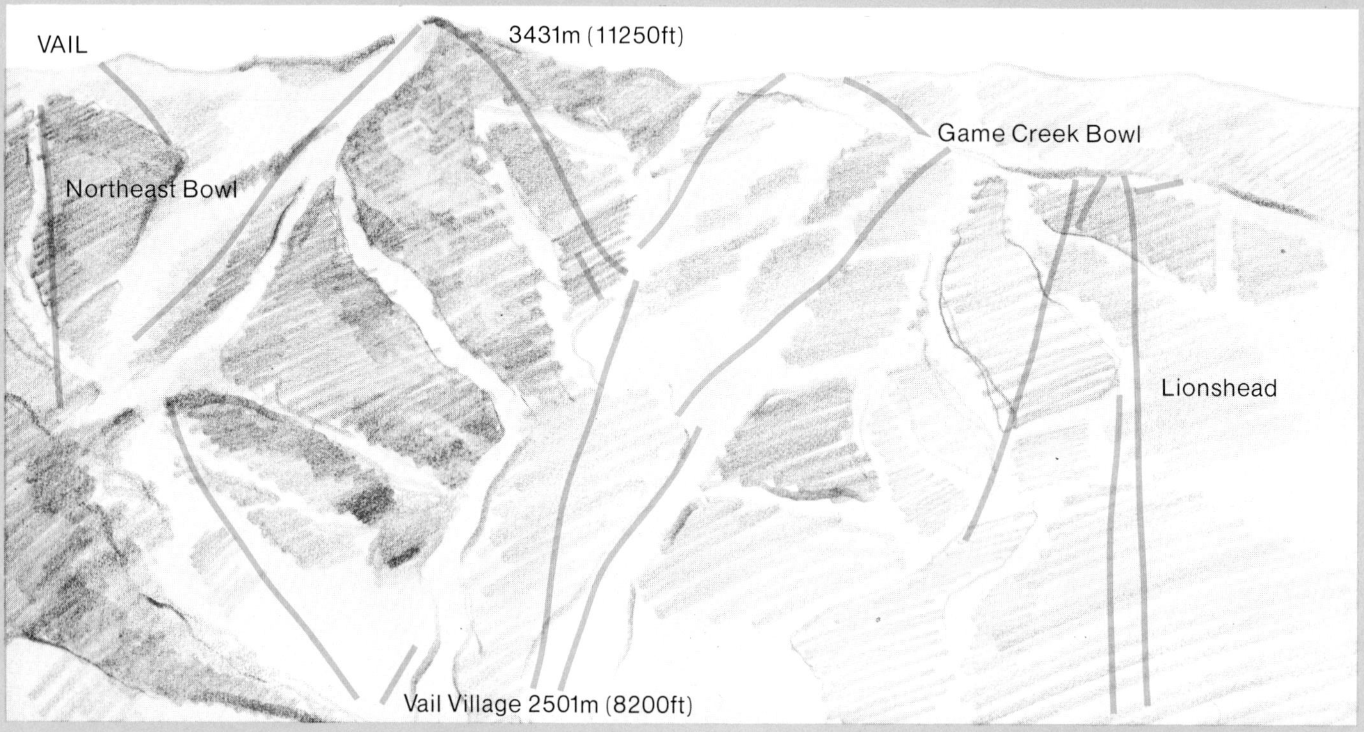

VAIL
3431m (11250ft)
Game Creek Bowl
Northeast Bowl
Lionshead
Vail Village 2501m (8200ft)

VAL D'ISERE
Aiguille Pers
3387m (11113ft)
Côte
3016m (9895ft)
Le Fornet
Val d'Isère

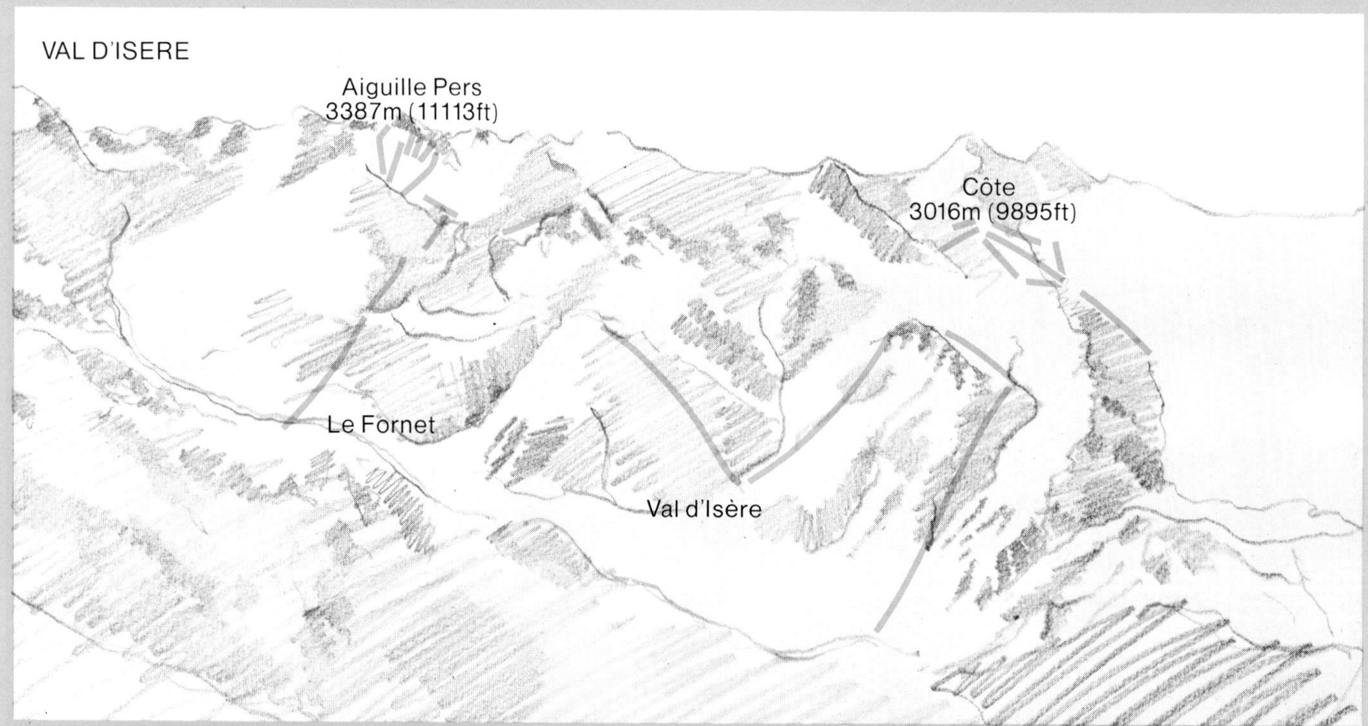

Vail, Colorado, USA
In the last fifteen years Vail has developed from a sheep farm to one of America's premier resorts. Its powder snow bowls are world famous and a vertical drop of 930m (3050ft) with steep slopes offers exciting courses.

Val d'Isère, France
France's main race centre, Val d'Isère has a continous programme of races throughout the winter and its slopes remain skiable through the summer. The first great event of the season, the Criterium de la Première Neige, takes place in December and the world watches for pointers to the rest of the season. A generous host, the Val d'Isère organization helps to sponsor many smaller races such as the Lowlander championships between the British, the Belgians, the Danes and the Dutch. It was also chosen for the first parallel slalom on the FIS calendar, the Daily Telegraph-Kandahar in 1974.

Val Gardena, Italy
In the Dolomites, this valley with a string of ski resorts served by cablecars up steep slopes offers excellent race courses. It hosted the 1970 World Championships and in 1975 held the final exciting World Cup events, in which Ingemar Stenmark was just beaten by the local hero, Gustavo Thoeni, in a parallel knock-out.

Voss, Norway *see overleaf*
The majority of Scandinavian resorts specialize in Nordic events, but Voss, in addition to first-rate cross country skiing, has the steep slopes and long drops which qualify it as a downhill course. For several years World Cup events were held on Bavallen, the finals taking place there in 1970.

Zakopane, Poland *see overleaf*
In 1929 the Polish Ski Association tried out the British rules for Alpine racing and included a downhill in the World Championship meeting at Zakopane. After making sure the meeting was open to all comers, two British women (Doreen Elliott and Audrey Sale-Barker) took part and delighted the crowds by finishing thirteenth and fourteenth, beating forty-five men. World Championships were held in Zakopane again in 1962.

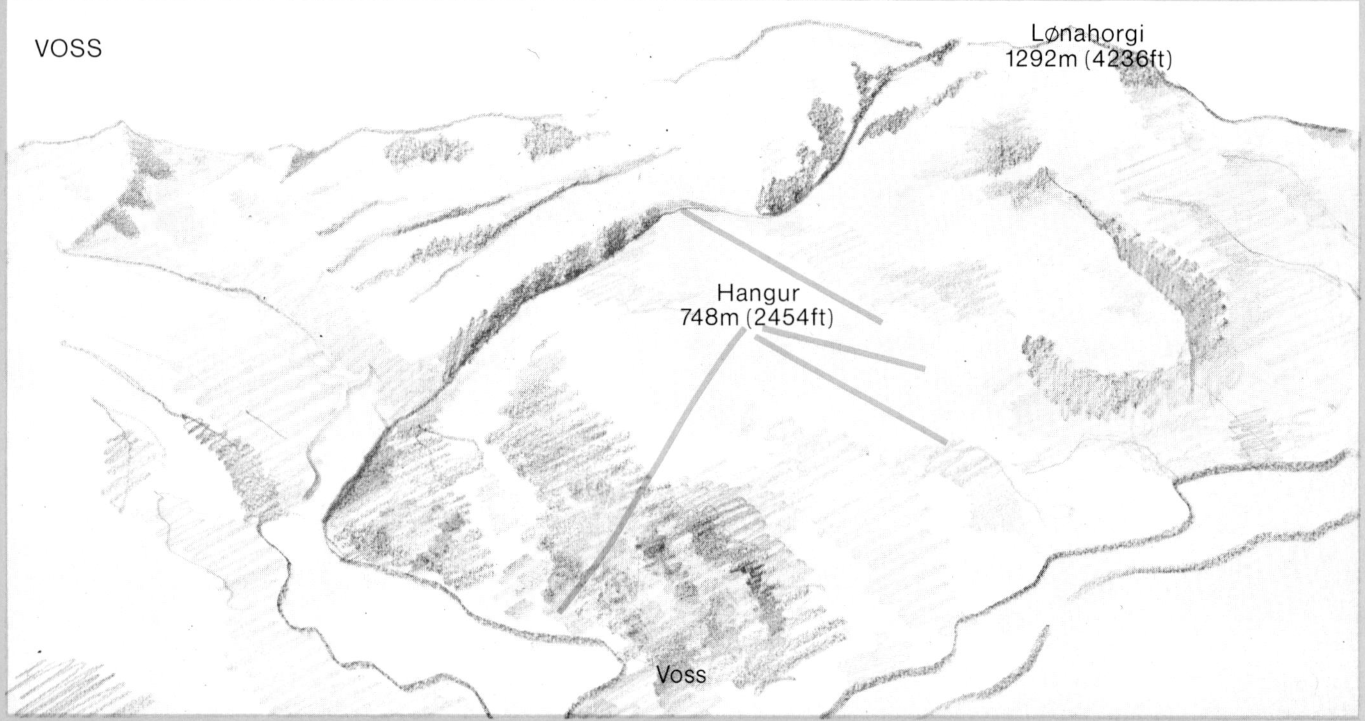

VOSS

Lønahorgi
1292m (4236ft)

Hangur
748m (2454ft)

Voss

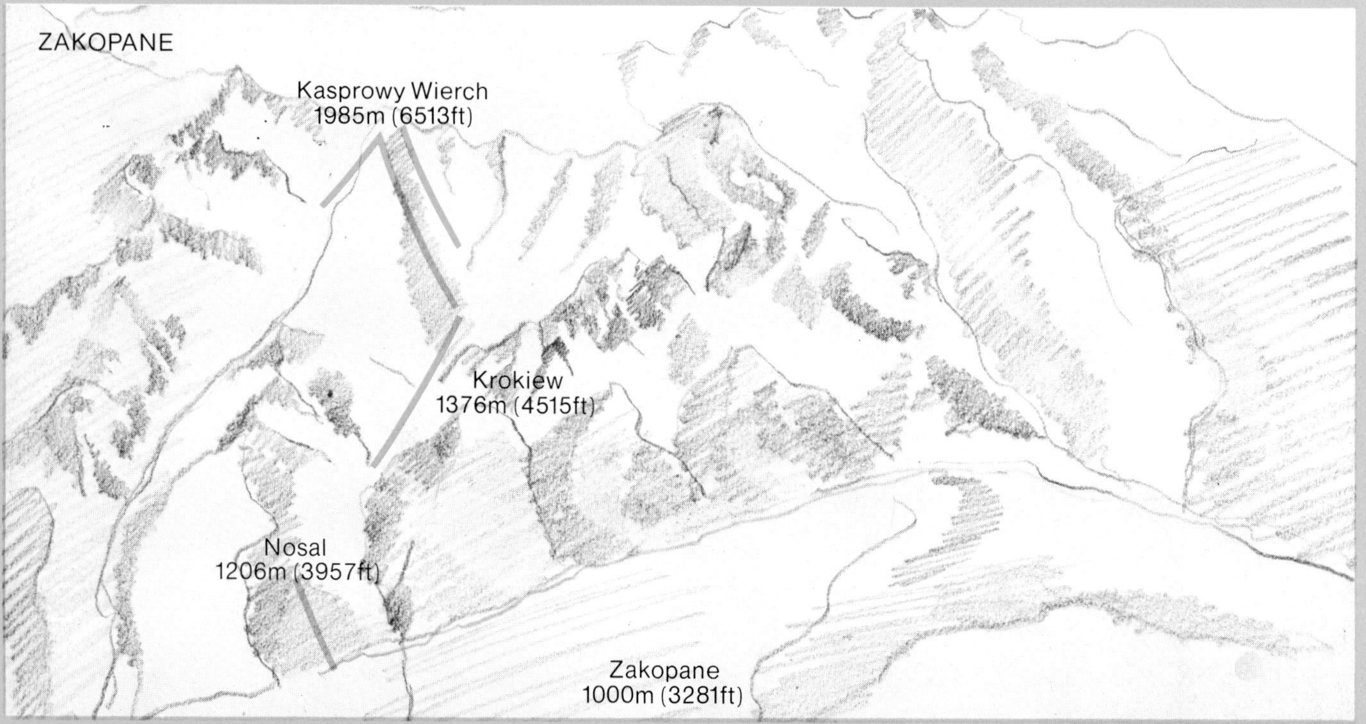

ZAKOPANE

Kasprowy Wierch
1985m (6513ft)

Krokiew
1376m (4515ft)

Nosal
1206m (3957ft)

Zakopane
1000m (3281ft)

Results

WINTER OLYMPIC GAMES

	Year	Place	Date
I	1924	Chamonix	Jan 24–Feb 4
II	1928	St Moritz	Feb 11–18
III	1932	Lake Placid	Feb 4–13
IV	1936	Garmisch-Partenkirchen	Feb 6–13
V	1948	St Moritz	Jan 30–Feb 8
VI	1952	Oslo	Feb 14–25
VII	1956	Cortina d'Ampezzo	Jan 26–Feb 5
VIII	1960	Squaw Valley	Feb 18–28
IX	1964	Innsbruck	Jan 29–Feb 9
X	1968	Grenoble	Feb 6–18
XI	1972	Sapporo	Feb 3–13
XII	1976	Innsbruck	Feb 4–15

WHERE WINTER MEDALS HAVE GONE

Country	Gold	Silver	Bronze
USSR	51	32	35
Norway	50	51	43
USA	30	38	40
Finland	23	35	21
Austria	22	31	27
Sweden	22	21	24
Switzerland	15	17	16
Germany (until 1964)	14	11	10
East Germany (after 1964)	12	10	16
France	12	9	13
Canada	11	7	14
Italy	10	7	7
Netherlands	9	13	9
West Germany (after 1964)	7	8	7
Great Britain	4	2	6
Czechoslovakia	2	5	5
Japan	1	2	1
Belgium	1	1	2
Poland	1	1	2
Spain	1	0	0
Hungary	0	1	4
North Korea	0	1	0
Liechtenstein	0	0	2
Rumania	0	0	1

SPEED SKATING (MEN)

500 METRES SPEED SKATING

Year	Gold	Silver	Bronze
1924	Charles Jewtraw (USA) 44s	Ole Olsen (Norway) 44.2s	Roald Larsen (Norway) & Clas Thunberg (Finland) 44.8s
1928	Clas Thunberg (Finland) & Bernt Evensen (Norway) 43.4s		John Farrell (USA) Roald Larsen (Norway) Jaakko Friman (Finland) 43.6s
1932	John Shea (USA) 43.4s	Bernt Evensen (Norway)	Alexander Hurd (Canada)
1936	Ivar Ballangrud (Norway) 43.4s	Georg Krog (Norway) 43.5s	Leo Freisinger (USA) 44s
1948	Finn Helgesen (Norway) 43.1s	Ken Bartholomew (USA), Thomas Byberg (Norway), Robert Fitzgerald (USA) 43.2s	
1952	Kenneth Henry (USA) 43.2s	Don McDermott (USA) 43.9s	Arne Johansen (Nor), Gorden Audley (Can) 44s
1956	Eugeny Grischin (USSR) 40.2s	Rafael Gratsch (USSR) 40.8s	Alv Gjestvang (Norway) 41s
1960	Eugeny Grischin (USSR) 40.2s	William Disney (USA) 40.3s	Rafael Gratsch (USSR) 40.4s
1964	Dick McDermott (USA) 40.1s	Eugeny Grischin (USSR), Alv Gjestvang (Norway) Vladimir Orlov (Poland) 40.6s	
1968	Erhard Keller (W. Germany) 40.3s	Magne Thomassen (Norway) 40.5s	Dick McDermott (USA) 40.5s
1972	Erhard Keller (W. Germany) 39.44s	Hasse Borjes (Sweden) 39.69s	Valery Muratov (USSR) 39.80s
1976	Eugeny Kulikov (USSR) 39.17s	Valery Muratov (USSR) 39.25s	Dan Immerfall (USA) 39.54s

1500 METRES SPEED SKATING

Year	Gold	Silver	Bronze
1924	Clas Thunberg (Finland) 2m 20.8s	Roald Larsen (Norway) 2m 22s	Sigurd Moen (Norway) 2m 25.6s
1928	Clas Thunberg (Finland) 2m 21.1s	Bernt Evensen (Norway) 2m 21.9s	Ivar Ballangrud (Norway) 2m 22.6s
1932	John Shea (USA) 2m 57.5s	Alexander Hurd (Canada)	William Logan (Canada)
1936	Charles Mathisen (Norway) 2m 19.2s	Ivar Ballangrud (Norway) 2m 20.2s	Birger Vasenius (Finland) 2m 20.9s
1948	Sverre Farstad (Norway) 2m 17.6s	Ake Seyffarth (Sweden) 2m 18.1s	Odd Lundberg (Norway) 2m 18.9s
1952	Hjalmar Andersen (Norway) 2m 20.4s	Willem van der Voort (Netherlands) 2m 10.6s	Roald Aas (Norway) 2m 21.6s
1956	Eugeny Grischin & Yuri Michailov (USSR) 2m 8.6s		Toivo Salonen (Finland) 2m 9.4s
1960	Roald Aas (Norway) & Eugeny Grischin (USSR) 2m 10.4s		Boris Stenin (USSR) 2m 11.5s
1964	Ants Antson (USSR) 2m 10.3s	Kees Verkerk (Netherlands) 2m 10.6s	Villy Haugen (Norway) 2m 11.2s
1968	Kees Verkerk (Netherlands) 2m 3.4s	Ard Schenk (Netherlands) & Ivar Eriksen (Norway) 2m 5s	
1972	Ard Schenk (Netherlands) 2m 2.96s	Roar Grönvold (Norway) 2m 4.26s	Goran Claesson (Sweden) 2m 5.89s

1976	Jan Egil Storholt (Norway) 1m 59.38s	Yuri Kondakov (USSR) 1m 59.97s	Hans van Helden (Netherlands) 2m 00.87s

5000 METRES SPEED SKATING

1924	Clas Thunberg (Finland) 8m 39s	Julius Skutnabb (Finland) 8m 48.4s	Roald Larsen (Norway) 8m 50.2s
1928	Ivar Ballangrud (Norway) 8m 50.5s	Julius Skutnabb (Finland) 8m 59.1s	Bernt Evensen (Norway) 9m 1.1s
1932	Irving Jaffee (USA) 9m 40.8s	Edward Murphy (USA)	William Logan (Canada)
1936	Ivar Ballangrud (Norway) 8m 19.6s	Birger Vasenius (Finland) 8m 23.3s	Antero Ojala (Finland) 8m 30.1s
1948	Reidar Liaklev (Norway) 8m 29.4s	Odd Lundberg (Norway) 8m 32.7s	Göthe Hedlund (Sweden) 8m 34.8s
1952	Hjalmar Andersen (Norway) 8m 10.6s	Cornelis Broekman (Netherlands) 8m 21.6s	Sverre Haugli (Norway) 8m 22.4s
1956	Boris Schilkov (USSR) 7m 48.7s	Sigvard Ericsson (Sweden) 7m 56.7s	Oleg Gontscharenko (USSR) 7m 57.5s
1960	Viktor Kositschkin (USSR) 7m 51.3s	Knut Johannesen (Norway) 8m 0.8s	Jan Pesman (Netherlands) 8m 5.1s
1964	Knut Johannesen (Norway) 7m 38.4s	Per Ivar Moe (Norway) 7m 38.6s	Fred Maier (Norway) 7m 42s
1968	Fred Maier (Norway) 7m 22.4s	Kees Verkerk (Netherlands) 7m 23.2s	Petrus Nottet (Netherlands) 7m 25.5s
1972	Ard Schenk (Netherlands) 7m 23.61s	Roar Grönvold (Norway) 7m 28.18s	Sten Stensen (Norway) 7m 33.39s
1976	Sten Stensen (Norway) 7m 24.48s	Piet Kleine (Netherlands) 7m 26.47s	Hans van Helden (Netherlands) 7m 26.54s

10000 METRES SPEED SKATING

1924	Julius Skutnabb (Finland) 18m 4.8s	Clas Thunberg (Finland) 18m 7.8s	Roald Larsen (Norway) 18m 12.2s
1932	Irving Jaffee (USA) 19m 13.6s	Ivar Ballangrud (Norway)	Frank Stack (Canada)
1936	Ivar Ballangrud (Norway) 17m 24.3s	Birger Vasenius (Finland) 17m 28.2s	Max Stiepl (Austria) 17m 30s
1948	Ake Seyffarth (Sweden) 17m 26.3s	Lauri Parkkinen (Finland) 17m 36s	Pentti Lammio (Finland) 17m 42.7s
1952	Hjalmar Andersen (Norway) 16m 45.8s	Cornelis Broekman (Netherlands) 17m 10.6s	Carl-Erik Asplund (Sweden) 17m 16.6s
1956	Sigvard Ericsson (Sweden) 16m 35.9s	Knut Johannesen (Norway) 16, 36.9s	Oleg Gontscharenko (USSR) 16m 42.3s
1960	Knut Johannesen (Norway) 15m 46.6s	Viktor Kositschkin (USSR) 15m 49.2s	Kjell Bäckman (Sweden) 16m 14.2s
1964	Johnny Nilsson (Sweden) 15m 50.1s	Fred Maier (Norway) 16m 6s	Knut Johannesen (Norway) 16m 6.3s
1968	Johnny Höeglin (Sweden) 15m 23.6s	Fred Maier (Norway) 15m 23.9s	Orjan Sandler (Sweden) 15m 31.8s
1972	Ard Schenk (Netherlands) 15m 1.35s	Kees Verkerk (Netherlands) 15m 4.70s	Sten Stensen (Norway) 15m 7.08s
1976	Piet Kleine (Netherlands) 14m 50.59s	Sten Stensen (Norway) 14m 53.30s	Hans van Helden (Netherlands) 15m 02.02s

SPEED SKATING (WOMEN)

500 METRES SPEED SKATING

1960	Helga Haase (Germany) 45.9s	Natalia Dontschenko (USSR) 46s	Jeanne Ashworth (USA) 46.1s
1964	Lydia Skoblikova (USSR) 45s	Irina Jegorova (USSR) 45.4s	Tatyana Sidorova (USSR) 45.5s
1968	Ljudmila Titova (USSR) 46.1s	Mary Meyers (USA) 46.3s	Diane Holum (USA) 46.3s
1972	Anne Henning (USA) 43.44s	Vera Krasnova (USSR) 44.01s	Ljudmila Titova (USSR) 44.45s
1976	Sheila Young (USA) 42.76s	Catherine Priestner (Canada) 43.12s	Tatiana Averina (USSR) 43.17s

1000 METRES SPEED SKATING

1960	Klara Guseva (USSR) 1m 34.1s	Helga Haase (Germany) 1m 34.3s	Tamara Rylova (USSR) 1m 34.8s
1964	Lydia Skoblikova (USSR) 1m 33.2s	Irina Yegorova (USSR) 1m 34.3s	Kaija Mustonen (Finland) 1m 34.8s
1968	Carolina Geijssen (Netherlands) 1m 32.6s	Ljudmila Titova (USSR) 1m 32.9s	Diane Holum (USA) 1m 33.4s
1972	Monika Pflug (W. Germany) 1m 31.4s	Atje Keulen-Deetstra (Netherlands) 1m 31.6s	Anne Henning (USA) 1m 31.6s
1976	Tatiana Averina (USSR) 1m 28.43s	Leah Poulos (USA) 1m 28.57	Sheila Young (USA) 1m 29.14s

1500 METRES SPEED SKATING

1960	Lydia Skoblikova (USSR) 2m 25.2s	Elvira Seroczynska (Poland) 2m 25.7s.	Helena Pilejczyk (Poland) 2m 27.1s
1964	Lydia Skoblikova (USSR) 2m 22.6s.	Kaija Mustonen (Finland) 2m 25.5s	Berta Kolokoltzeva (USSR) 2m 27.1s
1968	Kaija Mustonen (Finland) 2m 22.6s	Carolina Geijssen (Netherlands) 2m 22.7s	Stien Kaiser (Netherlands) 2m 24.5s
1972	Diane Holum (USA) 2m 20.85s	Stien Baas-Kaiser (Netherlands) 2m 21.05s	Atje Keulen-Deetstra (Netherlands) 2m 22.05s
1976	Galina Stepanskaya (USSR) 2m 16.58s	Sheila Young (USA) 2m 17.06s	Tatiana Averina (USSR) 2m 17.96s

3000 METRES SPEED SKATING

1960	Lydia Skoblikova (USSR) 5m 14.3s	Valentina Stenina (USSR) 5m 16.9s	Eevi Huttunen (Finland) 5m 21s
1964	Lydia Skoblikova (USSR) 5m 14.9s	Valentina Stenina (USSR) & Pil Hwa Han (N. Korea) 5m 18.5s	
1968	Johanna Schut (Netherlands) 4m 56.2s	Kaija Mustonen (Finland) 5m 1s	Stien Kaiser (Netherlands) 5m 1.3s
1972	Stien Baas-Kaiser (Netherlands) 4m 52.14s	Diane Holum (USA) 4m 58.67s	Atje Keulen-Deetstra (Netherlands) 4m 59.91s
1976	Tatiana Averina (USSR) 4m 45.19s	Andrea Mitscherlich (E. Germany) 4m 45.23s	Lisbeth Korsmo (Norway) 4m 45.24s

FIGURE SKATING

FIGURE SKATING (MEN)

1908	Ulrich Salchow (Sweden) 1,886.5	Richard Johansson (Sweden) 1,826	Per Thoren (Sweden) 1,787
1920	Gillis Grafström (Sweden) 2,575.25	Andreas Krogh (Norway) 2,634	Martin Stuxrud (Norway) 2,561
1924	Gillis Grafström (Sweden) 2,575.25	Willy Böckl (Austria) 2,518.75	Georg Gautschi (Switzerland) 2,223.5
1928	Gillis Grafström (Sweden) 2,698.25	Willy Böckl (Austria) 2,682.50	Robert van Zeebröck (Belgium) 2,578.75
1932	Karl Schäfer (Austria) 2,602	Gillis Grafström (Sweden) 2,514.5	Montgomery Wilson (Canada) 2,448.3
1936	Karl Schäfer (Austria) 2,959	Ernst Baier (Germany) 2,805.3	Felix Kasper (Austria) 2,801
1948	Richard Button (USA) 1,720.6	Hans Gerschwiler (Switzerland) 1,630.1	Edi Rada (Austria) 1,603.2
1952	Richard Button (USA) 1,730.3	Helmut Seibt (Austria) 1,621.3	James Grogan (USA) 1,627.4
1956	Hayes Alan Jenkins (USA) 1,497.75	Ronald Robertson (USA) 1,492.15	David Jenkins (USA) 1,465.41
1960	David Jenkins (USA) 1,440.2	Karol Divin (Czechoslovakia) 1,414.3	Donald Jackson (Canada) 1,401
1964	Manfred Schnelldorfer (Germany) 1,916.9	Alain Calmat (France) 1,876.5	Scott Allen (USA) 1,873.6
1968	Wolfgang Schwartz (Austria) 1,904.1	Tim Wood (USA) 1,891.6	Patrick Pera (France) 1,864.5
1972	Ondrej Nepela (Czech) 2,739.1	Sergei Chetverukhin (USSR) 2,672.4	Patrick Pera (France) 2,653.1
1976	John Curry (GB) 192.74	Vladimir Kovalev (USSR) 187.64	Toller Cranston (Canada) 187.38

FIGURE SKATING (WOMEN)

1908	Madge Syers (GB) 1,262.5pts	Elsa Rendschmidt (Germany) 1,055.0	D. Greenhough-Smith (GB) 960.5
1920	Magda Julin (Sweden) 887.75	Svea Noren (Sweden) 887.75	Theresa Weld (USA) 890.0
1924	Herma Planck-Szabo (Austria) 2,094.25	Beatrix Loughran (USA) 1,959.0	Ethel Muckelt (GB) 1,750.50
1928	Sonja Henie (Norway) 2,452.25	Fritzi Burger (Austria) 2,248.50	Beatrix Loughran (USA) 2,254.50
1932	Sonja Henie (Norway) 2,302.5	Fritzi Burger (Austria) 2,167.1	Maribel Vinson (USA) 2,158.5
1936	Sonja Henie (Norway) 2,971.4	Cecilia Colledge (GB) 2,926.8	Vivi-Anne Hulten (Sweden) 2,763.2
1948	Barbara Ann Scott (Canada) 1,467.7	Eva Pawlik (Austria) 1,418.3	Jeanette Altwegg (GB) 1,405.5
1952	Jeanette Altwegg (GB) 1,455.8	Tenley Albright (USA) 1,432.2	Jacqueline du Bief (France) 1,422.0
1956	Tenley Albright (USA) 1,868.39	Carol Heiss (USA) 1,848.24	Ingrid Wendl (Austria) 1,753.91
1960	Carol Heiss (USA) 1,490.1	Sjoukje Dijkstra (Netherlands) 1,424.8	Barbara Roles (USA) 1,414.9
1964	Sjoukje Dijkstra (Netherlands) 2,018.5	Regine Heitzer (Austria) 1,945.5	Petra Burka (Canada) 1,940.0
1968	Peggy Fleming (USA) 1,970.5	Gabriele Seyfert (E. Germany) 1,882.3	Hana Maskova (Czech) 1,828.8
1972	Trixi Schuba (Austria) 2,751.5	Karen Magnussen (Canada) 2,673.2	Janet Lynn Holmes (USA) 2,663.1
1976	Dorothy Hamill (USA) 193.80pts	Dianne de Leeuw (Netherlands) 190.24	Christine Errath (E. Germany) 188.16

FIGURE SKATING PAIRS

1908	Germany 56.0pts	GB 51.5	GB 48.0
1920	Finland 80.75pts	Norway 72.75	GB 66.25
1924	Austria 74.50pts	Finland 71.75	France 69.25
1928	France 100.50pts	Austria 99.25	Austria 93.25
1932	France 78.7pts	USA 77.5	Hungary 76.4
1936	Germany 103.3pts	Austria 102.7	Hungary 97.6
1948	Belgium 123.5pts	Hungary 122.2	Canada 121.0
1952	Germany 102.6pts	USA 100.6	Hungary 97.4
1956	Austria 101.8pts	Canada 101.7	Hungary 99.3
1960	Canada 80.4pts	Germany 76.8	USA 76.2
1964	USSR 104.4pts		Canada 98.5
1968	USSR 315.2pts	USSR 312.3	W. Germany 304.4
1972	USSR 420.4pts	USSR 419.4	E. Germany 411.8
1976	USSR 140.54pts	E. Germany 136.35	E. Germany 134.57

ICE DANCING

1976	Ljudmila Pakhomova Alexandr Gorshkov (USSR) 209.92pts	Irina Moiseeva Andrei Minenkov (USSR) 204.88	Colleen O'Connor Jim Millns (USA) 202.64

ICE HOCKEY

1920	Canada	USA	Czechoslovakia
1924	Canada	USA	GB
1928	Canada	Sweden	Switzerland
1932	Canada	USA	Germany
1936	GB	Canada	USA
1948	Canada	Czechoslovakia	Switzerland
1952	Canada	USA	Sweden
1956	USSR	USA	Canada
1960	USA	Canada	USSR
1964	USSR	Sweden	Czechoslovakia
1968	USSR	Czechoslovakia	Canada
1972	USSR	USA	Czechoslovakia
1976	USSR	Czechoslovakia	W. Germany

CROSS-COUNTRY SKIING (MEN)

18 KMS CROSS-COUNTRY

1924	Thorleif Haug (Norway) 1h 14m 31.0s	Johan Gröttumsbraaten (Norway) 1hr 15m 51.0s	Tapani Niku (Finland 1h 26m 26.0s
1928	Johan Gröttumsbraaten (Norway) 1h 37m 01.0s	Ole Hegge (Norway) 1h 39m 01.0s	Reidar Odegaard (Norway) 1h 40m 11.0s
1932	Sven Utterström (Sweden) 1h 23m 07.0s	Axel Wikström (Sweden) 1h 25m 07.0s	Veli Saarinen (Finland) 1h 25m 24.0s
1936	Erik-August Larsson (Sweden) 1h 14m 38.0s	Oddbjörn Hagen (Norway) 1h 15m 33.0s	Pekka Niemi (Finland) 1h 16m 59.0s
1948	Martin Lundström (Sweden) 1h 13m 50.0s	Nils Ostensson (Sweden) 1h 14m 22.0s	Gunnar Eriksson (Sweden) 1h 16m 06.0s
1952	Hallgeir Brenden (Norway) 1h 1m 34.0s	Tapio Mäkelä (Finland) 1h 2m 09.0s	Paavo Lonkila (Finland) 1h 2m 20.0s

15 KMS CROSS-COUNTRY

1956	Hallgeir Brenden (Norway) 49m 39s	Sixten Jernberg (Sweden) 50m 14.0s	Pavel Koltschin (USSR) 50m 17.0s
1960	Haakon Brusveen (Norway) 51m 55.5s	Sixten Jernberg (Sweden) 51m 58.6s	Veikko Hakulinen (Finland) 52m 03.0s
1964	Eero Mäntyranta (Finland) 50m 54.1s	Harald Grönningen (Norway) 51m 34.8s	Sixten Jernberg (Sweden) 51m 42.2s
1968	Harald Grönningen (Norway) 47m 54.2s	Eero Mäntyranta (Finland) 47m 56.1s	Gunnar Larsson (Sweden) 48m 33.7s
1972	Sven Ake Lundback (Sweden) 45m 28.24s	Fedor Simaschov (USSR) 46m 0.84s	Ivar Formo (Norway) 46m 2.68s
1976	Nicolai Bajukov (USSR) 43m 58.47s	Evgeniy Beliaev (USSR) 44m 01.10	Arto Koivisto (Finland) 44m 19.25s

30 KMS CROSS-COUNTRY

1956	Veikko Hakulinen (Finland) 1h 44m 06.0s	Sixten Jernberg (Sweden) 1h 44m 30.0s	Pavel Koltschin (USSR) 1h 45m 45.0s
1960	Sixten Jernberg (Sweden) 1h 51m 03.9s	Rolf Rämgard (Sweden) 1h 51m 16.9s	Nikolay Anikin (USSR) 1h 52m 28.2s
1964	Eero Mäntyranta (Finland) 1h 30m 50.7s	Harald Grönningen (Norway) 1h 32m 02.3s	Igor Voronchikin (USSR) 1h 32m 15.8s
1968	Franco Nones (Italy) 1h 35m 39.2s	Odd Martinsen (Norway) 1h 36m 28.9s	Eero Mäntyranta (Finland) 1h 36m 55.3s
1972	Vyacheslav Vedenin (USSR) 1h 36m 31.15s	Paul Tyldum (Norway) 1h 37m 25.30s	Johs Harviken (Norway) 1h 37m 32.24s
1976	Sergei Saveliev (USSR) 1h 30m 29.38s	Bill Koch (USA) 1h 30m 57.84s	Ivan Garanin (USSR) 1h 31m 09.29s

50 KMS CROSS-COUNTRY

1924	Thorleif Haug (Norway) 3h 44m 32.0s	Thoralf Stromstad (Norway) 3h 46m 23.0s	Johan Gröttumsbraaten (Norway) 3h 47m 46.0s
1928	Per Erik Hedlund (Sweden) 4h 52m 03.3s	Gustaf Jonsson (Sweden) 5h 05m 30.0s	Volger Andersson (Sweden) 5h 05m 46.0s
1932	Veli Saarinen (Finland) 4h 28m 00.0s	Väinö Likkanen (Finland) 4h 28m 20.0s	Arne Rustadstuen (Norway) 4h 31m 53s
1936	Elis Wiklund (Sweden) 3h 30m 11.0s	Axel Wikström (Sweden) 3h 33m 20.0s	Nils-Joel Englund (Sweden) 3h 34m 10.0s
1948	Nils Karlsson (Sweden) 3h 47m 48.0s	Harald Eriksson (Sweden) 3h 52m 20.0s	Benjamin Vanninen (Finland) 3h 57m 28.0s
1952	Veikko Hakulinen (Finland) 3h 33m 33.0s	Eero Kolehmainen (Finland) 3h 38m 11.0s	Magnar Estenstad (Norway) 3h 38m 28.0s
1956	Sixten Jernberg (Sweden) 2h 50m 27.0s	Veikko Hakulinen (Finland) 2h 51m 45.0s	Fyedor Terentyev (USSR) 2h 53m 32.0s
1960	Kalevi Hämäläinen (Finland) 2h 59m 06.3s	Veikko Hakulinen (Finland) 2h 59m 26.7s	Rolf Rämgård (Sweden) 3h 02m 46.7s
1964	Sixten Jernberg (Sweden) 2h 43m 52.6s	Assar Ronnlund (Sweden) 2h 44m 58.2s	Arto Tiainen (Finland) 2h 45m 30.4s
1968	Ole Ellefsaeter (Norway) 2h 28m 45.8s	Vyacheslav Vedenin (USSR) 2h 29m 02.5s	Josef Haas (Switz) 2h 29m 14.8s
1972	Paul Tyldum (Norway) 2h 43m 14.75s	Magne Myrmo (Norway) 2h 43m 29.45s	Vyacheslav Vedenin (USSR) 2h 44m 0.19s
1976	Ivar Formo (Norway) 2h 37m 30.05s	Gert-Dietmar Klause (E. Germany) 2h 38m 13.21s	Benny Soedergren (Sweden) 2h 39m 39.21s

RELAY RACE 4 × 10 KMS

1936	Finland 2h 41m 33.0s	Norway 2h 41m 39.0s	Sweden 2h 43m 03.0s
1948	Sweden 2h 32m 08.0s	Finland 2h 41m 06.0s	Norway 2h 44m 33.0s
1952	Finland 2h 20m 16.0s	Norway 2h 23m 13.0s	Sweden 2h 24m 13.0s
1956	USSR 2h 15m 30.0s	Finland 2h 16m 31.0s	Sweden 2h 17m 42.0s
1960	Finland 2h 18m 45.6s	Norway 2h 18m 46.4s	USSR 2h 21m 21.6s
1964	Sweden 2h 18m 34.6s	Finland 2h 18m 42.4s	USSR 2h 18m 46.4s
1968	Norway 2h 8m 33.5s	Sweden 2h 10m 13.2s	Finland 2h 10m 56.7s
1972	USSR 2h 4m 47.94s	Norway 2h 4m 57.06s	Switzerland 2h 7m 0.06s
1976	Finland 2h 7m 59.72s	Norway 2h 9m 58.36s	USSR 2h 10m 51.46s

CROSS-COUNTRY SKIING (WOMEN)

5 KMS CROSS COUNTRY

1964	Klaudia Boyarskikh (USSR) 17m 50.5s	Mirja Lehtonen (Finland) 17m 52.9s	Alevtina Koltchina (USSR) 18m 08.4s
1968	Toini Gustafsson (Sweden) 16m 45.2s	Galina Koulakova (USSR) 16m 48.4s	Alevtina Koltchina (USSR) 16m 51.6s
1972	Galina Koulakova (USSR) 17m 0.50s	Marjatta Kajosmaa (Finland) 17m 5.50s	Helena Sikolova (Czech) 17m 7.32s
1976	Helena Takalo (Finland) 15m 48.69	Raisa Smetanina (USSR) 15m 49.73s	Galina Koulakora (USSR) 16m 07.36s

10 KMS CROSS-COUNTRY (WOMEN)

1952	Lydia Wideman (Finland) 41m 40.0s	Mirja Heitamies (Finland) 42m 39.0s	Siiri Rantanen (Finland) 42m 50.0s
1956	Lyubov Kosyryeva (USSR) 38m 11.0s	Radya Yeroschina (USSR) 38m 16.0s	Sonja Edstrom (Sweden) 38m 32.0s
1960	Maria Gusakova (USSR) 39m 46.6s	Lyubov Baranova (USSR) 40m 04.2s	Radya Yeroschina (USSR) 40m 06.0s
1964	Klaudia Boyarskikh (USSR) 40m 24.3s	Judokija Mekshilo (USSR) 40m 26.6s	Maria Gusakova (USSR) 40m 46.6s
1968	Toini Gustafsson (Sweden) 36m 46.5s	Berit Mördre (Sweden) 37m 54.6s	Inger Aufles (Norway) 37m 59.9s
1972	Galina Koulakova (USSR) 34m 17.82s	Alevtina Olunina (USSR) 34m 54.11s	Marjatta Kajosmaa (Finland) 34m 56.45s
1976	Raisa Smetanina (USSR) 30m 13.41s	Helena Takalo (Finland) 30m 14.28s	Galina Koulakova (USSR) 30m 38.61s

RELAY RACE 3 × 5 KMS

Year	First	Second	Third
1956	Finland 1h 9m 01.0s	USSR 1h 9m 28.0s	Sweden 1h 9m 48.0s
1960	Sweden 1h 4m 21.4s	USSR 1h 5m 2.6s	Finland 1h 6m 27.5s
1964	USSR 59m 20.2s	Sweden 1h 1m 27.0s	Finland 1h 2m 45.1s
1968	Norway 57m 30.0s	Sweden 57m 51.0s	USSR 58m 13.6s
1972	USSR 48m 46.15s	Finland 49m 19.37s	Norway 49m 51.49s

RELAY RACE 4 × 5 KMS

Year	First	Second	Third
1976	USSR 1h 7m 49.75s	Finland 1h 8m 36.57s	E. Germany 1h 9m 57.95s

NORDIC COMBINED (CROSS-COUNTRY AND JUMPING)

Year	First	Second	Third
1924	Thorleif Haug (Norway) 18.906pts	Thoralf Strömstad (Norway) 18.219	Johan Gröttumsbraaten (Norway) 17.854
1928	Johan Gröttumsbraaten (Norway) 17,833pts	Hans Vinjarengen (Norway) 15,303	John Snersrud (Norway) 15,021
1932	Johan Gröttumsbraaten (Norway) 446.0pts	Ole Stenen (Norway) 436.05	Hans Vinjarengen (Norway) 434.60
1936	Oddbjörn Hagen (Norway) 430.30pts	Olaf Hoffsbakken (Norway) 419.80	Sverre Brodahl (Norway) 408.10
1948	Heikki Hasu (Finland) 448.80pts	Martti Huhtala (Finland) 433.65	Sfen Israelsson (Sweden) 433.40
1952	Simon Slättvik (Norway) 451.62pts	Heikki Hasu (Finland) 447.5	Sverre Stenersen (Norway) 436.335
1956	Sverre Stenersen (Norway) 454.0pts	Bengt Eriksson (Sweden) 437.4	F. Gron-Gasienica (Poland) 436.8
1960	Georg Thoma (Germany) 457.952pts	Tormod Knutsen (Norway) 453.0	Nikolai Gusokaw (USSR) 452.0
1964	Tormod Knutsen (Norway) 469.28pts	Nikolai Kiselev (USSR) 453.04	Georg Thoma (Germany) 452.88
1968	Franz Keller (W. Germany) 449.04pts	Alois Kälin (Switzerland) 447.94	Andreas Kunz (E. Germany) 444.10
1972	Ulrich Wehling (E. Germany) 413.34pts	Rauno Miettinen (Finland) 405.50	Karl Luck (E. Germany) 398.80
1976	Ulrich Wehling (E. Germany) 423.39pts	Urban Hettich (W. Germany) 418.90	Konrad Winkler (E. Germany) 417.47

BIATHLON

Year	First	Second	Third
1960	Klas Lestander (Sweden) 1h 33m 21.6s	Antti Tyrvainen (Finland) 1h 33m 57.7s	Aleksandr Privalov (USSR) 1h 34m 54.2s
1964	Vladimir Melyanin (USSR) 1h 20m 26.0s	Aleksandr Privalov (USSR) 1h 23m 42.5s	Olav Jordet (Norway) 1h 24m 38.8s
1968	Magnar Solberg (Norway) 1h 13m 45.9s	Alexandr Tikhonov (USSR) 1h 14m 40.4s	Vladimir Goundartsev (USSR) 1h 18m 27.4s
1972	Magnar Solberg (Norway) 1h 15m 55.50s	Hansjorg Knauthe (E. Ger) 1h 16m 7 60s	Lars Arvidson (Sweden) 1h 16m 27.03s
1976	Nicolai Kruglov (USSR) 1h 14m 12.26s	Hokki Ikola (Finland) 1h 15m 54.10s	Alexander Elizarov (USSR) 1h 16m 5.57s

BIATHLON-RELAY

Year	First	Second	Third
1968	USSR 2h 13m 2.4s	Norway 2h 14m 50.2s	Sweden 2h 17m 26.3s
1972	USSR 1hr 51m 44.92s	Finland 1h 54m 37.25s	E. Germany 1h 54m 37.67s
1976	USSR 1h 57m 55.64s	Finland 2h 1m 45.58s	E. Germany 2h 4m 8.61s

ALPINE SKI-ING (MEN)

GIANT SLALOM

Year	First	Second	Third
1952	Stein Eriksen (Norway) 2m 25.0s	Christian Pravda (Austria) 2m 26.9s	Toni Spiess (Austria) 2m 28.8s
1956	Anton Sailer (Austria) 3m 00.1s	Andreas Molterer (Austria) 3m 06.3s	Walter Schuster (Austria) 3m 07.2s
1960	Roger Staub (Switzerland) 1m 48.3s	Josef Stiegler (Austria) 1m 48.7s	Ernst Hinterseer (Austria) 1m 49.1s
1964	François Bonlieu (France) 1m 46.71s	Karl Schranz (Austria) 1m 47.09s	Josef Stiegler (Austria) 1m 48.05s
1968	Jean-Claude Killy (France) 3m 29.28s	Willy Favre (Switzerland) 3m 31.50s	Heinrich Messner (Austria) 3m 31.83s
1972	Gustavo Thoeni (Italy) 3m 9.62s	Edmund Bruggman (Switzerland) 3m 10.75s	Werner Mattle (Switzerland) 3m 10.90s
1976	Heini Hemmi (Switzerland) 3m 26.97s	Ernst Good (Switzerland) 3m 27.17s	Ingemar Stenmark (Sweden) 3m 27.41s

SLALOM

Year	First	Second	Third
1948	Edi Reinalter (Switzerland) 2m 10.3s	James Couttet (France) 2m 10.8s	Henri Oreiller (France) 2m 12.8s
1952	Othmar Schneider (Austria) 2m 00.0s	Stein Eriksen (Norway) 2m 01.2s	Guttorm Berge (Norway) 2m 01.7s
1956	Anton Sailer (Austria) 3m 14.7s	Chiharu Igaya (Japan) 3m 18.7s	Stig Sollander (Sweden) 3m 20.2s
1960	Ernst Hinterseer (Austria) 2m 08.9s	Matthias Leitner (Austria) 2m 10.3s	Charles Bozon (France) 2m 10.4s
1964	Josef Stiegler (Austria) 2m 11.13s	William Kidd (USA) 2m 11.27s	James Heuga (USA) 2m 11.52s
1968	Jean-Claude Killy (France) 1m 39.73s	Herbert Huber (Austria) 1m 39.82s	Alfred Matt (Austria) 1m 40.09s
1972	Francisco Ochoa (Spain) 1m 49.27s	Gustavo Thoeni (Italy) 1m 50.28s	Rolando Thoeni (Italy) 1m 50.30s
1976	Piero Gros (Italy) 2m 03.29s	Gustavo Thoeni (Italy) 2m 03.73s	Willy Frommelt (Liechtenstein) 2m 04.28s

DOWNHILL

1948	Henri Oreiller (France) 2m 55.0s	Franz Gabl (Austria) 2m 59.1s	K. Molitor & R. Olinger (Switzerland) 3m 00.3s
1952	Zeno Colo (Italy) 2m 30.8s	Othmar Schneider (Austria) 2m 32.0s	Christian Pravda (Austria) 2m 32.4s
1956	Anton Sailer (Austria) 2m 52.2s	Raymond Fellay (Switzerland) 2m 55.7s	Andreas Molterer (Austria) 2m 56.2s
1960	Jean Vuarnet (France) 2m 06.0s	Hans-Peter Lanig (Germany) 2m 06.5s	Guy Périllat (France) 2m 06.9s
1964	Egon Zimmermann (Austria) 2m 18.16s	Leo Lacroix (France) 2m 18.90s	Wolfgang Barteis (Germany) 2m 19.48s
1968	Jean-Claude Killy (France) 1m 59.85s	Guy Périllat (France) 1m 59.93s	Jean-Daniel Dätwyler (Switzerland) 2m 00.32s
1972	Bernhard Russi (Switzerland) 1m 51.43s	Roland Collombin (Switzerland) 1m 52.07s	Heinrich Messner (Austria) 1m 52.40s
1976	Franz Klamner (Austria) 1m 46.73s	Bernhard Russi (Switzerland) 1m 46.06s	Herbert Plank (Italy) 1m 46.59s

ALPINE SKI-ING (WOMEN)

GIANT SLALOM

1952	Andrea Lawrence (USA) 2m 06.8s	Dagmar Rom (Austria) 2m 09.0s	Annemarie Buchner (Germany) 2m 10s
1956	Ossi Reichert (Germany) 1m 56.5s	Josefine Frandl (Austria) 1m 57.8s	Dorothea Hochleitner (Austria) 1m 58.2s
1960	Yvonne Ruegg (Switzerland) 1m 39.9s	Penelope Pitou (USA) 1m 40.0s	Giuliana Minuzzo (Italy) 1m 40.2s
1964	Marielle Goitschel (France) 1m 52.24s	Christine Goitschel (France) & Jean Saubert (USA) 1m 53.11s	
1968	Nancy Greene (Canada) 1m 51.97s	Annie Famose (France) 1m 54.61s	Fernande Bochatay (Switzerland) 1m 54.74s
1972	Marie Therese Nadig (Switzerland) 1m 29.90s	Annemarie Proell (Austria) 1m 30.75s	Wiltrud Drexel (Austria) 1m 32.35s
1976	Kathy Kreiner (Canada) 1m 29.13s	Rosi Mittermaier (W. Germany) 1m 29.25s	Danielle Debernard (France) 1m 29.95s

SLALOM

1948	Gretchen Frazer (USA) 1m 57.2s	Antoinette Meyer (Switzerland) 1m 57.7s	Erika Mahringer (Austria) 1m 58.0s
1952	Andrea Lawrence (USA) 2m 10.6s	Ossi Reichert (Germany) 2m 11.4s	Annemarie Buchner (Germany) 2m 13.3s
1956	Renée Colliard (Switzerland) 1m 2.3s	Regina Schöpf (Austria) 1m 55.4s	Evginija Sidorova (USSR) 1m 56.7s
1960	Ann Heggtveit (Canada) 1m 49.6s	Betsy Snite (USA) 1m 52.9s	Barbara Henneberger (Germany) 1m 56.6s
1964	Christine Goitschel (France) 1m 29.86s	Marielle Goitschel (France) 1m 30.77s	Jean Saubert (USA) 1m 31.36s
1968	Marielle Goitschel (France) 1m 25.86s	Nancy Greene (Canada) 1m 26.15s	Annie Famose (France) 1m 27.89s
1972	Barbara Cochran (USA) 91.24s	Danielle Debernard (France) 91.26s	Florence Steurer (France) 92.69s
1976	Rosi Mittermaier (W. Germany) 1m 30.54s	C. Giordani (Italy) 1m 30.87s	Hanni Wenzel (Liechtenstein) 1m 32.20s

DOWNHILL

1948	Hedy Schlunegger (Switzerland) 2m 28.3s	Trude Beiser (Austria) 2m 29.1s	Resi Hammerer (Austria) 2m 30.2s
1952	Trude Beiser (Austria) 1m 47.1s	Annemarie Buchner (Germany) 1m 48.0s	Giuliana Minuzzo (Italy) 1m 49.0s
1956	Madeleine Berthod (Switzerland) 1m 40.7s	Frieda Dänzer (Switzerland) 1m 45.4s	Lucile Wheeler (Canada) 1m 45.9s
1960	Heidi Biebl (Germany) 1m 37.6s	Penelope Pitou (USA) 1m 38.6s	Gertrud Hecher (Austria) 1m 38.9s
1964	Christl Haas (Austria) 1m 55.39s	Edith Zimmerman (Austria) 1m 56.42s	Gertrud Hecher (Austria) 1m 56.66s
1968	Olga Pall (Austria) 1m 40.87s	Isabelle Mir (France) 1m 41.33s	Christl Haas (Austria) 1m 41.44s
1972	Marie-Therese Nadig (Switzerland) 1m 36.68s	Annemarie Proell (Austria) 1m 37s	Susan Corrock (USA) 1m 37.68s
1976	Rosi Mittermaier (W. Germany) 1m 46.16s	Brigitte Totschnig (Austria) 1m 46.68s	Cynthia Nelson (USA) 1m 47.50s

SKI JUMPING

SKI JUMPING

1924	Jacob Tullin-Thams (Norway)	Narve Bonna (Norway)	Thorleif Haug (Norway)
1928	Alf Andersen (Norway)	Sigmund Ruud (Norway)	Rudolf Purkert (Czechoslovakia)
1932	Birger Ruud (Norway)	Hans Beck (Norway)	Kaare Wahlberg (Norway)
1936	Birger Ruud (Norway)	Sven Eriksson (Sweden)	Reidar Anderson (Norway)
1948	Petter Hugsted (Norway)	Birger Ruud (Norway)	Thorleif Schjelderup (Norway)
1952	Arnfinn Bergmann (Norway)	Torbjorn Falkanger (Norway)	Karl Holmstrom (Sweden)
1956	Antti Hyvaringen (Finland)	Aulis Kellakorpl (Finland)	Harry Glass (Germany)
1960	Helmut Recknagel (Germany)	N. Halonen (Finland)	O. Leodolter (Austria)

SMALL HILL (70 METRES)

1964	Veikko Kankkonen (Finland) 229.90pts	Toralf Engan (Norway) 226.30	Torgeir Brandtzäg (Norway) 222.90
1968	Jiri Raska (Czech) 216.5pts	Reinhold Bachler (Austria) 214.2	Baldur Preiml (Austria) 212.6
1972	Yukio Kasaya (Japan) 244.2pts	Akitsugu Konno (Japan) 234.8	Seiji Aochi (Japan) 229.5
1976	Hans-Georg Aschenbach (E. Germany) 252.0pts	Jochen Danneberg (E. Germany) 246.0	Karl Schnabl (Austria) 242.0

BIG HILL (90 METRES)

1964	Toralf Engan (Norway) 230.7pts	Veikko Kankkonen (Finland) 228.9	Torgeir Brantzäg (Norway) 227.2
1968	Vladimir Beloussov (USSR) 231.3pts	Jiri Raska (Czech) 229.4	Lars Grini (Norway) 214.3
1972	Wojciech Fortuna (Poland) 219.9pts	Walter Steiner (Switzerland) 219.8	Rainer Schmidt (E. Germany) 219.3
1976	Karl Schnabel (Austria) 234.8pts	Anton Innauer (Austria) 232.9	Henry Glass (E. Germany) 221.7

BOBSLEIGH

2-MAN BOB

1932	USA 8m 14.74s	Switzerland 8m 16.28s	USA 8m 29.15s
1936	USA 5m 29.29s	Switzerland 5m 30.64s	USA 5m 33.96s
1948	Switzerland 5m 29.2s	Switzerland 5m 30.4s	USA 5m 35.3s
1952	Germany 5m 24.54s	USA 5m 26.89s	Switzerland 5m 27.71s
1956	Italy 5m 30.14s	Italy 5m 31.45s	Switzerland 5m 37.46s
1964	GB 4m 21.90s	Italy 4m 22.02s	Italy 4m 22.63s
1968	Italy 4m 41.54s	Germany 4m 41.54s	Rumania 4m 44.46s
1972	W. Germany 4m 57.07s	W. Germany 4m 58.84s	Switzerland 4m 59.33s
1976	E. Germany 3m 44.42s	W. Germany 3m 44.99s	Austria 3m 45.70s

4-MAN BOB

1924	Switzerland 5m 45.54s	GB 5m 48.83s	Belgium 6m 02.29s
1928	USA 3m 20.5s	USA 3m 21.0s	Germany 3m 21.9s
1932	USA 7m 53.68s	USA 7m 55.70s	Germany 8m 00.04s
1936	Switzerland 5m 19.85s	Switzerland 5m 22.73s	GB 5m 23.41s
1948	USA 5m 20.1s	Belgium 5m 21.3	USA 5m 21.5
1952	Germany 5m 07.84s	USA 5m 10.48s	Switzerland 5m 11.70s
1956	Switzerland 5m 10.44s	Italy 5m 12.10s	USA 5m 12.39s
1964	Canada 4m 14.46s	Austria 4m 15.48s	Italy 4m 15.60
1968	Italy 2m 17.39s	Austria 2m 17.48s	Switzerland 2m 18.04s
1972	Switzerland 3m 32.36s	Italy 3m 32.91s	W. Germany 3m 33.23s
1976	E. Germany 3m 40.43s	Switzerland 3m 40.89s	W. Germany 3m 41.37s

TOBOGGANING

SINGLE SEATER (MEN)

1964	Thomas Kohler (Germany) 3m 26.77s	Klaus Bonsack (E. Germany) 3m 27.04s	Hans Plenk (Germany) 3m 30.15s
1968	Manfred Schmid (Austria) 2m 52.48s	Thomas Kohler (E. Germany) 2m 52.66s	Klaus Bonsack (E. Germany) 2m 53.33s
1972	Wolfgang Sheidel (E. Germany) 3m 27.58s	Harald Ehrig (E. Germany) 3m 28.39s	Wolfram Fiedler (E. Germany) 3m 28.73s
1976	Detlef Guenther (E. Germany) 3m 27.69s	Josef Fendt (W. Germany) 3m 28.20s	Hans Rinn (E. Germany) 3m 28.57s

SINGLE SEATER (WOMEN)

1964	Ortrun Enderlein (Germany) 3m 24.67s	Lise Geisler (Germany) 3m 27.42s	Helene Thurner (Austria) 3m 29.06s
1968	Erica Lechner (Italy) 2m 28.66s	Christa Schmuck (W. Germany) 2m 29.37s	Angelika Dunhaupt (W. Germany) 2m 29.56s
1972	Anna Müller (E. Germany) 2m 59.18s	Ute Ruhrold (E. Germany) 2m 59.49s	Margit Schumann (E. Germany) 2h 59.54s
1976	Margit Schumann (E. Germany) 2m 50.62s	Ute Ruhrold (E. Germany) 2m 50.85s	E. Demleitner (W. Germany) 2m 51.06s

2 SEATER (MEN)

1964	Austria 1m 41.62s	Austria 1m 41.91s	Italy 1m 42.87s
1968	E. Germany 1m 35.85s	Austria 1m 36.34s	W. Germany 1m 37.29s
1972	Italy & E. Germany 1m 28.35s		E. Germany 1m 29.16s
1976	E. Germany 1m 25.60s	W. Germany 1m 25.89s	Austria 1m 25.92s

WORLD SPEED SKATING CHAMPIONSHIPS

OVERALL WINNERS (MEN)

Year	First	Second	Third
1893	Jaap Eden (Netherlands)		
1894	no champion declared		
1895	Jaap Eden (Netherlands)		
1896	Jaap Eden (Netherlands)		
1897	Jack K. McCulloch (Canada)		
1898	Peder Oestlund (Norway)		
1899	Peder Oestlund (Norway)		
1900	Edvard Engelsaas (Norway)		
1901	Franz Fredrik Wathèn (Finland)		
1902 and 1903 no champion declared			
1904	Sigurd Mathisen (Norway)		
1905	C. Coen de Koning (Netherlands)		
1906 and 1907 no champion declared			
1908	Oscar Mathisen (Norway)	Martin Saetherhang (Norway)	Moje Öholm (Sweden)
1909	Oscar Mathisen (Norway)	Oluf Steen (Norway)	Otto Andersson (Sweden)
1910	Nicolai Strunnikov (Russia)	Oscar Mathisen (Norway)	Martin Saetherhang (Norway)
1911	Nicolai Strunnikov (Russia)	Martin Saetherhang (Norway)	Henning Olsen (Norway)
1912	Oscar Mathisen (Norway)	Gunnar Strömsten (Finland)	Trygve Lundgreen (Norway)
1913	Oscar Mathisen (Norway)	Wasili Ippolitov (Russia)	Nikita Naidenov (Russia)
1914	Oscar Mathisen (Norway)	Wasili Ippolitov (Russia)	Wäiniö Wickström (Finland)
no world championships until			
1922	Harald Ström (Norway)	Roald Larsen (Norway)	Clas Thunberg (Finland)
1923	Clas Thunberg (Finland)	Harald Ström (Norway)	Jakob Melnikov (USSR)
1924	Roald Larsen (Norway)	Uno Pietilä (Finland)	Julius Skutnabb (Finland)
1925	Clas Thunberg (Finland)	Uno Pietilä (Finland)	Roald Larsen (Norway)
1926	Ivar Ballangrud (Norway)	Roald Larsen (Norway)	Bernt Evensen (Norway)
1927	Bernt Evensen (Norway)	Clas Thunberg (Finland)	Armand Carlsen (Norway)
1928	Clas Thunberg (Finland)	Ivar Ballangrud (Norway)	Bernt Evensen (Norway)
1929	Clas Thunberg (Finland)	Ivar Ballangrud (Norway)	Michael Staksrud (Norway)
1930	Michael Staksrud (Norway)	Ivar Ballangrud (Norway)	Adolf van der Scheer (Netherlands)
1931	Clas Thunberg (Finland)	Bernt Evensen (Norway)	Ivar Ballangrud (Norway)
1932	Ivar Ballangrud (Norway)	Michael Staksrud (Norway)	Bernt Evensen (Norway)
1933	Hans Engnestangen (Norway)	Michael Staksrud (Norway)	Ivar Ballangrud (Norway)
1934	Bernt Evensen (Norway)	Birger Wasenius (Finland)	Ivar Ballangrud (Norway)
1935	Michael Staksrud (Norway)	Ivar Ballangrud (Norway)	Hans Engnestangen (Norway)
1936	Ivar Ballangrud (Norway)	Birger Wasenius (Finland)	Eddie Schroeder (USA)
1937	Michael Staksrud (Norway)	Birger Wasenius (Finland)	Max Stiepl (Austria)
1938	Ivar Ballangrud (Norway)	Karl Wazulek (Austria)	Charles Mathisen (Norway)
1939	Birger Wasenius (Finland)	Alfons Berzins (USSR)	Charles Mathisen (Norway)
no world championships until			
1947	Lassi Parkkinen (Finland)	Sverre Farstad (Norway)	Ake Seyffarth (Sweden)
1948	Odd Lundberg (Norway)	John Werket (USA)	Henry Wahl (Norway)
1949	Kornél Pajor (Hungary)	Kees Broekmann (Netherlands)	Odd Lundberg (Norway)
1950	Hjalmar Andersen (Norway)	Odd Lundberg (Norway)	John Werket (USA)
1951	Hjalmar Andersen (Norway)	Johnny Cronshey (Great Britain)	Kornél Pajor (Hungary)
1952	Hjalmar Andersen (Norway)	Lassi Parkkinen (Finland)	Ivar Martinsen (Norway)
1953	Oleg Gontscharenko (USSR)	Boris Schilkov (USSR)	Willem van der Voort (Netherlands)
1954	Boris Schilkov (USSR)	Oleg Gontscharenko (USSR)	Eugeny Grischin (USSR)
1955	Sigvard Ericsson (Sweden)	Oleg Gontscharenko (USSR)	Boris Schilkov (USSR)
1956	Oleg Gontscharenko (USSR)	Robert Merkulov (USSR)	Eugeny Grischin (USSR)
1957	Knut Johannesen (Norway)	Boris Schilkov (USSR)	Boris Zybin (USSR)
1958	Oleg Gontscharenko (USSR)	Vladimir Schilikovski (USSR)	Roald Aas (Norway)
1959	Juhani Järvinen (Finland)	Toivo Salonen (Finland)	Robert Merkulov (USSR)
1960	Boris Stenin (USSR)	André Kouprianoff (France)	Helmut Kuhnert (East Germany)
1961	Henk van der Grifft (Netherlands)	Viktor Kositschkin (USSR)	Rudi Liebrechts (Netherlands)
1962	Victor Kositschkin (USSR)	Henk van der Grifft (Netherlands)	Ivar Nilsson (Sweden)
1963	Jonny Nilsson (Sweden)	Knut Johannesen (Norway)	Nils Aaness (Norway)
1964	Knut Johannesen (Norway)	Viktor Kositschkin (USSR)	Rudi Liebrechts (Netherlands)
1965	Per Ivar Moe (Norway)	Jouko Launonen (Finland)	Ard Schenk (Netherlands)
1966	Kees Verkerk (Netherlands)	Ard Shenk (Netherlands)	Jonny Nilsson (Sweden)
1967	Kees Verkerk (Netherlands)	Ard Schenk (Netherlands)	Fred Maier (Norway)
1968	Fred Maier (Norway)	Magne Thomassen (Norway)	Ard Schenk (Netherlands)
1969	Dag Fornaess (Norway)	Göran Claeson (Sweden)	Kees Verkerk (Netherlands)
1970	Ard Schenk (Netherlands)	Magne Thomassen (Norway)	Kees Verkerk (Netherlands)
1971	Ard Schenk (Netherlands)	Göran Claeson (Sweden)	Kees Verkerk (Netherlands)
1972	Ard Schenk (Netherlands)	Roar Grönvold (Norway)	Jan Bols (Netherlands)
1973	Göran Claeson (Sweden)	Sten Stensen (Norway)	Piet Kleine (Netherlands)
1974	Sten Stensen (Norway)	Harm Kuipers (Netherlands)	Göran Claeson (Netherlands)

1975	Harm Kuipers (Netherlands)	Vladimir Ivanov (USSR)	Juri Kondakov (USSR)
1976	Piet Kleine (Netherlands)	Sten Stensen (Norway)	Hans van Helden (Netherlands)

OVERALL WINNERS (WOMEN)

1936	Kit Klein (USA)	Verné Lesche (Finland)	Synnöve Lie (Norway)
1937	Laila Schou (Norway)	Synnöve Lie (Norway)	Verné Lesche (Finland)
1938	Laila Schou (Norway)	Verné Lesche (Finland)	Synnöve Lie (Norway)
1939	Verné Lesche (Finland)	Liisa Salmi (Finland)	Laura Tamminen (Finland)
no more championship until			
1947	Verné Lesche (Finland)	Else Marie Kristiansen (Norway)	Maggi Kvestad (Norway)
1948	Maria Isakova (USSR)	Lydia Selikova (USSR)	Zoia Kholtschevnikova (USSR)
1949	Maria Isakova (USSR)	Zoia Kholtschevnikova (USSR)	Rimma Zhukova (USSR)
1950	Maria Isakova (USSR)	Zinaida Krotova (USSR)	Rimma Zhukova (USSR)
1951	Eevi Huttunen (Finland)	Randi Thorvaldsen (Norway)	Ranghild Mikkelsen (Norway)
1952	Lydia Selikova (USSR)	Maria Anikanova (USSR)	Randi Thorvaldsen (Norway)
1953	Khalida Schegoleeva (USSR)	Rimma Zhukova (USSR)	Lydia Selikova (USSR)
1954	Lydia Selikova (USSR)	Rimma Zhukova (USSR)	Sofia Kondakova (USSR)
1955	Rimma Zhukova (USSR)	Tamara Rylova (USSR)	Sofia Kondakova (USSR)
1956	Sofia Kondakova (USSR)	Rimma Zhukova (USSR)	Tamara Rylova (USSR)
1957	Inga Artamonova (USSR)	Tamara Rylova (USSR)	Lydia Selikova (USSR)
1958	Inga Artamonova (USSR)	Tamara Rylova (USSR)	Sofia Kondakova (USSR)
1959	Tamara Rylova (USSR)	Valentina Stenina (USSR)	Lydia Skoblikova (USSR)
1960	Valentina Stenina (USSR)	Tamara Rylova (USSR)	Lydia Skoblikova (USSR)
1961	Valentina Stenina (USSR)	Albina Tuzova (USSR)	Lydia Skoblikova (USSR)
1962	Inga Artamonova (USSR)	Lydia Skoblikova (USSR)	Albina Tuzova (USSR)
1963	Inga Artamonova (USSR)	Lydia Skoblikova (USSR)	Valentina Stenina (USSR)
1964	Lydia Skoblikova (USSR)	Inga Artamonova (USSR)	Tamara Rylova (USSR)
1965	Inga Artamonova (USSR)	Valentina Stenina (USSR)	Stien Kaiser (Netherlands)
1966	Valentina Stenina (USSR)	Song Soon Kim (N. Korea)	Stien Kaiser (Netherlands)
1967	Stien Kaiser (Netherlands)	Lasma Kauniste (USSR)	Diane Holum (USA)
1968	Stien Kaiser (Netherlands)	Johanna Schut (Netherlands)	Carolina Geijssen (Netherlands)
1969	Lasma Kauniste (USSR)	Stien Kaiser (Netherlands)	Johanna Schut (Netherlands)
1970	Atje Keulen-Deetstra (Netherlands)	Stien Kaiser (Netherlands)	Sigrid Sundby (Norway)
1971	Nina Statkevich (USSR)	Stien Kaiser (Netherlands)	Ljudmila Titova (USSR)
1972	Atje Keulen-Deetstra (Netherlands)	Stien Baas-Kaiser (Netherlands)	Diane Holum (USA)
1973	Atje Keulen-Deetstra (Netherlands)	Tatiana Schelekova (USSR)	Trijnie Rep (Netherlands)
1974	Atje Keulen-Deetstra (Netherlands)	Nina Statkevich (USSR)	Tatiana Schelekova (USSR)
1975	Karin Kessow (East Germany)	Tatiana Averina (USSR)	Sheila Young (USSR) (USA)
1976	Sylvia Burka (Canada)	Tatiana Averina (USSR)	Sheila Young (USA)

EUROPEAN SPEED SKATING CHAMPIONSHIPS

1891	no champion declared		
1892	Franz Schilling (Austria)		
1893	Rudolf Ericsson (Sweden)		
1894	no champion declared		
1895	Alfred Naess (Norway)		
1896	Julius Seyler (Germany)		
1897	Julius Seyler (Germany)		
1898	Gustav Estlander (Finland)		
1899	Peder Oestlund (Norway)		
1900	Peder Oestlund (Norway)		
1901	Rudolf Gundersen (Norway)		
1902	Johan Schwartz (Norway)		
1903	no champion declared		
1904	Rudolf Gundersen (Norway)		
1905	Johan Wikander (Finland)		
1906	Rudolf Gundersen (Norway)		
1907	Moje Öholm (Sweden)		
1908	Moje Öholm (Sweden)		
1909	Oscar Mathisen (Norway)	Thomas Bohrer (Austria)	Moje Öholm (Sweden)
1910	Nicolai Strunnikov (Russia)	Magnus Johansen (Norway)	Oscar Mathisen (Norway)
1911	Nicolai Strunnikov (Russia)	Thomas Bohrer (Austria)	Otto Andersson (Sweden)
1912	Oscar Mathisen (Norway)	Gunnar Strömsten (Finland)	Martin Saetherhang (Norway)
1913	Wasili Ippolitov (Russia)	Oscar Mathisen (Norway)	Nikita Naidenov (Russia)
1914	Oscar Mathisen (Norway)	Wasili Ippolitov (Russia)	Bjarne Frang (Norway)
no more championships until			
1922	Clas Thunberg (Finland)	Ole Olsen (Norway)	Asser Walenius (Finland)
1923	Harald Ström (Norway)	Clas Thunberg (Finland)	Roald Larsen (Norway)
1924	Roald Larsen (Norway)	Clas Thunberg (Finland)	Oscar Olsen (Norway)
1925	Otto Polaczek (Austria)	Roald Larsen (Norway)	Oscar Olsen (Norway)
1926	Julius Skutnabb (Finland)	Otto Polaczek (Austria)	Uno Pietilä (Finland)
1927	Bernt Evensen (Norway)	Clas Thunberg (Finland)	Ivar Ballangrud (Norway)
1928	Clas Thunberg (Finland)	Bernt Evensen (Norway)	Roald Larsen (Norway)
1929	Ivar Ballangrud (Norway)	Clas Thunberg (Finland)	Thorstein Stenbeck (Norway)
1930	Ivar Ballangrud (Norway)	Michael Staksrud (Norway)	Thorstein Stenbeck (Norway)
1931	Clas Thunberg (Finland)	Ossi Blomqvist (Finland)	Adolf van der Scheer (Netherlands)
1932	Clas Thunberg (Finland)	Ossi Blomqvist (Finland)	Rudolf Riedl (Austria)
1933	Ivar Ballangrud (Norway)	Birger Wasenius (Finland)	Kalle Paananen (Finland)
1934	Michael Staksrud (Norway)	Max Stiepl (Austria)	Karl Wazulek (Austria)
1935	Karl Wazulek (Austria)	Bernt Evensen (Norway)	Birger Wasenius (Finland)
1936	Ivar Ballangrud (Norway)	Charles Mathisen (Norway)	Harry Haraldsen (Norway)
1937	Michael Staksrud (Norway)	Hans Engnestangen (Norway)	Birger Wasenius (Finland)
1938	Charles Mathisen (Norway)	Harry Haraldsen (Norway)	Ivar Ballangrud (Norway)
1939	Alfons Berzins (Latvia USSR)	Charles Mathisen (Norway)	Åge Johansen (Norway)
1947	Ake Seyffarth (Sweden)	Göthe Hedlund (Sweden)	Sverre Farstad (Norway)
1948	Reidar Liaklev (Norway)	Göthe Hedlund (Sweden)	Odd Lundberg (Norway)
1949	Sverre Farstad (Norway)	Hjalmar Andersen (Norway)	Kornél Pajor (Hungary)
1950	Hjalmar Andersen (Norway)	Reidar Liaklev (Norway)	Sverre Haugli (Norway)
1951	Hjalmar Andersen (Norway)	Willem van der Voort (Netherlands)	Henry Wahl (Norway)
1952	Hjalmar Andersen (Norway)	Kees Broekmann (Netherlands)	Kornél Pajor (Hungary)
1953	Kees Broekmann (Netherlands)	Willem van der Voort (Netherlands)	Ivar Martinsen (Norway)
1954	Boris Schillkov (USSR)	Hjalmar Andersen (Norway)	Sigvard Ericsson (Sweden)
1955	Sigvard Ericsson (Sweden)	Oleg Gontscharenko (USSR)	Dmitri Sakunenko (USSR)
1956	Eugeny Grischin (USSR)	Knut Johannesen (Norway)	Siggvard Ericsson (Sweden)
1957	Oleg Gontscharenko (USSR)	Knut Johannesen (Norway)	Roald Aas (Norway)
1958	Oleg Gontscharenko (USSR)	Vladimir Shilikovski (USSR)	Knut Johannesen (Norway)
1959	Knut Johannesen (Norway)	Juhani Järvinen (Finland)	Toivo Salonen (Finland)
1960	Knut Johannesen (Norway)	Boris Stenin (USSR)	Roald Aas (Norway)
1961	Viktor Kositschkin (USSR)	Henk van der Grifft (Netherlands)	André Kouprianoff (Netherlands)
1962	Robert Merkulov (USSR)	André Kouprianoff (Netherlands)	Boris Stenin (USSR)
1963	Nils Aaness (Norway)	Knut Johannesen (Norway)	Per Ivar Moe (Norway)
1964	Ants Antson (USSR)	Juri Jumasjev (USSR)	Per Ivar Moe (Norway)
1965	Eduard Matusevich (USSR)	Per Ivar Moe (Norway)	Victor Kositschkin (USSR)
1966	Ard Schenk (Netherlands)	Kees Verkerk (Netherlands)	Valeri Kaplan (USSR)
1967	Kees Verkerk (Netherlands)	Valeri Kaplan (USSR)	Eduard Matusevich (USSR)
1968	Fred Maier (Norway)	Eduard Matusevich (USSR)	Magne Thomassen (Norway)
1969	Dag Fornaess (Norway)	Kees Verkerk (Netherlands)	Göran Claeson (Sweden)
1970	Ard Schenk (Netherlands)	Dag Fornaess (Norway)	Göran Claeson (Sweden)
1971	Dag Fornaess (Norway)	Ard Schenk (Netherlands)	Göran Claeson (Sweden)
1972	Ard Schenk (Netherlands)	Roar Grönvold (Norway)	Jan Bols (Netherlands)
1973	Göran Claeson (Sweden)	Hans van Helden (Netherlands)	Harm Kuipers (Netherlands)
1974	Göran Claeson (Sweden)	Amund Sjøbrend (Norway)	Hans van Helden (Netherlands

1975	Sten Stensen (Norway)	Harm Kuipers (Netherlands)	Piet Kleine (Netherlands)
1976	Kay Arne Stenshjemmet (Norway)	Sten Stenson (Norway)	Jan Egil Storholt (Norway)

WORLD CHAMPIONSHIPS – FIGURE SKATING

FIGURE SKATING (MEN)

1896	Gilbert Fuchs (Germany)	Gustav Hügel (Austria)	Georg Sanders (Russia)
1897	Gustav Hügel (Austria)	Ulrich Salchow (Sweden)	Johan Lefstad (Norway)
1898	Henning Grenander (Sweden) 10	Gustav Hügel (Austria) 13	Gilbert Fuchs (Germany) 13
1899	Gustav Hügel (Austria) 7	Ulrich Salchow (Sweden) 8	Edgar Syers (Great Britain) 15
1900	Gustav Hügel (Austria) 7	Ulrich Salchow (Sweden) 8	
1901	Ulrich Salchow (Sweden) 9	Gilbert Fuchs (Germany) 9	
1902	Ulrich Salchow (Sweden) 5	Mrs Madge Syers-Cave (Great Britain) 13	Martin Gordon (Germany) 15
1903	Ulrich Salchow (Sweden) 6	Nicolai Panin (Russia) 12	Max Bohatsch (Austria) 12
1904	Ulrich Salchow (Sweden) 5	Heinrich Burger (Germany) 12	Martin Gordan (Germany) 13
1905	Ulrich Salchow (Sweden) 8	Max Bohatsch (Austria) 14	Per Thoren (Sweden) 21
1906	Gilbert Fuchs (Germany) 5	Heinrich Burger (Germany) 14	Bror Meyer (Sweden) 17
1907	Ulrich Salchow (Sweden) 8	Max Bohatsch (Austria) 11	Gilbert Fuchs (Germany) 12
1908	Ulrich Salchow (Sweden) 9	Gilbert Fuchs (Germany) 12	Heinrich Burger (Germany) 21
1909	Ulrich Salchow (Sweden) 7	Per Thoren (Sweden) 10	Ernest Herz (Austria) 16
1910	Ulrich Salchow (Sweden) 11	Werner Rittberger (Germany) 17	Andor Szende (Hungary) 20
1911	Ulrich Salchow (Sweden) 14	Werner Rittberger (Germany) 17	Fritz Kachler (Austria) 20
1912	Fritz Kachler (Austria) 8	Werner Rittberger (Germany) 16	Andor Szende (Hungary) 18
1913	Fritz Kachler (Austria) 5	Willy Böckl (Austria) 14	Andor Szende (Hungary) 16
1914	Gösta Sandahl (Sweden) 12	Fritz Kachler (Austria) 17	Willy Böckl (Austria) 17
no world championships until			
1922	Gillis Graftström (Sweden) 7	Fritz Kachler (Austria) 8	Willy Böckl (Austria) 15
1923	Fritz Kachler (Austria) 7	Willy Böckl (Austria) 12	Gösta Sandahl (Sweden) 16
1924	Gillis Graftström (Sweden) 5	Willy Böckl (Austria) 10	Ernst Oppacher (Austria) 22
1925	Willy Böckl (Austria) 8	Fritz Kachler (Austria) 8	Otto Preissecker (Austria) 14
1926	Willy Böckl (Austria) 7	Otto Preissecker (Austria) 11	John Page (Great Britain) 18
1927	Willy Böckl (Austria) 11	Otto Preissecker (Austria) 15	Karl Schäfer (Austria) 24
1928	Willy Böckl (Austria) 5½	Karl Schäfer (Austria) 11½	Dr Hugo Distler (Austria) 22
1929	Gillis Graftström (Sweden) 6	Karl Schäfer (Austria) 9	Ludwig Wrede (Austria) 18
1930	Karl Schäfer (Austria) 5	Roger Turner (USA) 11	Georg Gautschi (Switzerland) 19
1931	Karl Schäfer (Austria) 8	Roger Turner (USA) 26	Ernst Baier (Germany) 33
1932	Karl Schäfer (Austria) 7	Montgomery Wilson (Canada) 14	Ernst Baier (Germany) 25
1933	Karl Schäfer (Austria) 5	Ernst Baier (Germany) 11	Markus Nikkanen (Finland) 17
1934	Karl Schäfer (Austria) 7	Ernst Baier (Germany) 26	Erich Erdos (Austria) 26
1935	Karl Schäfer (Austria) 5	Jack Dunn (Great Britain) 15	Dénes Pataky (Hungary) 15

1936	Karl Schäfer (Austria) 6	Graham Sharp (Great Britain) 10	Felix Kaspar (Austria) 17
1937	Felix Kaspar (Austria) 5	Graham Sharp (Great Britain) 10	Elemér Tertak (Hungary) 17
1938	Felix Kaspar (Austria) 9	Graham Sharp (Great Britain) 12	Herbert Alward (Austria) 32
1939	Graham Sharp (Great Britain) 5	Freddie Tomlins (Great Britain) 11	Horst Faber (Germany) 15
no world championships until			
1947	Hans Gerschwiler (Switzerland) 7	Richard Button (USA) 8	Arthur Apfel (Great Britain) 16
1948	Richard Button (USA) 11	Hans Gerschwiler (Switzerland) 19	Ede Kiraly (Hungary) 28
1949	Richard Button (USA) 5	Ede Kiraly (Hungary) 12	Edi Rada (Austria) 13
1950	Richard Button (USA) 7	Ede Kiraly (Hungary) 14	Hayes Alan Jenkins (USA) 22
1951	Richard Button (USA) 7	James Grogan (USA) 17	Helmut Seibt (Austria) 22
1952	Richard Button (USA) 7	James Grogan (USA) 19	Hayes Alan Jenkins (USA) 21
1953	Hayes Alan Jenkins (USA) 13	James Grogan (USA) 16	Carlo Fassi (Italy) 36
1954	Hayes Alan Jenkins (USA) 5	James Grogan (USA) 12	Alain Giletti (France) 18
1955	Hayes Alan Jenkins (USA) 11	Ronald Robertson (USA) 16	David Jenkins (USA) 18
1956	Hayes Alan Jenkins (USA) 10	Ronald Robertson (USA) 17	David Jenkins (USA) 28
1957	David Jenkins (USA) 7	Tim Brown (USA) 16	Charles Snelling (Canada) 22
1958	David Jenkins (USA) 9	Tim Brown (USA) 28	Alain Giletti (France) 26
1959	David Jenkins (USA) 7	Donald Jackson (Canada) 18	Tim Brown (USA) 19
1960	Alain Giletti (France) 9	Donald Jackson (Canada) 12	Alain Calmat (France) 25
1961	no world championship held owing to an air crash involving the American team		
1962	Donald Jackson (Canada) 13	Karol Divin (Czechoslovakia) 17	Alain Calmat (France) 25
1963	Donald McPherson (Canada) 13	Alain Calmat (France) 22	Manfred Schnelldorfer (W. Germany) 22
1964	Manfred Schnelldorfer (W. Germany) 10	Alain Calmat (France) 23	Karol Divin (Czechoslovakia) 38
1965	Alain Calmat (France) 9	Scott Allen (USA) 27	Donald Knight (Canada) 29
1966	Emmerich Danzer (Austria) 11	Wolfgang Schwartz (Austria) 25	Gary Visconti (USA) 28
1967	Emmerich Danzer (Austria) 16	Wolfgang Schwartz (Austria) 16	Gary Visconti (USA) 35
1968	Emmerich Danzer (Austria) 12	Tim Wood (USA) 15	Patrick Pera (France) 38
1969	Tim Wood (USA) 9	Ondrej Nepela (Czechoslovakia) 22	Patrick Pera (France) 27
1970	Tim Wood (USA) 12	Ondrej Nepela (Czechoslovakia) 15	Günter Zöller (East Germany) 32
1971	Ondrej Nepela (Czechoslovakia) 12	Patrick Pera (France) 16	Sergei Chetverukhin (USSR) 34
1972	Ondrej Nepela (Czechoslovakia) 9	Sergei Chetverukhin (USSR) 19	Vladimir Kovalev (USSR) 34
1973	Ondrej Nepela (Czechoslovakia) 10	Sergei Chetverukhin (USSR) 17	Jan Hoffmann (East Germany) 35
1974	Jan Hoffmann (East Germany) 11	Sergei Volkov (USSR) 27	Toller Cranston (Canada) 26
1975	Sergei Volkov (USSR) 13	Vladimir Kovalev (USSR) 27	John Curry (Great Britain) 23
1976	John Curry (Great Britain) 13	Vladimir Kovalev (USSR) 15	Jan Hoffman (East Germany) 29

FIGURE SKATING (WOMEN)

1906	Madge Syers-Cave (Great Britain) 5	Jenny Herz (Austria) 13	Lily Kronberger (Hungary) 13½
1907	Madge Syers-Cave (Great Britain) 5	Jenny Herz (Austria) 12	Lily Kronberger (Hungary) 13
1908	Lily Kronberger (Hungary) 5	Elsa Rendschmidt (Germany) 10	
1909	Lily Kronberger (Hungary) 5		
1910	Lily Kronberger (Hungary) 5	Elsa Rendschmidt (Germany) 10	
1911	Lily Kronberger (Hungary) 7	Opika von Méray Horvath (Hungary) 14	Ludowika Eilers (Germany) 21
1912	Opika von Méray Horvath (Hungary) 7	D. Greenhough-Smith (Great Britain) 14	Phyllis Johnson (Great Britain) 18
1913	Opika von Méray Horvath (Hungary) 5	Phyllis Johnson (Great Britain) 17	Svea Noren (Sweden) 17
1914	Opika von Méray Horvath (Hungary) 6	Angela Hanka (Austria) 10	Phyllis Johnson (Great Britain) 18
no world championships until			
1922	Herma Planck-Szabo (Austria) 5	Svea Noren (Sweden) 11	Margot Moe (Norway) 14
1923	Herma Planck-Szabo (Austria) 6	Gisela Reichmann (Austria) 12	Svea Noren (Sweden) 16
1924	Herma Planck-Szabo (Austria) 5	Ellen Brockhöfft (Germany) 12	Beatrix Loughran (USA) 16
1925	Herma Jaross-Szabo (Austria)	Ellen Brockhöfft (Germany) 12	Elisabeth Böckel (Germany) 18
1926	Herma Jaross-Szabo (Austria) 5	Sonja Henie (Norway) 10	Kathleen Shaw (Great Britain) 16
1927	Sonja Henie (Norway) 7	Herma Jaross-Szabo (Austria) 8	Karen Simensen (Norway) 17
1928	Sonja Henie (Norway) 6	Maribel Vinson (USA) 13	Fritzi Burger (Austria) 15
1929	Sonja Henie (Norway) 5	Fritzi Burger (Austria) 12	Melitta Brunner (Austria) 13
1930	Sonja Henie (Norway) 5	Cecil Smith (Canada) 12	Maribel Vinson (USA) 16
1931	Sonja Henie (Norway) 8	Hilde Holovsky (Austria) 17	Fritzi Burger (Austria) 21
1932	Sonja Henie (Norway) 7	Fritzi Burger (Austria) 22	Constance Samuel (Canada) 24
1933	Sonja Henie (Norway) 5	Vivi-Anne Hulten (Sweden) 14	Hilde Holovsky (Austria) 15
1934	Sonja Henie (Norway) 7	Megan Taylor (Great Britain) 19	Liselotte Landbeck (Austria) 20
1935	Sonja Henie (Norway) 7	Cecilia Colledge (Great Britain) 17	Vivi-Anne Hulten (Sweden) 22
1936	Sonja Henie (Norway) 7	Megan Taylor (Great Britain) 15	Vivi-Anne Hulten (Sweden) 21
1937	Cecilia Colledge (Great Britain) 7	Megan Taylor (Great Britain) 14	Vivi-Anne Hulten (Sweden) 25½
1938	Megan Taylor (Great Britain) 7	Cecilia Colledge (Great Britain) 8	Hedy Stenuf (USA) 21
1939	Megan Taylor (Great Britain) 5	Hedy Stenuf (USA) 14	Daphne Walker (Great Britain) 15
1947	Barbara Ann Scott (Canada) 10	Daphne Walker (Great Britain) 22	Gretchen Merrill (USA) 32
1948	Barbara Ann Scott (Canada) 11	Eva Pawlik (Austria) 25	Jirina Nekolova (Czecholslovakia) 32
1949	Alena Vrzanova (Czechoslovakia) 7	Yvonne Sherman (USA) 17	Jeanette Altwegg (Great Britain) 18
1950	Alena Vrzanova (Czechoslovakia) 12	Jeanette Altwegg (Great Britain) 18	Yvonne Sherman (USA) 23
1951	Jeanette Altwegg (Great Britain) 8	Jacqueline du Bief (France) 14	Sonya Klopfer (USA) 23
1952	Jacqueline du Bief (France) 9	Sonya Klopfer (USA) 21	Virginia Baxter (USA) 24
1953	Tenley Albright (USA) 7	Grundi Busch (Germany) 16	Valda Osborn (Great Britain) 28
1954	Grundi Busch (Germany) 9	Tenley Albright (USA) 12	Erica Batchelor (Great Britain) 26

1955	Tenley Albright (USA) 9	Carol Heiss (USA) 28	Hanna Eigel (Austria) 29
1956	Carol Heiss (USA) 13	Tenley Albright (USA) 14	Ingrid Wendl (Austria) 33
1957	Carol Heiss (USA) 7	Hanna Eigel (Austria) 17	Ingrid Wendl (Austria) 21
1958	Carol Heiss (USA) 9	Ingrid Wendl (Austria) 19	Hanna Walter (Austria) 41½
1959	Carol Heiss (USA) 7	Hanna Walter (Austria) 20	Sjoukje Dijkstra (Netherlands) 24
1960	Carol Heiss (USA) 9	Sjoukje Dijkstra (Netherlands) 19	Barbara Roles (USA) 26
1961	no world championship held owing to an air crash involving the American team		
1962	Sjoukje Dijkstra (Netherlands) 9	Wendy Griner (Canada) 21	Regine Heitzer (Austria) 42
1963	Sjoukje Dijkstra (Netherlands) 9	Regine Heitzer (Austria) 22	Nicole Hassler (France) 30
1964	Sjoukje Dijkstra (Netherlands) 9	Regine Heitzer (Austria) 21	Petra Burka (Canada) 24
1965	Petra Burka (Canada) 9	Regine Heitzer (Austria) 23	Peggy Fleming (USA) 28
1966	Peggy Fleming (USA) 9	Gabiele Seyfert (East Germany) 22	Petra Burka (Canada) 23
1967	Peggy Fleming (USA) 9	Gabriele Seyfert (East Germany) 21	Hana Maskova (Czechoslovakia) 29
1968	Peggy Fleming (USA) 9	Gabriele Seyfert (East Germany) 19	Hana Maskova (Czechoslovakia) 29
1969	Gabriele Seyfert (East Germany) 9	Beatrix Schuba (Austria) 24	Zsuzsa Almassy (Hungary) 27
1970	Gabriele Seyfert (East Germany) 9	Beatrix Schuba (Austria) 21	Janet Lynn Holmes (USA) 38
1971	Beatrix Schuba (Austria) 10	Janet Lynn Holmes (USA) 24½	Karen Magnussen (Canada) 27
1972	Beatrix Schuba (Austria) 13	Karen Magnussen (Canada) 16	Janet Lynn Holmes (United States) 25
1973	Karen Magnussen (Canada) 9	Janet Lynn Holmes (USA) 18	Christine Errath (East Germany) 31
1974	Christine Errath (East Germany) 12	Dorothy Hamill (USA) 15	Dianne de Leeuw (Netherlands) 27
1975	Dianne de Leeuw (Netherlands) 9	Dorothy Hamill (USA) 25	Christine Errath (East Germany) 31
1976	Dorothy Hamill (USA) 10	Christine Errath (East Germany) 22	Dianne de Leeuw (Netherlands) 41

FIGURE SKATING (PAIRS)

1908	Anna Hübler Heinrich Burger (Germany) 5	Phyllis Johnson James H. Johnson (Great Britain) 11½	A. L. Fischer L. P. Popowa (Russia) 13½
1909	Phyllis Johnson James H. Johnson (Great Britain) 5½	Valborg Lindahl Nils Rosenius (Sweden) 9½	Gertrud Ström Richard Johanson (Sweden) 16
1910	Anna Hübler Heinrich Burger (Germany) 8½	Ludowika Eilers Walter Jacobsson (Germany/Finland) 14	Phyllis Johnson James H. Johnson (Great Britain) 19½
1911	Ludowika Eilers Walter Jacobsson (Germany/Finland) 7		
1912	Phyllis Johnson James H. Johnson (Great Britain) 8½	Ludowika Jacobsson-Eilers Walter Jacobsson-Eilers (Finland) 10	Alexia Bryn-Schöyen Yngvar Bryn-Schöyen (Norway) 14
1913	Helene Engelmann Karl Mejstrick (Austria) 9	Ludowika Jacobsson-Eilers Walter Jacobsson-Eilers (Finland) 10	Christa von Szabo Leo Horwitz (Austria) 11½
1914	Ludowika Jacobsson-Eilers Walter Jacobsson-Eilers (Finland) 7	Helene Engelmann Karl Mejstrick (Austria) 11	Christa von Szabo Leo Horwitz (Austria) 12
no world championships until			
1922	Helene Engelmann Alfred Berger (Austria) 6	Ludowika Jacobsson-Eilers Walter Jacobsson-Eilers (Finland) 12½	Margaret Metzner Paul Metzner (Germany) 17½
1923	Ludowika Jacobsson-Eilers Walter Jacobsson-Eilers (Finland) 6½	Alexia Bryn-Schöyen Yngvar Bryn-Schöyen (Norway) 10½	Elna Henrikson Kaj af Ekström (Sweden) 14
1924	Helene Engelmann Alfred Berger (Austria) 5	Ethel Muckett John F. Page (Great Britain) 10	Elna Henrikson Kaj af Ekström (Sweden) 15
1925	Herma Jaross-Szabo Ludwig Wrede (Austria) 10	Andrée Joly Pierre Brunet (France) 10½	Lilly Scholz Otto Kaiser (Austria) 14½
1926	Andrée Brunet Pierre Brunet (France) 12	Lilly Scholz Otto Kaiser (Austria) 22	Herma Jaross-Szabo Ludwig Wrede (Austria) 26
1927	Herma Jaross-Szabo Ludwig Wrede (Austria) 6½	Lilly Scholz Otto Kaiser (Austria) 9	Else Hoppe Oscar Hoppe (Czechoslovakia) 14½
1928	Andrée Brunet Pierre Brunet (France) 7	Lilly Scholz Otto Kaiser (Austria) 8	Melitta Brunner Ludwig Wrede (Austria) 18
1929	Lilly Scholz Otto Kaiser (Austria)	Melitta Brunner Ludwig Wrede (Austria)	Olga Organista Sandor Szalay (Hungary)
1930	Andrée Brunet Pierre Brunet (France) 6½	Melitta Brunner Ludwig Wrede (Austria) 13½	Beatrix Loughran Sherwin Badger (USA) 16
1931	Emilie Rotter Laszlo Szollas (Hungary) 13½	Olga Organista Sandor Szalay (Hungary) 14½	Idi Papez Karl Zwack (Austria) 23½
1932	Andrée Brunet Pierre Brunet (France) 9	Emilie Rotter Laszlo Szollas (Hungary) 16	Beatrix Loughran Sherwin Badger (USA) 22½
1933	Emilie Rotter Laszlo Szollas (Hungary) 7	Idi Papez Karl Zwack (Austria) 8	Randi Bakke Christen Christensen (Norway) 18
1934	Emilie Rotter Laszlo Szollas (Hungary) 12	Idi Papez Karl Zwack (Austria) 8	Maxi Herber Ernst Baier (Germany) 18
1935	Emilie Rotter Laszlo Szollas (Hungary) 5	Ilse Pausin Erich Pausin (Austria) 12½	Lucy Gallo Reszö Dillinger (Hungary) 14½
1936	Maxi Herber Ernst Baier (Germany) 5	Ilse Pausin Erich Pausin (Austria) 11	Violet Cliff Leslie Cliff (Great Britain) 19
1937	Maxi Herber Ernst Baier (Germany) 8½	Ilse Pausin Erich Pausin (Austria) 14½	Violet Cliff Leslie Cliff (Great Britain) 24½
1938	Maxi Herber Ernst Baier (Germany) 12	Ilse Pausin Erich Pausin (Austria) 16	Inge Koch Günther Noack (Germany) 30
1939	Maxi Herber Ernst Baier (Germany) 8	Ilse Pausin Erich Pausin (Austria) 13	Inge Koch Günther Noack (Germany) 24
no world championships until			
1947	Micheline Lannoy Pierre Baugniet (Belgium) 16	Karol Kennedy Peter Kennedy (USA) 19½	Suzanne Diskeuve Edmond Verbustel (Belgium) 25½
1948	Micheline Lannoy Pierre Baugniet (Belgium) 13½	Andrea Kékesy Ede Kiraly (Hungary) 24½	Suzanne Morrow Wallace Diestelmeyer (Canada) 26
1949	Andrea Kékesy Ede Kiraly (Hungary) 7	Karol Kennedy Peter Kennedy (USA) 14½	Ann Davies Carleton Hoffner (USA) 31½

1950	Karol Kennedy Peter Kennedy (USA) 15	Jennifer Nicks John Nicks (Great Britain) 28½	Marianne Nagy Laszlo Nagy (Hungary) 32
1951	Ria Baran Paul Falk (Germany) 10	Karol Kennedy Peter Kennedy (USA) 11½	Jennifer Nicks John Nicks (Great Britain) 20½
1952	Ria Falk Paul Falk (Germany) 9	Karol Kennedy Peter Kennedy (USA) 23½	Jennifer Nicks John Nicks (Great Britain) 29
1953	Jennifer Nicks John Nicks (Great Britain) 10½	Frances Dafoe Norris Bowden (Canada) 16	Marianne Nagy Laszlo Nagy (Hungary) 23½
1954	Frances Dafoe Norris Bowden (Canada) 9½	Silvia Grandjean Michel Grandjean (Switzerland) 17½	Sissy Schwarz Kurt Oppelt (Austria) 21
1955	Frances Dafoe Norris Bowden (Canada) 17½	Sissy Schwarz Kurt Oppelt (Austria) 17½	Marianne Nagy Laszlo Nagy (Hungary) 28
1956	Sissy Schwarz Kurt Oppelt (Austria) 14	Frances Dafoe Norris Bowden (Canada) 15	Marika Kilius Franz Ningel (West Germany) 30
1957	Barbara Wagner Robert Paul (Canada) 8	Marika Kilius Franz Ningel (West Germany) 16½	Maria Jelinek Otto Jelinek (Canada) 17½
1958	Barbara Wagner Robert Paul (Canada) 10	Vera Suchankova Zdenek Dolezal (Czechoslovakia) 26	Maria Jelinek Otto Jelinek (Canada) 28
1959	Barbara Wagner Robert Paul (Canada) 9	Marika Kilius Hans Jürgen Bäumler (West Germany) 19	Nancy Ludington-Rouillard Ronald Ludington-Rouillard (USA) 35½
1960	Barbara Wagner Robert Paul (Canada) 9	Maria Jelinek Otto Jelinek (Canada) 21	Marika Kilius Hans Jürgen Bäumler (West Germany) 24
1961	no world championship held owing to an air crash involving the American team		
1962	Maria Jelinek Otto Jelinek (Canada) 15	Ljudmila Belousova Oleg Protopopov (USSR) 16½	Margaret Göbl Franz Ningel (West Germany) 25½
1963	Maria Kilius Hans Jürgen Bäumler (West Germany) 9	Ljudmila Belousova Oleg Protopopov (USSR) 20	Tatiana Zhuk Alexandr Gavrilov (USSR) 31
1964	Maria Kilius Hans Jürgen Bäumler (West Germany) 13	Ljudmila Belousova Oleg Protopopov (USSR) 14	Debbi Wilkes Guy Revell (Canada) 28
1965	Ljudmila Belousova Oleg Protopopov (USSR) 9	Vivian Joseph Ronald Joseph (USA) 19	Tatiana Zhuk Alexandr Gorelik (USSR) 32
1966	Ljudmila Belousova Oleg Protopov (USSR) 13	Tatiana Zhuk Alexandr Gorelik (USSR) 14	Cynthia Kauffmann Ronald Kauffmann (USA) 30
1967	Ljudmila Belousova Oleg Protopopov (USSR) 9	Margot Glockshuber Wolfgang Danne (West Germany) 25	Cynthia Kauffmann Ronald Kauffmann (USA) 27
1968	Ljudmila Belousova Oleg Protopopov (USSR)	Tatiana Zhuk Alexandr Gorelik (USSR) 19	Cynthia Kauffmann Ronald Kauffmann (USA) 27
1969	Irina Rodnina Alexsei Ulanov (USSR) 9	Tamara Moskvina Alexei Mishin (USSR) 23	Ljudmila Belousova Oleg Protopopov (USSR) 26
1970	Irina Rodnina Alexsei Ulanov (USSR) 11	Ljudmila Smirnova Andrei Suraikin (USSR) 16	Heidemarie Walther-Steiner Heinz Ulrich Walther (East Germany) 27
1971	Irina Rodnina Alexsei Ulanov (USSR) 11	Ljudmila Smirnova Andrei Suraikin (USSR) 17	Jo Jo Starbuck Kenneth Shelly (USA) 29
1972	Irina Rodnina Alexsei Ulanov (USSR) 9	Ljudmila Smirnova Andrei Suraikin (USSR)	Jo Jo Starbuck Kenneth Shelly (USA) 28½
1973	Irina Rodnina Alexandr Zaitsev (USSR) 9	Ljudmila Smirnova Alexsei Ulanov (USSR) 18	Manuela Gross Uwe Kagelmann (East Germany) 29
1974	Irina Rodnina Alexandr Zaitsev (USSR) 9	Ljudmila Smirnova Alexsei Ulanov (USSR) 21	Romy Kermer Rolf Österreich (East Germany) 25
1975	Irina Rodnina Alexandr Zaitsev (USSR) 9	Romy Kermer Rolf Österreich (East Germany) 19	Manuela Gross Uwe Kagelmann (East Germany) 27
1976	Irina Rodnina Alexandr Zaitsev (USSR) 9	Romy Kermer Rolf Österreich (East Germany) 23	Irina Vorobieva Alexandr Vlasov (USSR) 28

ICE DANCING

1952	Jean Westwood Lawrence Demmy (Great Britain) 7	Joan Dewhirst John Slater (Great Britain) 14	Carol Peters Daniel Ryan (USA) 23
1953	Jean Westwood Lawrence Demmy (Great Britain) 6	Joan Dewhirst John Slater (Great Britain) 10	Carol Peters Daniel Ryan (USA) 16
1954	Jean Westwood Lawrence Demmy (Great Britain) 5	Nesta Davies Paul Thomas (Great Britain) 14	Carmel Bodel Edward Bodel (USA) 18
1955	Jean Westwood Lawrence Demmy (Great Britain) 7	Pamela Weight Paul Thomas (Great Britain) 14	Barbara Radford Raymond Lockwood (Great Britain) 21
1956	Pamela Weight Paul Thomas (Great Britain) 7	June Markham Courtney Jones (Great Britain) 15	Barbara Thompson Gerard Rigby (Great Britain) 29
1957	June Markham Courtney Jones (Great Britain) 5	Geraldine Fenton William McLachlan (Canada) 11	Sharon McKenzie Bert Wright (USA) 16
1958	June Markham Courtney Jones (Great Britain) 9	Geraldine Fenton William McLachlan (Canada) 25	Andrée Anderson Donald Jacoby (USA) 35
1959	Doreen Denny Courtney Jones (Great Britain) 6	Andrée Jacoby-Anderson Donald Jacoby-Anderson (USA) 12	Geraldine Fenton William McLachlan (Canada) 14
1960	Doreen Denny Courtney Jones (Great Britain) 7	Virginia Thompson William McLachlan (Canada) 16	Christiane Guhel Jean Paul Guhel (France) 22
1961	no world championship held owing to an air crash involving the American team		
1962	Eva Romanova Pavel Roman (Czechoslovakia) 15	Chritiane Guhel Jean Paul Guhel (France) 26	Virginia Thompson William McLachlan (Canada) 23
1963	Eva Romanova Pavel Roman (Czechoslovakia) 14	Linda Shearman Michael Phillips (Great Britain) 15	Paulette Doan Kenneth Ormsby (Canada) 26
1964	Eva Romanova Pavel Roman (Czechoslovakia) 8	Paulette Doan Kenneth Ormsby (Canada) 20	Janet Sawbridge David Hickinbottom (Great Britain) 18
1965	Eva Romanova Pavel Roman (Czechoslovakia) 7	Janet Sawbridge David Hickinbottom (Great Britain) 18	Lorna Dyer John Carrell (USA) 26
1966	Diana Towler Bernard Ford (Great Britain) 9	Kristin Fortune Dennis Sveum (United States) 17	Lorna Dyer John Carrell (USA) 17
1967	Diana Towler Bernard Ford (Great Britain) 9	Lorna Dyer John Carrell (USA) 12	Yvonne Suddick Malcolm Cannon (Great Britain) 21
1968	Diana Towler Bernard Ford (Great Britain) 9	Yvonne Suddick Malcolm Cannon (Great Britain) 24	Janet Sawbridge Jon Lane (Great Britain) 24

1969	Diana Towler Bernard Ford (Great Britain) 7	Ljudmila Pakhomova Alexandr Gorshkov (USSR) 16	Judy Schwomeyer James Sladky (USA) 24
1970	Ljudmila Pakhomova Alexandr Gorshkov (USSR) 14	Judy Schwomeyer James Sladky (USA) 15	Angelika Buck Erich Buck (West Germany) 25
1971	Ljudmila Pakhomova Alexandr Groshkov (USSR) 16	Angelika Buck Erich Buck (West Germany) 21	Judy Schwomeyer James Sladky (USA) 20
1972	Ljudmila Pakhomova Alexandr Groshkov (USSR) 14	Angelika Buck Erich Buck (West Germany) 17	Judy Schwomeyer James Sladky (USA) 24
1973	Ljudmila Pakhomova Alexandr Gorshkov (USSR) 9	Angelika Buck Erich Buck (West Germany) 18	Hilary Green Glynn Watts (Great Britain) 29
1974	Ljudmila Pakhomova Alexandr Gorshkov (USSR) 9	Hilary Green Glynn Watts (Great Britain) 18	Natalya Linichuk Gennadi Karponosov (USSR) 28
1975	Irina Moiseeva Andrei Minenkov (USSR) 13	Colleen O'Connor Jim Millns (USA) 19	Hilary Green Glynn Watts (Great Britain) 30
1976	Ljudmila Pakhomova Alexandr Gorshkov (USSR) 9	Irina Moiseeva Andrei Minenkov (USSR) 19	Colleen O'Connor Jim Millns (USA) 28

EUROPEAN CHAMPIONSHIPS

FIGURE SKATING

FIGURE SKATING (MEN)

1891	Oskar Uhlig (Germany) $146\frac{6}{9}$	A. Schmitson (Germany) $114\frac{7}{9}$	Franz Zilly (Germany) $101\frac{3}{9}$
1892	Eduard Engelmann (Austria) $\frac{1}{1}$	Tibor von Földváry (Hungary) $\frac{2}{3}$	Georg Zachariades (Austria) $\frac{3}{6}$
1893	Eduard Engelmann (Austria) 11	Henning Grenander (Sweden) 16	Georg Zachariades (Austria) 21
1894	Eduard Engelmann (Austria) $\frac{1}{1}$	Gustav Hügel (Austria) $\frac{3}{2}$	Tibor von Földváry (Hungary) $\frac{2}{3}$
1895	Tibor von Földváry (Hungary) 6	Gustav Hügel (Austria) 11	Gilbert Fuchs (Germany) 13
1896 and 1897 no European championship			
1898	Ulrich Salchow (Sweden) 7	Johan Lefstad (Norway) 8	Oscar Holthe (Norway) 15
1899	Ulrich Salchow (Sweden) 7	Gustav Hügel (Austria) 10	Ernst Fellner (Austria) 12
1900	Ulrich Salchow (Sweden) $\frac{1}{2}$	Gustav Hügel (Austria) $\frac{2}{1}$	Oscar Holthe (Norway) $\frac{3}{3}$
1901	Gustav Hügel (Austria) 5	Gilbert Fuchs (Germany) 11	Ulrich Salchow (Sweden) 14
1902 and 1903 no European championships			
1904	Ulrich Salchow (Sweden) 8	Max Bohatsch (Austria) 13	Nicolai Panin (Russia) 21
1905	Max Bohatsch (Austria) 5	Heinrich Burger (Germany) 10	Karl Zenger (Germany) 15
1906	Ulrich Salchow (Sweden) 5	Ernst Herz (Austria) 13	Per Thoren (Sweden) 18
1907	Ulrich Salchow (Sweden) 6	Gilbert Fuchs (Germany) 10	Ernst Herz (Austria) 14
1908	Ernst Herz (Austria) 5	Nicolai Panin (Russia) 10	S. Przedrzymirski (Russia) 15
1909	Ulrich Salchow (Sweden) 9	Gilbert Fuchs (Germany) 15	Per Thoren (Sweden) 18
1910	Ulrich Salchow (Sweden) 7	Werner Rittberger (Germany) 14	Per Thoren (Sweden) 22
1911	Per Thoren (Sweden) 15	Karl Ollow (Russia) 17	Werner Rittberger (Germany) 21
1912	Gösta Sandahl (Sweden) 6	Ivan Malinin (Russia) 9	Martin Stixrud (Norway) 15
1913	Ulrich Salchow (Sweden) 12	Andor Szende (Hungary) 14	Willy Böckl (Austria) 19
1914	Fritz Kachler (Austria) 8	Andreas Krogh (Norway) 12	Willy Böckl (Austria) 13
no European championships until			
1922	Willy Böckl (Austria) 10	Fritz Kachler (Austria) 11	Ernst Oppacher (Austria) 14
1923	Willy Böckl (Austria) 5	Martin Stixrud (Norway) 10	Gunnar Jakobsson (Finland) 15
1924	Fritz Kachler (Austria) 5	Ludwig Wrede (Austria) 16	Werner Rittberger (Germany) 18
1925	Willy Böckl (Austria) 7	Werner Rittberger (Germany) 10	Otto Preissecker (Austria) 16
1926	Willy Böckl (Austria) 7	Otto Preissecker (Austria) 10	Georg Gautschi (Switzerland) 15
1927	Willy Böckl (Austria) 5	Hugo Distler (Austria) 12	Karl Schäfer (Austria) 14
1928	Willy Böckl (Austria) 6	Karl Schäfer (Austria) 11	Otto Preissecker (Austria) 13
1929	Karl Schäfer (Austria) 5	Georg Gautschi (Switzerland) 12	Ludwig Wrede (Austria) 14
1930	Karl Schäfer (Austria) 5	Otto Gold (Czechoslovakia) 20	Markus Nikkanen (Finland) 17
1931	Karl Schäfer (Austria) 5	Ernst Baier (Germany) 10	Hugo Distler (Austria) 15
1932	Karl Schäfer (Austria) 5	Ernst Baier (Germany) 11	Erich Erdös (Austria) 18

1933	Karl Schäfer (Austria) 5	Ernst Baier (Germany) 10	Erich Erdös (Austria) 15
1934	Karl Schäfer (Austria) 5	Dénes Pataky (Hungary) 14	Elemer Tertak (Hungary) 22
1935	Karl Schäfer (Austria) 8	Felix Kaspar (Austria) 18	Ernst Baier (Germany) 22
1936	Karl Schäfer (Austria) 7	Graham Sharp (Great Britain) 20	Ernst Baier (Germany) 23
1937	Felix Kaspar (Austria) 5	Graham Sharp (Great Britain) 10	Elemér Tertak (Hungary) 20
1938	Felix Kaspar (Austria) 6	Graham Sharp (Great Britain) 9	Herbert Alward (Austria) 17
1939	Graham Sharp (Great Britain) 7	Freddie Tomlins (Great Britain) 11	Horst Faber (Germany) 12
no European championships until			
1947	Hans Gerschwiler (Switzerland) 7	Vladislav Cáp (Czechoslovakia) 18	Fernand Leemans (Belgium) 21
1948	Richard Button (United States) 11	Hans Gerschwiler (Switzerland) 18	Edi Rada (Austria) 20
1949	Edi Rada (Austria) 6	Ede Kiraly (Hungary) 9	Helmut Seibt (Austria) 15
1950	Ede Kiraly (Hungary) 7	Helmut Seibt (Austria) 14	Carlo Fassi (Italy) 25
1951	Helmut Seibt (Austria) 7	Horst Faber (Germany) 8	Carlo Fassi (Italy) 16
1952	Helmut Seibt (Austria) 11	Carlo Fassi (Italy) 18	Michael Carrington (Great Britain) 27
1953	Carlo Fassi (Italy) 9	Alain Giletti (France) 12	Freimut Stein (Germany) 25
1954	Carlo Fassi (Italy) 8	Alain Giletti (France) 16	Karol Divin (Czechoslovakia) 24
1955	Alain Giletti (France) 8	Michael Booker (Great Britain) 17	Karol Divin (Czechoslovakia) 21
1956	Alain Giletti (France) 12	Michael Booker (Great Britain) 22	Karol Divin (Czechoslovakia) 22
1957	Alain Giletti (France) $\frac{1}{4}$1	Karol Divin (Czechoslovakia) $\frac{3}{1}$2	Michael Booker (Great Britain) $\frac{2}{2}$3
1958	Karol Divin (Czechoslovakia) 10	Alain Giletti (France) 12	Alain Calmat (France) 23
1959	Karol Divin (Czechoslovakia) 10	Alain Giletti (France) 20	Norbet Felsinger (Austria) 30
1960	Alain Giletti (France) 11	Norbet Felsinger (Austria) 20	Manfred Schnelldorfer (West Germany) 31
1961	Alain Giletti (France) 9	Alain Calmat (France) 22	Manfred Schnelldorfer (West Germany) 23
1962	Alain Calmat (France) 14	Karol Divin (Czechoslovakia) 16	Manfred Schnelldorfer (West Germany) 25
1963	Alain Calmat (France) 10	Manfred Schnelldorfer (West Germany) 17	Emmerich Danzer (Austria) 40
1964	Alain Calmat (France) 10	Manfred Schnelldorfer (West Germany) 20	Karol Divin (Czechoslovakia) 33
1965	Emmerich Danzer (Austria) 14	Alain Calmat (France) 16	Peter Jonas (Austria) 29
1966	Emmerich Danzer (Austria) 11	Wolfgang Schwartz (Austria) 16	Ondrej Nepela (Czechoslovakia) 29
1967	Emmerich Danzer (Austria) 9	Wolfgang Schwartz (Austria) 23	Ondrej Nepela (Czechoslovakia) 26
1968	Emmerich Danzer (Austria) 9	Wolfgang Schwartz (Austria) 18	Ondrej Nepela (Czechoslovakia) 29
1969	Ondrej Nepela (Czechoslovakia) 9	Patrick Pera (France) 18	Sergei Chetverukhin (USSR) 27
1970	Ondrej Nepela (Czechoslovakia) 9	Patrick Pera (France) 21	Gunther Zöller (East Germany) 24
1971	Ondrej Nepela (Czechoslovakia) 9	Sergei Chetverukhin (USSR) 19	Haig Oundjian (Great Britain) 31
1972	Ondrej Nepela (Czechoslovakia) 9	Sergei Chetverukhin (USSR) 23	Patrick Pera (France) 25
1973	Ondrej Nepela (Czechoslovakia) 12	Sergei Chetverukhin (USSR) 20	Jan Hoffmann (East Germany) 22
1974	Jan Hoffmann (East Germany) 11	Sergei Volkov (USSR) 23	John Curry (Great Britain) 27
1975	Vladimir Kovalev (USSR) 11	John Curry (Great Britain) 20	Yuri Ovchinnikov (USSR) 27
1976	John Curry (Great Britain) 15	Vladimir Kovalev (USSR) 16	Jan Hoffmann (East Germany) 23

FIGURE SKATING (WOMEN)

1930	Fritzi Burger (Austria) 5	Ilse Hornung (Austria) 10	Vivi-Anne Hulten (Sweden) 22
1931	Sonja Henie (Norway) 7	Fritzi Burger (Austria) 14	Hilde Holovsky (Austria) 23
1932	Sonja Henie (Norway) 6	Fritzi Burger (Austria) 12	Vivi-Anne Hulten (Sweden) 16
1933	Sonja Henie (Norway) 5	Cecilia Colledge (Great Britain) 13	Fritzi Burger (Austria) 16
1934	Sonja Henie (Norway) 8	Liselotte Landbeck (Austria) 15	Maribel Vinson (United States) 23
1935	Sonja Henie (Norway) 7	Liselotte Landbeck (Austria) 17	Cecilia Colledge (Great Britain) 21
1936	Sonja Henie (Norway) 7	Cecilia Colledge (Great Britain) 16	Megan Taylor (Great Britain) 21
1937	Cecilia Colledge (Great Britain) 5	Megan Taylor (Great Britain) 10	Emmy Putzinger (Austria) 16
1938	Cecilia Colledge (Great Britain) 7	Megan Taylor (Great Britain) 14	Emmy Putzinger (Austria) 27
1939	Cecilia Colledge (Great Britain) 6	Megan Taylor (Great Britain) 9	Daphne Walker (Great Britain) 17
no more championships until			
1947	Barbara Ann Scott (Canada) 9	Gretchen Merrill (United States) 20	Daphne Walker (Great Britain) 23
1948	Barbara Ann Scott (Canada) 7	Eva Pawlik (Austria) 22	Alena Vrzanova (Czechoslovakia) 23
1949	Eva Pawlick (Austria) 10	Alena Vrzanova (Czechoslovakia) 16	Jeanette Altwegg (Great Britain) 16
1950	Alena Vrzanova (Czechoslovakia) 7	Jeanette Altwegg (Great Britain) 14	Jacqueline du Bief (France) 25
1951	Jeanette Altwegg (Great Britain) 9	Jacqueline du Bief (France) 12	Barbara Wyatt (Great Britain) 22
1952	Jeanette Altwegg (Great Britain) 11	Jacqueline du Bief (France) 16	Barbara Wyatt (Great Britain) 32
1953	Valda Osborn (Great Britain) 10	Grundi Busch (Germany) 11	Erica Batchelor (Great Britain) 27
1954	Grundi Busch (Germany) 11	Erica Batchelor (Great Britain) 18	Yvonne Sugden (Great Britain) 22
1955	Hanna Eigel (Austria) 11	Yvonne Sugden (Great Britain) 14	Erica Batchelor (Great Britain) 17
1956	Ingrid Wendl (Austria) 13	Yvonne Sugden (Great Britain) 16	Erica Batchelor (Great Britain) 25
1957	Hanna Eigel (Austria) $\frac{2}{5}$1	Ingrid Wendl (Austria) $\frac{1}{6}$2	Hanna Walter (Austria) $\frac{3}{2}$3
1958	Ingrid Wendl (Austria) 10	Hanna Walter (Austria) 17	Joan Haanappel (Netherlands) 27
1959	Hanna Walter (Austria) 11$\frac{1}{2}$	Sjoukje Dijkstra (Netherlands) 26	Joan Haanappel (Netherlands) 26$\frac{1}{2}$
1960	Sjoukje Dijkstra (Netherlands) 9	Regine Heitzer (Austria) 20	Joan Haanappel (Netherlands) 28
1961	Sjoukje Dijkstra (Netherlands) 9	Regine Heitzer (Austria) 21	Jana Mrazkova (Czechoslovakia) 26
1962	Sjoukje Dijkstra (Netherlands) 9	Regine Heitzer (Austria) 18	Karin Frohner (Austria) 30
1963	Sjoukje Dijkstra (Netherlands) 9	Nicole Hassler (France) 25	Regine Heitzer (Austria) 27
1964	Sjoukje Dijkstra (Netherlands) 9	Regine Heitzer (Austria) 21	Nicole Hassler (France) 24
1965	Regine Heitzer (Austria) 9	Sally-Ann Stapleford (Great Britain) 26	Nicole Hassler (France) 30
1966	Regine Heitzer (Austria) 9	Gabriele Seyfert (East Germany) 21	Nicole Hassler (France) 29

1967	Gabriele Seyfert (East Germany) 10	Hana Maskova (Czechoslovakia) 17	Zsuzsa Almassy (Hungary) 31
1968	Hana Maskova (Czechoslovakia) 10	Gabriele Seyfert (East Germany) 21	Beatrix Schuba (Austria) 27
1969	Gabriele Seyfert (East Germany) 9	Hana Maskova (Czechoslovakia) 22	Beatrix Schuba (Austria) 23
1970	Beatrix Schuba (Austria) 10	Gabriele Seyfert (East Germany) 17	Zsuzsa Almassy (Hungary) 27
1971	Beatrix Schuba (Austria) 9	Zsuzsa Almassy (Hungary) 22	Rita Trapanese (Italy) 23
1972	Beatrix Schuba (Austria) 9	Rita Trapanese (Italy) 22	Sonja Morgenstern (East Germany) 29
1973	Christine Errath (East Germany) 9	Jean Scott (Great Britain) 22	Karin Iten (Switzerland) 34
1974	Christine Errath (East Germany) 10	Dianne de Leeuw (Netherlands) 26	Liana Drahova (Czechoslovakia) 27
1975	Christine Errath (East Germany) 13	Dianne de Leeuw (Netherlands) 14	Anett Poetzsch (East Germany) 28
1976	Dianne de Leeuw (Netherlands) 10	Anett Poetzsch (East Germany) 21	Christine Errath (East Germany) 24

FIGURE SKATING (PAIRS)

1930	Olga Organista Sandor Szalay (Hungary) 6	Emilie Rotter Laszlo Szollas (Hungary) 15	Gisela Hochhaltinger Otto Preissecker (Austria) 15
1931	Olga Organista Sandor Szalay (Hungary) 8	Emilie Rotter Laszlo Szollas (Hungary) $14\frac{1}{4}$	Lilly Gaillard Willy Petter (Austria) $19\frac{1}{2}$
1932	Andrée Brunet Pierre Brunet (France) 6	Lilly Gaillard Willy Petter (Austria) 11	Idi Papez Karl Zwack (Austria) 13
1933	Idi Papez Karl Zwack (Austria) $5\frac{1}{2}$	Lilly Scholz-Gaillard Willy Peter (Austria) $9\frac{1}{2}$	Mollie Phillips Rodney Murdoch (Great Britain) 15
1934	Emilie Rotter Laszlo Szollas (Hungary) 7	Idi Papez Karl Zwack (Austria) 9	Zofja Bilorowna Tadeusz Kowalski (Poland) 16
1935	Maxi Herber Ernst Baier (Germany) 11	Idi Papez Karl Zwack (Austria) 15	Lucy Gallo Reszö Dillinger (Hungary) $31\frac{1}{2}$
1936	Maxi Herber Ernst Baier (Germany) 7	Violet Cliff Leslie Cliff (Great Britain) 18	Piroska Szekrényessy Attila Szekrényessy (Hungary) 19
1937	Maxi Herber Ernst Baier (Austria) 9	Ilse Pausin Erich Pausin (Austria) 12	Piroska Szekrényessy Attila Szekrényessy (Hungary) $23\frac{1}{2}$
1938	Maxi Herber Ernst Baier (Austria) 6	Ilse Pausin Erich Pausin (Austria) 10	Inge Koch Günther Noack (Germany) 17
1939	Maxi Herber Ernst Baier (Austria) 5	Ilse Pausin Erich Pausin (Austria) 10	Inge Koch Günther Noack (Germany) 17
1947	Micheline Lannoy Pierre Baugniet (Belgium) 9	Winifred Silverthorne Dennis Silverthorne (Great Britain) $19\frac{1}{2}$	Suzanne Diskeuve Edmond Verbustel (Belgium) 19
1948	Andrea Kékesy Ede Kiraly (Hungary) 5	Blazena Knittlova Karel Vosatka (Czechoslovakia) 15	Herta Ratzenhofer Emil Ratzenhofer (Austria) 17
1949	Andrea Kékesy Ede Kiraly (Hungary) 5	Marianne Nagy Laszlo Nagy (Hungary) 21	Herta Ratzenhofer Emil Ratzenhofer (Austria) 17
1950	Marianne Nagy Laszlo Nagy (Hungary) 6	Eliane Steinemann André Calame (Switzerland) $12\frac{1}{2}$	Jennifer Nicks John Nicks (Great Britain) 13
1951	Ria Baran Paul Falk (Germany) 8	Eliane Steinemann André Calame (Switzerland) $18\frac{1}{2}$	Jennifer Nicks John Nicks (Great Britain) 20
1952	Ria Baran Paul Falk (Germany) 8	Jennifer Nicks John Nicks (Great Britain) 19	Marianne Nagy Laszlo Nagy (Hungary) 20
1953	Jennifer Nicks John Nicks (Great Britain) 10	Marianne Nagy Laszlo Nagy (Hungary) $11\frac{1}{2}$	Sissy Schwarz Kurt Oppelt (Austria) 25
1954	Silvia Grandjean Michel Grandjean (Switzerland) 9	Sissy Schwarz Kurt Oppelt (Austria) $8\frac{1}{2}$	Sonja Balunova Miroslov Balun (Czechoslovakia) 20
1955	Marianne Nagy Laszlo Nagy (Hungary) 5	Vera Suchankova Zdenek Dolezal (Czechoslovakia) 13	Marika Kilius Franz Ningel (Germany) $22\frac{1}{2}$
1956	Sissy Schwarz Kurt Oppelt (Austria) 9	Marianne Nagy Laszlo Nagy (Hungary) 23	Marika Kilius Franz Ningel (Germany) 23
1957	Vera Suchankova Zdenek Dolezal (Czechoslovakia)	Marianne Nagy Laszlo Nagy (Hungary)	Marika Kilius Franz Ningel (Germany)
1958	Vera Suchankova Zdenek Dolezal (Czechoslovakia) 7	Nina Zhuk Stanislav Zhuk (USSR) $28\frac{1}{2}$	Joyce Coates Anthony Holles (Great Britain) $33\frac{1}{2}$
1959	Marika Kilius Hans Jürgen Bäumler (West Germany) 11	Nina Zhuk Stanislav Zhuk (USSR) 14	Joyce Coates Anthony Holles (Great Britain) $20\frac{1}{2}$
1960	Marika Kilius Hans Jürgen Bäumler (West Germany) 10	Nina Zhuk Stanislav Zhuk (USSR) 13	Margret Göbl Franz Ningel (West Germany)
1961	Marika Kilius Hans Jürgen Bäumler (West Germany) 13	Margret Göbl Franz Ningel (West Germany) 20	Margrit Senf Peter Göbel (East Germany) $38\frac{1}{2}$
1962	Marika Kilius Hans Jürgen Bäumler (West Germany) 15	Ljudmila Belousova Oleg Protopopov (USSR) 19	Margret Göbl Franz Ningel (West Germany) 20
1963	Marika Kilius Hans Jürgen Bäumler (West Germany) 9	Ljudmila Belousova Oleg Protopopov (USSR) 18	Tatiana Zhuk Alexandr Gavrilov (USSR) 33
1964	Marika Kilius Hans Jürgen Bäumler (West Germany) 11	Ljudmila Belousova Oleg Protopopov (USSR) 16	Tatiana Zhuk Alexandr Gavrilov (USSR) 32
1965	Ljudmila Belousova Oleg Protopopov (USSR) 9	Gerda Johner Ruedi Johner (Switzerland) 18	Tatiana Zhuk Alexandr Gorelik (USSR) 28
1966	Ljudmila Belousova Oleg Protopopov (USSR) 9	Tatiana Zhuk Alexandr Gorelik (USSR) 18	Margot Glockshuber Wolfgang Danne (West Germany) 29
1967	Ljudmila Belousova Oleg Protopopov (USSR) 10	Margot Glockshuber Wolfgang Danne (West Germany) 18	Heidemarie Steiner Heinz Ulrich Walther (East Germany) 29
1968	Ljudmila Belousova Oleg Protopopov (USSR) 9	Tamara Moskvina Aleksei Mishin (USSR) 30	Heidemarie Steiner Heinz Ulrich Walther (East Germany) 28
1969	Irina Rodnina Alexsei Ulanov (USSR) 10	Ljudmila Belousova Oleg Protopopov (USSR) 19	Tamara Moskvina Aleksei Mishin (USSR) 27
1970	Irina Rodnina Alexsei Ulanov (USSR) 9	Ljudmila Smirnova Andrei Suraikin (USSR) $24\frac{1}{2}$	Heidemarie Walther Steiner Heinz Ulrich Walther (East Germany) 27
1971	Irina Rodnina Alexsei Ulanov (USSR) 10	Ljudmila Smirnova Andrei Suraikin (USSR) 18	Galina Karelina Georgei Proskurin (USSR) 31
1972	Irina Rodnina Alexsei Ulanov (USSR) 10	Ljudmila Smirnova Andrei Suraikin (USSR) 17	Manuela Gross Uwe Kagelmann (East Germany) 27
1973	Irina Rodnina Alexandr Zaitsev (USSR) 9	Ljudmila Smirnova Alexsei Ulanov (USSR) 21	Almut Lehmann Herbert Wiesinger (West Germany) 28
1974	Irina Rodnina Alexandr Zaitsev (USSR) 9	Romy Kermer Rolf Österreich (East Germany) 27	Ljudmila Smirnova Alexsei Ulanov (USSR) 30

1975	Irina Rodnina Alexandr Zaitsev (USSR) 9	Romy Kermer Rolf Österreich (East Germany) 18	Manuela Gross Uwe Kagelmann (East Germany) 33
1976	Irina Rodnina Alexandr Zaitsev (USSR) 9	Romy Kermer Rolf Österreich (East Germany) 22	Irina Vorobieva Alexandr Vlasov (USSR) 27.5

ICE DANCING

1954	Jean Westwood Lawrence Demmy (Great Britain) 5	Nesta Davies Paul Thomas (Great Britain) 10	Barbara Radford Raymond Lockwood (Great Britain) 15
1955	Jean Westwood Lawrence Demmy (Great Britain) 5	Pamela Weight Paul Thomas (Great Britain) 11	Barbara Radford Raymond Lockwood (Great Britain) 14
1956	Pamela Weight Paul Thomas (Great Britain) 8	June Markham Courtney Jones (Great Britain) 13	Barbara Thompson Gerard Rigby (Great Britain) 23
1957	June Markham Courtney Jones (Great Britain) 7	Barbara Thompson Gerard Rigby (Great Britain) 14	Catherine Morris Michael Robinson (Great Britain) 24
1958	June Markham Courtney Jones (Great Britain) 5	Catherine Morris Michael Robinson (Great Britain) 12	Barbara Thompson Gerard Rigby (Great Britain) 15
1959	Doreen Denny Courtney Jones (Great Britain) 7	Catherine Morris Michael Robinson (Great Britain) 15	Christiane Guhel Jean Paul Guhel (France) 20
1960	Doreen Denny Courtney Jones (Great Britain) 7	Christiane Guhel Jean Paul Guhel (France) 14	Mary Parry Roy Mason (Great Britain) 23
1961	Doreen Denny Courtney Jones (Great Britain) 7	Christiane Guhel Jean Paul Guhel (France) 14	Linda Shearman Michael Philipps (Great Britain) 25
1962	Christiane Guhel Jean Paul Guhel (France) 10	Linda Shearman Michael Philipps (Great Britain) 12	Eva Romanova Pavel Roman (Czechoslovakia) 21
1963	Linda Shearman Michael Philipps (Great Britain) 10	Eva Romanova Pavel Roman (Czechoslovakia) 11	Janet Sawbridge David Hickinbottom (Great Britain) 21
1964	Eva Romanova Pavel Roman (Czechoslovakia) 7	Janet Sawbridge David Hickinbottom (Great Britain) 14	Yvonne Suddick Roger Kennerson (Great Britain) 26
1965	Eva Romanova Pavel Roman (Czechoslovakia) 7	Janet Sawbridge David Hickinbottom (Great Britain) 14	Yvonne Suddick Roger Kennerson (Great Britain) 25
1966	Diane Towler Bernard Ford (Great Britain) 10½	Yvonne Suddick Roger Kennerson (Great Britain) 16½	Jitka Babicka Joromir Holan (Czechoslovakia) 35
1967	Diane Towler Bernard Ford (Great Britain) 9	Yvonne Suddick Roger Kennerson (Great Britain) 20	Brigitte Martin Francis Gamichon (France) 32
1968	Diane Towler Bernard Ford (Great Britain) 9	Yvonne Suddick Roger Kennerson (Great Britain) 18	Janet Sawbridge Jon Lane (Great Britain) 27
1969	Diane Towler Bernard Ford (Great Britain) 7	Janet Sawbridge Jon Lane (Great Britain) 17	Ljudmila Pakhomova Alexandr Gorshkov (USSR) 18
1970	Ljudmila Pakhomova Alexandr Gorshkov (USSR) 9	Angelika Buck Erich Buck (West Germany) 19	Tatiana Voitiuk Viacheslav Zhigalin (USSR) 32
1971	Ljudmila Pakhomova Alexandr Gorshkov (USSR) 15	Angelika Buck Erich Buck (West Germany) 15	Susan Getty Roy Bradshaw (Great Britain) 24
1972	Angelika Buck Erich Buck (West Germany) 13	Ljudmila Pakhomova Alexandr Gorschkov (USSR) 16	Janet Sawbridge David Hickinbottom (Great Britain) 27
1973	Ljudmila Pakhomova Alexandr Gorshkov (USSR) 9	Angelika Buck Erich Buck (West Germany) 19	Hilary Green Glynn Watts (Great Britain) 27
1974	Ljudmila Pakhomova Alexandr Gorshkov (USSR) 9	Hilary Green Glynn Watts (Great Britain) 18	Natalia Linichuk Gennadi Karponosov (USSR) 29
1975	Ljudmila Pakhomova Alexandr Gorshkov (USSR) 9	Hilary Green Glynn Watts (Great Britain) 20	Natalia Linichuk Gennadi Karponosov (USSR) 29
1976	Ljudmila Pakhomova Alexandr Gorshkov (USSR) 9	Irina Moiseeva Andrei Minenkov (USSR) 19	Natalia Linichuk Gennadi Karponosov (USSR) 30

FIS SKI WORLD CHAMPIONSHIPS

MEN

Year	Event	Winner	Country
1925	18kms cross-country	O. Nemecky	Czechoslovakia
	50kms cross-country	F. Donth	Czechoslovakia
	Jumping	W. Dick	Czechoslovakia
	Nordic combined	O. Nemecky	Czechoslovakia
1926	30kms cross-country	M. Raivio	Finland
	50kms cross-country	M. Raivio	Finland
	Jumping	J. T.-Thams	Norway
	Nordic combined	J. Gröttumsbraaten	Norway
1927	18kms cross-country	J. Lindgren	Sweden
	50kms cross-country	J. Lindgren	Sweden
	Jumping	T. Edman	Sweden
	Nordic combined	R. Purkert	Czechoslovakia
1929	18kms cross-country	V. Saarinen	Finland
	50kms cross-country	A. Knuttila	Finland
	Jumping	S. Ruud	Norway
	Nordic combined	H. Vinjarengen	Norway
1930	18kms cross-country	A. Rustadstuen	Norway
	50kms cross-country	S. Utterström	Sweden
	Jumping	G. Andersen	Norway
	Nordic combined	H. Vinjarengen	Norway
1931	18kms cross-country	J. Gröttumsbraaten	Norway
	50kms cross-country	O. Stenen	Norway
	Jumping	B. Ruud	Norway
	Nordic combined	J. Gröttumsbraaten	Norway
	Downhill	W. Prager	Switzerland
	Slalom	D. Zogg	Switzerland
1932	Downhill	G. Lantschner	Austria
	Slalom	F. Dauber	Germany
	Alpine combined	O. Fürrer	Switzerland
1933	18kms cross-country	N. Englund	Sweden
	50kms cross-country	V. Saarinen	Finland
	40kms cross-country relay		Sweden
	Jumping	M. Reymond	Switzerland
	Nordic combined	S. Eriksson	Sweden
	Downhill	W. Prager	Switzerland
	Slalom	A. Seelos	Austria
	Alpine combined	A. Seelos	Austria
1934	18kms cross-country	S. Nurmela	Finland
	50kms cross-country	E. Viklund	Sweden
	40kms cross-country relay		Finland
	Jumping	K. Johansen	Norway
	Nordic combined	O. Hagen	Norway
	Downhill	D. Zogg	Switzerland
	Slalom	F. Pfnür	Germany
	Alpine combined	D. Zogg	Switzerland
1935	18kms cross-country	K. Karppinen	Finland
	50kms cross-country	N. Englund	Sweden
	40kms cross-country relay		Finland
	Jumping	B. Ruud	Norway
	Nordic combined	O. Hagen	Norway
	Downhill	F. Zingerle	Austria
	Slalom	A. Seelos	Austria
	Alpine combined	A. Seelos	Austria
1936	Downhill	R. Rominger	Switzerland
	Slalom	R. Matt	Austria
	Alpine combined	R. Rominger	Switzerland
1937	18kms cross-country	L. Bergendahl	Norway
	50kms cross-country	P. Niemi	Finland
	40kms cross-country relay		Norway
	Jumping	B. Ruud	Norway
	Nordic combined	S. Röen	Norway
	Downhill	E. Allais	France
	Slalom	E. Allais	France
	Alpine combined	E. Allais	France
1938	18kms cross-country	P. Pietikäinen	Finland
	50kms cross-country	K. Jalkanen	Finland
	40kms cross-country relay		Finland
	Jumping	A. Ruud	Norway
	Nordic combined	O. Hoffsbakken	Norway
	Downhill	J. Couttet	France
	Slalom	R. Rominger	Switzerland
	Alpine combined	E. Allais	France
1939	18kms cross-country	J. Kurikkala	Finland
	50kms cross-country	L. Bergendahl	Norway
	40kms cross-country relay		Finland
	Jumping	J. Bradl	Austria
	Nordic combined	H. Beraur	Czechoslovakia
	Downhill	H. Lantschner	Germany
	Slalom	R. Rominger	Switzerland
	Alpine combined	J. Jennewein	Germany
1950	50–18kms cross-country	K.-E. Aaström	Sweden
	50kms cross-country	G. Erikksson	Sweden
	40kms cross-country relay		Sweden
	Jumping	H. Björnstad	Norway
	Nordic combined	H. Hasu	Finland
	Downhill	Z. Colo	Italy
	Slalom	G. Schneider	Switzerland
	Giant slalom	Z. Colo	Italy
1954	15kms cross-country	V. Häkulinen	Finland
	30kms cross-country	V. Kusin	USSR
	50kms cross-country	V. Kusin	USSR
	40kms cross-country relay		Finland
	Jumping	M. Pietikäinen	Finland
	Nordic combined	S. Stenersen	Norway
	Downhill	C. Pravda	Austria
	Slalom	S. Eriksen	Norway
	Giant slalom	S. Eriksen	Norway
	Alpine combined	S. Eriksen	Norway
1958	15kms cross-country	V. Häkulinen	Finland
	30kms cross-country	K. Hämäläinen	Finland
	50kms cross-country	S. Jernberg	Sweden
	40kms cross-country relay		Sweden
	Jumping	J. Kärkinen	Finland
	Nordic combined	P. Korhonen	Finland
	Downhill	A. Sailer	Austria
	Slalom	J. Rieder	Austria
	Giant slalom	A. Sailer	Austria
	Alpine combined	A. Sailer	Austria
1962	15kms cross-country	A. Rönnlund	Sweden
	30kms cross-country	E. Mäntyranta	Finland
	50kms cross-country	S. Jernberg	Sweden
	40kms cross-country relay		Sweden
	Jumping—70 metres	T. Engan	Norway
	Jumping—90 metres	H. Recknagel	Germany
	Nordic combined	A. Larsen	Norway
	Downhill	K. Schranz	Austria
	Slalom	C. Bozon	France
	Giant slalom	E. Zimmerman	Austria
	Alpine combined	K. Schranz	Austria
1966	15kms cross-country	G. Eggen	Norway
	30kms cross-country	E. Mäntyranta	Finland
	50kms cross-country	G. Eggen	Norway
	40kms cross-country relay		Norway
	Jumping—70 metres	B. Wirkola	Norway
	Jumping—90 metres	B. Wirkola	Norway
	Nordic combined	G. Thoma	Germany
	Downhill	J.-C. Killy	France
	Slalom	C. Senoner	Italy
	Giant slalom	G. Périllat	France
	Alpine combined	J.-C. Killy	France

1970	15kms cross-country	L. G. Aslund	Sweden
	30kms cross-country	V. Vedenin	USSR
	50kms cross-country	K. Oikarainen	Finland
	40kms cross-country relay		USSR
	Jumping—70 metres	G. Napalkov	USSR
	Jumping—90 metres	G. Napalkov	USSR
	Nordic combined	L. Rygl	Czechoslovakia
	Downhill	B. Russi	Switzerland
	Slalom	J.-N. Augert	France
	Giant slalom	K. Schranz	Austria
	Alpine combined	W. Kidd	USA
1974	15kms cross-country	M. Myrmo	Norway
	30kms cross-country	T. Magnuson	Sweden
	50kms cross-country	Gerhard Grimmer	East Germany
	40kms cross-country relay		East Germany
	Jumping—70 metres	H.-G. Aschenbach	East Germany
	Jumping—90 metres	H.-G. Aschenbach	East Germany
	Nordic combined	Ullrich Wehling	East Germany
	Downhill	D. Zwilling	Austria
	Slalom	G. Thoeni	Italy
	Giant slalom	G. Thoeni	Italy

WOMEN

Year	Event	Winner	Country
1931	Slalom	E. M. Mackinnon	Great Britain
	Downhill	E. M. Mckinnon	Great Britain
1932	Slalom	R. Streiff	Switzerland
	Downhill	P. Wiesinger	Italy
	Alpine combined	R. Streiff	Switzerland
1933	Slalom	I. Wersin-Lantschner	Austria
	Downhill	I. Wersin-Lantschner	Austria
	Alpine combined	I. Wersin-Lantschner	Austria
1934	Slalom	C. Cranz	Germany
	Downhill	A. Rüegg	Switzerland
	Alpine combined	C. Cranz	Germany
1935	Slalom	I. Rüegg	Switzerland
	Downhill	C. Cranz	Germany
	Alpine combined	C. Cranz	Germany
1936	Slalom	G. Paumgarten	Austria
	Downhill	E. Pinching	Great Britain
	Alpine combined	E. Pinching	Great Britain
1937	Slalom	C. Cranz	Germany
	Downhill	C. Cranz	Germany
	Alpine combined	C. Cranz	Germany
1938	Slalom	C. Cranz	Germany
	Downhill	L. Resch	Germany
	Alpine combined	C. Cranz	Germany
1939	Slalom	C. Cranz	Germany
	Downhill	C. Cranz	Germany
	Alpine combined	C. Cranz	Germany
1950	Slalom	D. Rom	Austria
	Giant slalom	D. Rom	Austria
	Downhill	T. Jochum-Beiser	Austria
1954	10kms cross-country	L. Kozyreva	USSR
	15kms cross-country relay		USSR
	Slalom	T. Klecker	Austria
	Giant slalom	L. Schmit	France
	Downhill	I. Schopfer	Switzerland
	Alpine combined	I. Schopfer	Switzerland
1958	10kms cross-country	A. Koltjina	USSR
	15kms cross-country relay		USSR
	Slalom	I. Björnbakken	Norway
	Giant slalom	L. Wheeler	Canada
	Downhill	L. Wheeler	Canada
	Alpine combined	F. Dänzer	Switzerland
1962	5kms cross-country	A. Koltjina	USSR
	10kms cross-country	A. Koltjina	USSR
	15kms cross-country relay		USSR
	Slalom	M. Jahn	Austria
	Giant slalom	M. Jahn	Austria
	Downhill	C. Haas	Austria
	Alpine combined	M. Goitschel	France
1966	5kms cross-country	A. Koltjina	USSR
	10kms cross-country	C. Boyarskikh	USSR
	15kms cross-country relay		USSR
	Slalom	A. Famose	France
	Giant slalom	M. Goitschel	France
	Downhill	E. Schinegger	Austria
	Alpine combined	M. Goitschel	France
1970	5kms cross-country	G. Kulakova	USSR
	10kms cross-country	A. Oljunia	USSR
	15kms cross-country relay		USSR
	Slalom	I. Lafforgue	France
	Giant slalom	B. Clifford	Canada
	Downhill	A. Zyrd	Switzerland
	Alpine combined	M. Jacot	France
1974	5kms cross-country	G. Kulakova	USSR
	10kms cross-country	G. Kulakova	USSR
	20kms cross-country relay		USSR
	Slalom	H. Wenzel	Liechtenstein
	Giant slalom	F. Serrat	France
	Downhill	A. Moser-Proell	Austria
	Alpine combined	F. Serrat	France

FIS CHAMPIONSHIP SITES

1925 Johannisbad, Czechoslovakia
1926 Lahti, Finland
1927 Cortina d'Ampezzo, Italy
1929 Zakopane, Poland
1930 Oslo, Norway
1931 Oberhof, Germany (Nordic events); Mürren, Switzerland (Alpine events)
1932 Cortina d'Ampezzo, Italy
1933 Innsbruck, Austria
1934 Solleftea, Sweden (Nordic events); St Mortiz, Switzerland (Alpine events)
1935 Strebski Pleso, Czechoslovakia (Nordic events); Mürren, Switzerland (Alpine events)
1936 Innsbruck, Austria
1937 Chamonix, France
1938 Lahti, Finland (Nordic events); Engelberg, Switzerland (Alpine events)
1939 Zakopane, Poland
1950 Lake Placid, USA (Nordic events); Aspen, USA (Alpine events)
1954 Falun, Sweden (Nordic events); Are, Sweden (Alpine events)
1958 Lahti, Finland (Nordic events); Bad Gastein, Austria (Alpine events)
1962 Zakopane, Poland (Nordic events); Chamonix, France (Alpine events)
1966 Oslo, Norway (Nordic events); Portillo, Chile (Alpine events)
1970 Strebski Pleso, Czechoslovakia (Nordic events); Val Gardena, Italy (Alpine events)
1974 Falun, Sweden (Nordic events); St Mortiz, Switzerland (Alpine events)

WORLD CUP

OVERALL CHAMPIONS (MEN)

1967	Jean-Claude Killy (France)	Heini Messner (Austria)	Guy Périllat (France)
1968	Jean-Claude Killy (France)	Dumenc Giovanoli (Switzerland)	Herbert Huber (Austria)
1969	Karl Schranz (Austria)	Jean-Noël Augert (France)	Reinhard Tritscher (Austria)
1970	Karl Schranz (Austria)	Patrick Russel (France)	Gustavo Thoeni (Italy)
1971	Gustavo Thoeni (Italy)	Henri Duvillard (France)	Patrick Russel (France)
1972	Gustavo Thoeni (Italy)	Henri Duvillard (France)	Edmund Bruggmann (Switzerland)
1973	Gustavo Thoeni (Italy)	David Zwilling (Austria)	Roland Colombin (Switzerland)
1974	Piero Gros (Italy)	Gustavo Thoeni (Italy)	Hans Hinterseer (Austria)
1975	Gustavo Thoeni (Italy)	Ingemar Stenmark (Sweden)	Franz Klammer (Austria)

OVERALL CHAMPIONS (WOMEN)

1967	Nancy Greene (Canada)	Marielle Goitschel (France)	Annie Famose (France)
1968	Nancy Greene (Canada)	Isabelle Mir (France)	Florence Steurer (France)
1969	Gertrude Gabl (Austria)	Florence Steurer (France)	Wiltrud Drexel (Austria)
1970	Michèle Jacot (France)	Françoise Macchi (France)	Florence Steurer (France)
1971	Annemarie Proell (Austria)	Michèle Jacot (France)	Françoise Macchi (France)
1972	Annemarie Proell (Austria)	Françoise Macchi (France)	Britt Lafforgue (France)
1973	Annemarie Proell (Austria)	Monika Kaserer (Austria)	Patricia Emonet (France)
1974	Annemarie Moser-Proell (Austria)	Monika Kaserer (Austria)	Hanni Wenzel (Liechtenstein)
1975	Annemarie Moser-Proell (Austria)	Bernadette Zurbriggen (Switzerland)	Marie-Therese Nadig (Switzerland)

WORLD CUP RACES

MEN

Location	Slalom	Giant Slalom	Downhill
1967			
Berchtesgaden, Germany	Heini Messner (Austria)	Georges Maiduit (France)	
Adelboden, Switzerland		Jean-Claude Killy (France)	
Wengen, Switzerland	Jean-Claude Killy (France)		Jean-Claude Killy (France)
Kitzbühel, Austria	Jean-Claude Killy (France)		Jean-Claude Killy (France)
Megève, France	Guy Périllat (France)		Jean-Claude Killy (France)
Madonna, Italy	Guy Périllat (France)		
Sestriere, Italy			Jean-Claude Killy (France)
Franconia, New Hampshire, USA	Jean-Claude Killy (France)	Jean-Claude Killy (France)	Jean-Claude Killy (France)
Jackson Hole, Wyoming, USA		Jean-Claude Killy (France)	
Vail, Colorado, USA		Jean-Claude Killy (France)	
1968			
Hindelang, Germany		Edi Bruggmann (Switzerland)	
Adelboden, Switzerland		Jean-Claude Killy (France)	
Wengen, Switzerland	Dumenc Giovanoli (Switzerland)		Gerhard Nenning (Austria)
Kitzbühel, Austria	Dumenc Giovanoli (Switzerland)		Gerhard Nenning (Austria)
Megève, France	Alain Penz (France)	Bernard Orcel (France)	
Chamonix, France	Reinhard Tritscher (Austria)		
Oslo, Norway	Patrick Russel (France)	Werner Bleiner (Austria)	
Grenoble, France	Jean-Claude Killy (France)	Jean-Claude Killy (France)	Jean-Claude Killy (France)

Location	Slalom	Giant Slalom	Downhill
1969			
Val d'Isère, France (1968)	Karl Schranz (Austria)	I. Gerhard Nenning (Austria) II. Jean-Claude Killy (France)	
Berchtesgaden, Germany	Alfred Matt (Austria)		
Adelboden, Switzerland		Jean-Noël Augert (France)	
Wengen, Switzerland	Reinhard Tritscher (Austria)		Karl Schranz (Austria)
Kiltzbühel, Austria	Patrick Russel (France)		Karl Schranz (Austria)
Megève, France	Alain Penz (France)		Henri Duvillard (France)
St Anton, Austria			Karl Schranz (Austria)
Cortina, Italy			Josuah Minsch (Switzerland)
Are, Sweden	Patrick Russel (France)	Jean-Noël Augert (France)	
Val Gardena, Italy			Jean-Daniel Dätwyler (Switzerland)
Kranjska Gora, Yugoslavia	Edmund Bruggmann (Switzerland)	Reinhard Tritscher (Austria)	
Squaw Valley, California, USA	William Kidd (USA)		
Mont Ste Anne, Quebec, Canada	Alfred Matt (Austria)	Karl Schranz (Austria)	
Waterville Valley, New Hampshire, USA	Jean-Noël Augert (France)	Dumenc Giovanoli (Switzerland)	

Location	Slalom	Giant Slalom	Downhill
1970			
Val d'Isère, France		Gustavo Thoeni (Italy)	Malcolm Milne (Australia)
Lienz, Austria	Jean-Noël Augert (France)	Patrick Russel (France)	
Hindelang, Germany	Gustavo Thoeni (Italy)		
Adelboden, Switzerland		Karl Schranz (Austria)	
Wengen, Switzerland	Patrick Russel (France)		Henri Duvillard (France)
Morzine, France	Gerhard Riml (Austria)		Bernard Grosfilley (France)
Villars-sur-Ollon, Switzerland	Manfrid Jocoker (Switzerland)		Paul Mitterer (Austria)
Kitzbühel, Austria	Patrick Russel (France)	Dumenc Giovanoli (Switzerland)	
Kranjska Gora, Yugoslavia	Peter Frei (Switzerland)	Dumenc Giovanoli (Switzerland)	
Megève, France	Patrick Russel (France)		Karl Schranz (Austria)
Madonna, Italy	Henri Brechu (France)	Gustavo Thoeni (Italy)	
Garmisch-Partenkirchen, Germany			Karl Schranz (Austria)
Val Gardena, Italy	Jean-Noël Augert (France)	Karl Schranz (Austria)	Bernhard Russi (Switzerland)
Saalbach, Austria	Herald Rofner (Austria)		Kurt Huggler (Switzerland)
Jackson Hole, Wyoming, USA	Alain Penz (France)		Karl Cordin (Austria)
Chamonix, France			Rudi Sailer (Austria)
Grouse Mt., B.C., Canada	Alain Penz (France)	Alain Penz (France)	
Leysin, Mosses, Diablerets, Switzerland	Kurt Schnider (Switzerland)	Josef Loidl (Austria)	
Heavenly Valley, California, USA	Alain Penz (France)	Patrick Russel (France)	
Voss, Bergen, Norway	Patrick Russel (France)	Werner Bleiner (Austria)	

Location	Slalom	Giant slalom	Downhill
1971			
Sestriere, Italy			Henri Duvillard (France)
Val d'Isère, France		Patrick Russel (France)	Karl Cordin (Austria)
Berchtesgaden, Germany	Jean-Noël Augert (France)	Edmund Bruggmann (Switzerland)	
Madonna, Italy	Gustavo Thoeni (Italy)	Henri Duvillard (France)	
Wengen, Switzerland	Tyler Palmer (United States)		Walter Tresch (Switzerland)
Adelboden, Switzerland		Patrick Russel (France)	
Kitzbühel, Austria	Jean-Noël Augert (France)		
Megève, France	Jean-Noël Augert (France)		I Jean-Daniel Dätwyler (Switzerland) II Bernhard Russi (Switzerland)
Mürren, Switzerland	Jean-Noël Augert (France)		
Mont Ste Anne, Quebec, Canada	Patrick Russel (France)	Bernhard Russi (Switzerland)	
Sugarloaf, Maine, USA		Gustavo Thoeni (Italy)	I Bernhard Russi (Italy) II Stefano Anzi (Italy)
Heavenly Valley, California, USA	Gustavo Thoeni (Italy)	Gustavo Thoeni (Italy)	
Are, Sweden	Jean-Noël Augert (France)	David Zwilling (Austria)	
1972			
St Moritz, Switzerland			Bernhard Russi (Switzerland)
Val d'Isère, France		Erich Haker (Netherlands)	Karl Schranz (Austria)
Sestriere, Italy	Tyler Palmer (USA)		
Berchtesgaden, Germany	Henri Duvillard (France)	Roger Rossat-Mignod (France)	
Kitzbühel, Austria	Jean-Noël Augert (France)		I Karl Schranz (A-K) (Austria) II Karl Schranz (Austria)
Wengen, Switzerland	Jean-Noël Augert (France)		
Banff, Alberta, Canada	Andrzej Bachleda (Poland)	Erich Haker (Netherlands)	
Crystal Mountain, Washington, USA			I Bernhard Russi (Switzerland) II Franz Vogler (West Germany)
Heavenly Valley, California, USA		Gustavo Thoeni (Italy)	
St Christina, Italy		Edmund Bruggmann (Switzerland)	
Madonna di Campiglio, Italy	Roland Thoeni (Italy)		
Pra Loup, France	Roland Thoeni (Italy)	Edmund Bruggmann (Switzerland)	

Location	Slalom	Giant Slalom	Downhill
1973			
Val d'Isère, France		Piero Gros (Italy)	Reinhard Tritscher (Austria)
Madonna di Campiglio, Italy	Piero Gros (Italy)	David Zwilling (Austria)	
Selva, Italy			Roland Colombin (Switzerland)
Garmisch-Partenkirchen, Germany			I Roland Colombin (Switzerland) II Roland Colombin (Switzerland)
Adelboden, Switzerland		Gustavo Thoeni (Italy)	
Wengen, Switzerland	Christian Neureuther (West Germany)		Bernhard Russi (Switzerland)
Megève, France	Christian Neureuther (West Germany)	Henri Duvillard (France)	
Kitzbühel, Austria	Jean-Noël Augert (France)		Roland Colombin (Switzerland)
St Anton, Austria	Gustavo Thoeni (Italy)		Bernhard Russi (Switzerland)
Mont Ste Anne, Quebec, Canada	Gustavo Thoeni (Italy)	Max Rieger (West Germany)	
St Moritz, Switzerland			Werner Grissman (Austria)
Naeba, Japan	Jean-Noël Augert (France)	Erik Haker (Ne)	
Heavenly Valley, California, USA	Jean-Noël Augert (France)	Bob Cochran (USA)	
1974			
Val d'Isère, France		Hans Hinterseer (Austria)	Herbert Plank (Italy)
Vitipeno, Italy		Hubert Berchtold (Austria)	
Zell-am-See, Austria			Karl Cordin (Austria)
Schladming, Austria			Franz Klammer (Austria)
Garmisch-Partenkirchen, Germany	Christian Neureuther (West Germany)		Roland Colombin (Switzerland)
Berchtesgaden, Germany		Piero Gros (Italy)	
Morzine, France		Piero Gros (Italy)	Roland Colombin (Switzerland)
Wengen, Switzerland	Christian Neureuther (West Germany)		Roland Colombin (Switzerland)
Adelboden, Switzerland		Gustavo Thoeni (Italy)	
Kitzbühel, Austria	Hans Hinterseer (Austria)		Roland Colombin (Switzerland)
Voss, Norway	Piero Gros (Italy)	Gustavo Thoeni (Italy)	
Zakopane, Poland	Fernandez Ochoa (Spain)		
Vysoke Tatry, Czechoslovakia	Gustavo Thoeni (Italy)	Piero Gros (Italy)	

Location	Slalom	Giant slalom	Downhill
1975			
Val d'Isère, France		Piero Gros (Italy)	Franz Klammer (Austria)
St Moritz, Switzerland			Franz Klammer (Austria)
Madonna, Italy	Ingemar Stenmark (Sweden)	Piero Gros (Italy)	
Garmisch-Partenkirchen, Germany	Piero Gros (Italy)		Franz Klammer (Austria)
Wengen, Switzerland	Ingemar Stenmark (Sweden)		Franz Klammer (Austria)
Adelboden, Switzerland		Piero Gros (Italy)	
Kitzbühel, Austria	Piero Gros (Italy)		Franz Klammer (Austria)
Fulpmes, Austria		Erik Haker (Norway)	
Innsbruck, Austria			Franz Klammer (Austria)
Megève-Chamonix, France	Gustavo Thoeni (Italy)		Walter Vesti (Switzerland)
Naeba, Japan	Hans Hinterseer (Austria)	Ingemar Stenmark (Sweden)	
Vancouver-Garibaldi, Canada		Ingemar Stenmark (Sweden)	
Jackson Hole, Wyoming, USA			Franz Klammer (Austria)
Sun Valley, Idaho, USA	Gustavo Thoeni (Italy)	Ingemar Stenmark (Sweden)	
Val Gardena, Italy			Franz Klammer (Austria)

WOMEN

Location	Slalom	Giant Slalom	Downhill
1967			
Oberstaufen, Germany	Nancy Greene (Canada)	Nancy Greene (Canada)	
Grindelwald, Switzerland	Annie Famose (France)	Nancy Greene (Canada)	Nancy Greene (Canada)
Schruns, Austria			Marielle Goitschel (France)
St Gervais, France	Annie Famose (France)	Erika Schinegger (Austria)	
Monte Bondone, Italy	Brugl Farbiner (W. Germany)		
Sestriere, Italy			Marielle Goitschel (France) Giustina Demetz (Italy)
Franconia, New Hampshire, USA	Marielle Goitschel (France)	Christine Beranger (France)	Isabelle Mir (France)
Jackson Hole, Wyoming, USA	Nancy Greene (Canada)	Nancy Greene (Canada)	
Vail, Colorado, USA		Nancy Greene (Canada)	
1968			
Oberstaufen, Germany	Marielle Goitschel (France)	Fernande Bochatay (Switzerland)	
Grindelwald, Switzerland	Gertrud Gabl (Austria)	Nancy Greene (Canada)	
Badgastein, Austria	Florence Steurer (France)		Olga Pall (Austria)
St Gervais France	Fernande Bochatay (Switzerland)		Isabelle Mir (France)
Chamonix, France	Nancy Greene (Canada)		Nancy Greene (Canada)
Oslo, Norway	Kiki Cutter (USA)	Fernande Bochatay (Switzerland)	
Grenoble, France	Marielle Goitschel (France)	Nancy Greene (Canada)	Olga Pall (Austria)
1969			
Val d'Isère, France	Isabelle Mir (France)	Florence Steurer (France)	
Oberstaufen, Germany	Gertrud Gabl (Austria)	Christina Cutter (USA)	
Grindelwald, Switzerland	Gertrud Gabl (Austria)		Wiltrud Drexel (Austria)
Schruns, Austria	Rosl Mittermaier (W. Germany)		Wiltrud Drexel (Austria)
St Gervais, France	Ingrid Lafforgue (France)		Isabelle Mir (France)
St Anton, Austria			Olga Pall (Austria)
Vipiteno, Italy	Judy Nagel (USA)	Michèle Jacot (France)	
Vysoke-Tatry, Czechoslovakia	Gertrud Gabl (Austria)	Gertrud Gabl (Austria)	
Squaw Valley, California, USA	Bernie Rauter (Austria)	Florence Steurer (France)	
Mont Ste Anne, Quebec, Canada	Christina Cutter (USA)	Michèle Jacot (France)	
Waterville Valley, New Hampshire, USA	Christina Cutter (USA)	Bernie Rauter (Austria)	

Location	Slalom	Giant Slalom	Downhill
1970			
Val d'Isère, France	Michèle Jacot (France)	Françoise Macchi (France)	
Lienz, Austria	Judy Nagel (USA)	Judy Nagel (USA)	
Oberstaufen, Germany	Bernie Rauter (Austria)	Michèle Jacot (France)	
Grindelwald, Switzerland	Michèle Jacot (France)		Isabelle Mir (France)
Badgastein, Austria	Ingrid Lafforgue (France)		Isabelle Mir (France)
Maribor, Yugoslavia	Barbara Cochran (USA)	Annemarie Proell (Austria)	
Saint Gervals, France	Kiki Cutter (USA)	Françoise Macchi (France)	
Garmisch-Partenkirchen, Germany			Françoise Macchi (France)
Abetone, Italy	Ingrid Lafforgue (France)	Britt Lafforgue (France)	
Val Gardena, Italy	Ingrid Lafforgue (France)	Betsy Clifford (Canada)	Anneroesli Zyrd (Switzerland)
Grouse Mt., B.C., Canada	Michèle Jacot (France)		
Voss, Bergen, Norway	Rosi Mittermaier (Germany)	Ingrid Lafforgue (France)	
Jackson Hole, Wyoming, USA	Ingrid Lafforgue (France)		Isabelle Mir (France)
1971			
Sestriere, Italy			Françoise Macchi (France)
Val d'Isère, France	Betsy Clifford (Canada)		Isabelle Mir (France)
Maribor, Yugoslavia	Annemarie Proell (Austria)	Françoise Macchi (France)	
Oberstaufen, Germany	Michèle Jacot (France)	Michèle Jacot (France)	
Grindelwald, Switzerland	Britt Lafforgue (France)		
Montafon, Austria	Betsy Clifford (Canada)		Michèle Jacot (France)
Pra Loup, France			Wiltrud Drexel (Austria)
St Gervais, France	Annemarie Proell (Austria)		
Mürren, Switzerland	Britt Lafforgue (France)		
Mont Ste Anne, Quebec, Canada	Marilyn Cochran (United States)	Isabelle Mir (France)	
Sugarloaf, Maine, USA		Michèle Jacot (France)	I Annemarie Proell (Austria) II Annemarie Proell (Austria)
Heavenly Valley, California, USA	Barbara Cochran (United States)	Barbara Cochran (United States)	
Abetone, Italy		I Annemarie Proell (Austria) II Annemarie Proell (Austria)	
Are, Sweden		Annemarie Proell (Austria)	

Location	Slalom	Giant Slalom	Downhill
1972			
St Moritz, Switzerland			Annemarie Proell (Austria)
Val d'Isère, France			Jacqueline Rouvier (France)
Sestriere, Italy	Françoise Macchi (France)		Annemarie Proell (Austria)
Oberstaufen, Germany	Françoise Macchi (France)	Françoise Macchi (France)	
Marburg, Germany		Françoise Macchi (France)	
Badgastein, Austria	Britt Lafforgue (France)		Annemarie Proell (Austria)
Grindelwald, Switzerland			Annemarie Proell (Austria)
St Gervais, France		Annemarie Proell (Austria)	
Grindelwald, Switzerland	Britt Lafforgue (France)		
Banff, Alberta, Canada	Britt Lafforgue (France)	Annemarie Proell (Austria)	
Crystal Mountain, Washington, USA			I Annemarie Proell (Austria) II Wiltrud Drexel (Austria)
Heavenly Valley, California, USA		Annemarie Proell (Austria)	
Pra Loup, France	Danielle Debernard (France)	I Danielle Debernard (France) II Britt Lafforgue (France)	
1973			
Val d'Isère, France	Pamela Behr (West Germany)		Annemarie Proell (Austria)
Saalbach, Austria		Annemarie Proell (Austria)	Annemarie Proell (Austria)
Pfronten, Germany			I Annemarie Proell (Austria) II Annemarie Proell (Austria)
Les Contamines, France		Monika Kaserer (Austria)	
St Gervais, France		Annemarie Proell (Austria)	
Grindelwald, Switzerland	Monika Kaserer (Austria)		Annemarie Proell (Austria)
Chamonix, France	Marylin Cochran (USA)		Annemarie Proell (Austria)
Abetone, Italy		Monika Kaserer (Austria)	
Schruns-Tschaguns, Austria	Rosi Mittermaier (West Germany)		Annemarie Proell (Austria)
Mont Ste Anne, Quebec, Canada	Patricia Emonet (France)		Annemarie Proell (Austria)
St Moritz, Switzerland			Annemarie Proell (Austria)
Anchorage, Alaska, USA		Bernadette Zurbriggen (Switzerland)	
Naeba, Japan	Danielle Debernard (France)	Marylin Cochran (USA)	
Heavenly Valley, California, USA	Patricia Emonet (France)	Patricia Emonet (France)	

Location	Slalom	Giant Slalom	Downhill
1974			
Val d'Isère, France	Christa Zechmeister (West Germany)		Annemarie Moser-Proell (Austria)
Zell-am-See, Austria		Hanni Wenzel (Liechtenstein)	Annemarie Moser-Proell (Austria)
Pfronten, Germany		Kathy Kreiner (Canada)	Annemarie Moser-Proell (Austria)
Les Gets, France	Christa Zechmeister (West Germany)	Claudia Giordani (Italy)	
Grindelwald, Switzerland		Monika Kasserer (Austria)	Cindy Nelson (United States)
Les Diablerets, Switzerland	Christa Zechmeister (West Germany)		
Badgastein, Austria	Christa Zechmeister (West Germany)	Fabienne Serrat (France)	Annemarie Moser-Proell (Austria)
Abetone, Italy	Rosi Mittermaier (West Germany)		
Vysoke Tatry, Poland	Rosi Mittermaier (West Germany)	Monika Kasserer (Austria)	
1975			
Val d'Isère France		Annemarie Moser-Proell (Austria)	Wiltrud Drexel (Austria)
Cortina, Italy	Annemarie Moser-Proell (Austria)		Annemarie Moser-Proell (Austria)
Saalbach, Austria			Cindy Nelson (USA)
Garmisch-Partenkirchen, Germany	Lise-Marie Morerod (Switzerland)		
Grindelwald, Switzerland		Annemarie Moser-Proell (Austria)	Annemarie Moser-Proell (Austria)
Schruns-Tschagguns, Austria	Christa Zechmeister (West Germany)		Bernadette Zurbriggen (Switzerland)
Jahorina, Yugoslavia		Annemarie Moser-Proell (Austria)	
Axamer Lizum Austria			Marie-Therese Nadig (Switzerland)
St Gervais, France	Lise-Marie Morerod (Switzerland)		
Chamonix, France			Bernadette Zurbriggen (Switzerland)
Naeba, Japan	Hanni Wenzel (Lichtenstein)	Annemarie Moser-Proell (Austria)	
Vancouver-Garibaldi, Canada		Cindy Nelson (USA)	
Jackson Hole, Wyoming, USA			Marie-Therese Nadig (Switzerland)
Sun Valley, Idaho, USA	Hanni Wenzel (Liechtenstein)	Lise-Marie Morerod (Switzerland)	
Val Gardena, Italy	Lise-Marie Morerod (Switzerland)		

ARLBERG-KANDAHAR

Year	Winner (Men)	Nationality	Winner (Women)	Nationality	Locale of Race
1928	Benno Leubner	Austria	Lisbeth Poland	Austria	St Anton
1929	Karl Neuner	Germany	Audrey Sale-Barker	England	St Anton
1930	Walter Prager	Switzerland	Inge Lantschner	Austria	St Anton
1931	Otto Fürrer	Switzerland	Audrey Sale-Barker	England	Mürren
1932	Otto Fürrer	Switzerland	Hedi Lantschner	Austria	St Anton
1933	Walter Prager	Switzerland	Esmé Mackinnon	England	Mürren
1934	Otto Fürrer	Switzerland	Jeannette Kessler	England	Mürren
1935	Arnold Glatthard	Switzerland	Anny Rüegg	Switzerland	St Anton
1936	Friedl Pfeiffer	Austria	Gerda Paumgarten	Austria	St Anton
1937	Emile Allais	France	Christel Cranz	Germany	Mürren
1938	Race canceled				
1939	Rudolf Rominger	Switzerland	Marian Steedman	England	Mürren
1947	James Couttet	France	Celina Seghi	Italy	Mürren
1948	James Couttet	France	Celina Seghi	Italy	Chamonix
1949	Zeno Colo	Italy	F. Martell	France	St Anton
1950	James Couttet	France	Marisette Agnel	France	Mürren
1951	Zeno Colo	Italy	F. Martell	France	Sestriere
1952	Fritz Huber, Jr.	Austria	Erika Mahringer	Austria	Chamonix
1953	Anderl Molterer	Austria	Trude Klecker	Austria	St Anton
1954	Anderl Molterer	Austria	A. Buchner-Fischer	Germany	Garmisch
1955	Walter Schuster	Austria	Hilde Hofheer	Austria	Mürren
1956	Anderl Molterer	Austria	M. Berthod	France	Sestriere
1957	Karl Schranz	Austria	Lotti Blattl	Austria	Chamonix
1958	Karl Schranz	Austria	Putzi Frandl	Austria	St Anton
1959	Karl Schranz	Austria	Anne Heggtveit	Canada	Garmisch
1960	Adrien Duvillard	France	Marianne Jahn	Austria	Sestriere
1961	Guy Périllat	France	Heidi Biebl	Germany	Mürren
1962	Karl Schranz	Austria	Traudel Hecher	Austria	Sestriere
1963	François Bonlieu	France	Traudel Hecher	Austria	Chamonix
1964	James Heuga	USA	Marielle Goitschel	France	Garmisch
1965	Gerhard Nenning	Austria	Marielle Goitschel	France	St Anton
1966	Jean-Claude Killy	France	Christl Haas	Austria	Mürren
1967	Jean-Claude Killy	France	Marielle Goitschel	France	Sestriere
1968	Guy Périllat	France	Nancy Greene	Canada	Chamonix
1969	Karl Schranz	Austria	Gertrude Gabl	Austria	St Anton
1970	Karl Schranz	Austria	Michèle Jacot	France	Garmisch
1971	Patrick Russel	France	Britt Lafforge	France	Mürren
1972	Oreste Peccedi	Italy	Françoise Macchi	France	St Anton
1973	Gustavo Thoeni	Italy	Annemarie Moser-Proell	Austria	St Anton
1974	David Zwilling	Austria		Austria	Garmisch
1975	Gustavo Thoeni	Italy	Annemarie Moser-Proell		Chamonix St Gervais, Megève

WORLD CURLING CHAMPIONSHIPS

1959 Regina, Canada:
Ernie, Arnold, Sam and Wes Richardson
1960 Regina, Canada:
Ernie, Arnold, Sam and Wes Richardson
1961 Edmonton, Canada:
Hec Gervais, Ray Werner, Vic Raymer, Wally Ursuliak
1962 Regina, Canada:
Ernie, Arnold, Sam and Wes Richardson
1963 Regina, Canada:
Ernie, Arnold and Sam Richardson, Mel Perry
1964 Vancouver, Canada:
Lyall Dagg, Leo Herbert, Fred Britton, Barry Naimark
1965 Superior, USA:
Bud Somerville, Bill Strum, Al Gagne, Tom Wright
1966 Calgary, Canada:
Ron Northcott, George Fink, Bernie Sparkes, Fred Storey
1967 Perth, Scotland:
Chuck Hay, John Bryden, Alen Glen, David Howie
1968 Calgary, Canada:
Ron Northcott, Jim Shields, Bernie Sparkes, Fred Storey
1969 Calgary, Canada:
Ron Northcott, Dave Gerlach, Bernie Sparkes, Fred Storey
1970 Winnipeg, Canada:
Don Duguid, Rod Hunter, Jim Pettapiece, Bryan Wood
1971 Winnipeg, Canada:
Don Duguid, Rod Hunter, Jim Pettapiece, Bryan Wood
1972 Winnipeg, Canada:
Orest Meleschuk, Dave Romano, John Hanesiak, Pat Hailley
1973 Stockholm, Sweden:
Kjell Oscarius, Bengt Oscarius, Tom Schaeffer, Claes-Goran Carlman
1974 Superior, USA:
Bud Somerville, Bill Nichols, Bill Strum, Tom Locken
1975 Zurich, Switzerland:
Otto Danieli, Roland Schneider, Rolf Gautschi, Ueli Mulli
1976 Hibbing, USA:
Bruce Roberts, Joe Roberts, Gary Kleffman, Jerry Scott

CRESTA RUN

GRAND NATIONAL WINNERS
(Cresta Run race from Top)

1885 C. Austin
1886 P. Minsch
1887 G. Guthrie
1888 E. Cohen
1889 J. Vansittart
1890 R. Towle
1891 J. Patterson
1892 H. Topham
1893 H. Gibson
1894 H. Topham
1895 H. Topham
1896 H. Gibson
1897 B. Dwyer
1898 R. Bird
1899 B. Dwyer
1900 P. Spence
1901 J. Bott
1902 J. Bott
1903 E. Thoma-Badrutt
1904 C. Martin
1905 J. Bott
1906 J. Bott
1907 J. Bott
1908 G. Slater
1909 G. Slater
1910 G. Slater
1911 C. Webb-Bowen
1912 E. Quicke
1913 No competition
1914 V. Gibbs
1915–20 No competition
1921 H. Giles
1922 W. Bodmer
1923 L. Smithers
1924 H. Goodrich
1925 No competition
1926 Lord Northesk
1927 J. Heaton
1928 Lord Northesk
1929 J. Heaton
1930 R. Capadrutt
1931 J. Coats
1932 No competition
1933 J. Coats
1934 J. Coats
1935 J. Coats
1936 W. Fiske
1937 J. Coats
1938 W. Fiske
1939 Baron Gevers
1940–46 No competition
1947 W. Hirogoyen
1948–54 No competition
1955 D. Connor
1956 No competition
1957 D. Connor
1958 No competition
1959 C. Mitchell
1960 N. Bibbia
1961 N. Bibbia
1962 N. Bibbia
1963 N. Bibbia
1964 N. Bibbia
1965 C. Mitchell
1966 N. Bibbia
1967 H. Küderli
1968 N. Bibbia
1969 B. Bischofberger
1970 H. Küderli
1971 B. Bischofberger
1972 B. Bischofberger
1973 N. Bibbia
1974 P. Felder
1975 P. Berchtold
1976 R. Gansser

CURZON CUP WINNERS
(Cresta Run race from Junction)

1910 G. Slater
1911 C. Bacon
1912 E. Thoma-Badrutt
1913 V. Gibbs
1914 V. Gibbs
1915–19 No competition
1920 J. Moore-Brabazon
1921 H. Giles
1922 J. Moore-Brabazon
1923 W. Bodmer
1924 N. Marsden
1925 N. Marsden
1926 Lord Northesk
1927 J. Moore-Brabazon
1928 Lord Northesk
1929 R. Hawkes
1930 J. Heaton
1931 A. Lanfranchi
1932 Lord Grimthorpe
1933 J. Heaton
1934 C. Holland-Moritz
1935 W. Fiske
1936 B. Bathurst
1937 W. Fiske
1938 J. Crammond
1939 W. Keddie
1940–46 No competition
1947 R. Bott
1948–49 No competition
1950 N. Bibbia
1951 C. Holland
1952 P. Arnold
1953 P. Arnold
1954 C. Mitchell
1955 D. Connor
1956 D. Connor
1957 N. Bibbia
1958 N. Bibbia
1959 C. Mitchell
1960 N. Bibbia
1961 H. Küderli
1962 N. Bibbia
1963 N. Bibbia
1964 N. Bibbia
1965 L. Ciparisso
1966 L. Ciparisso
1967 L. Ciparisso
1968 J. Glattfelder
1969 N. Bibbia
1970 J. Glattfelder
1971 P. Gallian
1972 B. Bischofberger
1973 B. Bischofberger
1974 P. Felder
1975 P. Berchtold
1976 R. Gansser

ICE HOCKEY WORLD CHAMPIONSHIPS

Year	First	Second	Third	Place
1920	Canada	USA	Czechoslovakia	Antwerp
1924	Canada	USA	Great Britain	Chamonix
1928	Canada	Sweden	Switzerland	St Moritz
1930	Canada	Germany	Switzerland	Chamonix-Berlin
1931	Canada	USA	Austria	Krynica
1932	Canada	USA	Germany	Lake Placid
1933	USA	Canada	Czechoslovakia	Prague
1934	Canada	USA	Germany	Milan
1935	Canada	Switzerland	Great Britain	Davos
1936	Great Britain	Canada	USA	Garmisch
1937	Canada	Great Britain	Switzerland	London
1938	Canada	Great Britain	Czechoslovakia	Prague
1939	Canada	USA	Switzerland	Zurich-Basle
1947	Czechoslovakia	Sweden	Austria	Prague
1948	Canada	Czechoslovakia	Switzerland	St Moritz
1949	Czechoslovakia	Canada	USA	Stockholm
1950	Canada	USA	Switzerland	London
1951	Canada	Sweden	Switzerland	Paris
1952	Canada	USA	Sweden	Oslo
1953	Sweden	West Germany	Switzerland	Zurich-Basle
1954	USSR	Canada	Sweden	Stockholm
1955	Canada	USSR	Czechoslovakia	West Germany
1956	USSR	USA	Canada	Cortina
1957	Sweden	USSR	Czechloslovakia	Moscow
1958	Canada	USSR	Sweden	Oslo
1959	Canada	USSR	Czechoslovakia	Czechoslovakia
1960	USA	Canada	USSR	Squaw Valley
1961	Canada	Czechoslovakia	USSR	Geneva-Lausanne
1962	Sweden	Canada	USA	Col. Springs-Denver
1963	USSR	Sweden	Czechoslovakia	Stockholm
1964	USSR	Sweden	Czechoslovakia	Innsbruck
1965	USSR	Czechoslovakia	Sweden	Tampere (A)
1966	USSR	Czechoslovakia	Canada	Ljubljana (A)
1967	USSR	Sweden	Canada	Vienna
1968	USSR	Czechoslovakia	Canada	Grenoble
1969	USSR	Sweden	Czechoslovakia	Stockholm (A)
1970	USSR	Sweden	Czechoslovakia	Stockholm (A)
1971	USSR	Czechoslovakia	Sweden	Bern-Geneva (A)
1972	Czechoslovakia	USSR	Sweden	Prague (A)
1973	USSR	Sweden	Czechoslovakia	Moscow
1974	USSR	Czechoslovakia	Sweden	Helsinki (A)
1975	USSR	Czechoslovakia	Sweden	Munich/ Dusseldorf (A)
1976	Czechoslovakia	USSR	Sweden	Kotowice

EUROPEAN CHAMPIONSHIPS

Year	First	Second	Third	Place
1910	Great Britain	Germany	Belgium	Les Avants
1911	Bohemia	Germany	Belgium	Berlin
1912	Bohemia	Germany	Austria	Prague-Annulled
1913	Belgium	Bohemia	Germany	Munich
1914	Bohemia	Germany	Belgium	Berlin
1921	Sweden	Czechoslovakia		Stockholm
1922	Czechoslovakia	Sweden	Switzerland	St Moritz
1923	Sweden	France	Czechoslovakia	Antwerp
1924	France	Sweden	Belgium-Switzerland	Milan
1925	Czechoslovakia	Austria	Switzerland	Prague
1926	Switzerland	Czechoslovakia	Austria	Davos
1927	Austria	Belgium	Germany	Vienna
1928	Sweden	Switzerland	Great Britain	St Moritz
1929	Czechoslovakia	Poland	Austria	Budapest
1930	Germany	Switzerland	Austria	Chamonix-Berlin
1931	Austria	Poland	Czechoslovakia	Krynica
1932	Sweden	Austria	Switzerland	Berlin
1933	Czechoslovakia	Austria	Germany-Switzerland	Prague
1934	Germany	Switzerland	Czechoslovakia	Milan
1935	Switzerland	Great Britain	Czechoslovakia	Davos
1936	Great Britain	Czechoslovakia	Sweden-Germany	Garmisch
1937	Great Britain	Switzerland	Germany	London
1938	Great Britain	Czechoslovakia	Germany	Prague
1939	Switzerland	Czechoslovakia	Germany	Zurich-Basle
1940–1946 No championships				
1947	Czechoslovakia	Sweden	Austria	Prague
1948	Czechoslovakia	Switzerland	Sweden	St Moritz
1949	Czechoslovakia	Sweden	Switzerland	Stockholm
1950	Switzerland	Great Britain	Sweden	London
1951	Sweden	Switzerland	Norway	Paris
1952	Sweden	Czechoslovakia	Switzerland	Oslo
1953	Sweden	West Germany	Switzerland	Zurich-Basle
1954	USSR	Sweden	Czechoslovakia	Stockholm
1955	USSR	Czechoslovakia	Sweden	West Germany
1956	USSR	Sweden	Czechoslovakia	Cortina
1957	Sweden	USSR	Czechoslovakia	Moscow
1958	USSR	Sweden	Czechoslovakia	Oslo
1959	USSR	Czechoslovakia	Sweden	Czechoslovakia
1960	USSR	Czechoslovakia	Sweden	Squaw Valley
1961	Czechoslovakia	USSR	Sweden	Geneva-Lausanne
1962	Sweden	Finland	Norway	Col. Springs-Denver
1963	USSR	Sweden	Czechoslovakia	Stockholm
1964	USSR	Sweden	Czechoslovakia	Innsbruck
1965	USSR	Czechoslovakia	Sweden	Tampere (A)
1966	USSR	Czechoslovakia	Sweden	Ljubljana (A)
1967	USSR	Sweden	Czechoslovakia	Vienna
1968	USSR	Czechoslovakia	Sweden	Grenoble
1969	USSR	Sweden	Czechoslovakia	Stockholm (A)
1970	USSR	Sweden	Czechoslovakia	Stockholm (A)
1971	Czechoslovakia	USSR	Sweden	Bern-Geneva (A)
1972	Czechoslovakia	USSR	Sweden	Prague (A)
1973	USSR	Sweden	Czechoslovakia	Moscow (A)
1974	USSR	Czechoslovakia	Sweden	Helsinki (A)
1975	USSR	Czechoslovakia	Sweden	Munich/Düsseldorf (A)
1976	Czechoslovakia	USSR	Sweden	Kotowice

Index

Figures in italics refer to illustration page numbers

Acknowledgements

Front cover – Transworld. 2-3 – Jakob Vaage. 7 – Transworld. 10, 11 – National Gallery, London. 12 – Radio Times Hulton Picture Library. 13 – Mary Evans. 14 – National Gallery, London (*centre*); Mary Evans (*bottom*). 15, 16, 17 – Mary Evans. 18, 19 – Radio Times Hulton Picture Library. 20 – Jakob Vaage. 21 – Jakob Vaage (*top right*); Mansell (*bottom*). 23 – Jakob Vaage. 24-5 – Mary Evans. 26 – Jakob Vaage. 27 – Radio Times Hulton Picture Library. 28 – Jakob Vaage. 29 – Mary Evans. 30 – Radio Times Hulton Picture Library. 31 – St Moritz Tourist Board. 33 – Mary Evans. 34 – Swiss National Tourist Office. 35 – Radio Times Hulton Picture Library (*left*); Mary Evans (*right*). 36 – Mary Evans. 37 – St Moritz Tourist Board. 38, 39 – Swiss National Tourist Office. 41, 42-3 – Mary Evans. 44 – Mansell. 45 – Radio Times Hulton Picture Library. 46 – Ernst Schudel (*top*); Mary Evans (*bottom*). 47 – Swiss National Tourist Office (*top*); Mary Evans (*bottom*). 49 – Ernst Schudel. 50 – Radio Times Hulton Picture Library. 51, 53 – Mary Evans. 54 – Camera Press (*top*); Popperfoto (*centre and bottom*). 55 – Royal Caledonian Curling Club. 56 – Jakob Vaage. 57 – Swiss National Tourist Office. 58, 60-61 – Jakob Vaage. 62 – Swiss National Tourist Office. 65, 67 – Swiss National Tourist Office. 69 – Ernst Schudel. 70, 71 – St Moritz Tourist Board. 72, 73 – Popperfoto. 75 – Radio Times Hulton Picture Library. 76, 77 – Jakob Vaage. 79 – Swiss National Tourist Office. 80 – St Moritz Tourist Board (*top*); Ski Club of Great Britain (*bottom*). 84 – Jakob Vaage. 85 – Ski Club of Great Britain. 86, 89 – Radio Times Hulton Picture Library. 91 – Ski Club of Great Britain. 95 – Radio Times Hulton Picture Library. 96 – Swiss National Tourist Office. 97, 98 – Radio Times Hulton Picture Library. 99 – Mary Evans. 100 – Radio Times Hulton Picture Library (*top*); Mary Evans (*bottom*). 101 – Swiss National Tourist Office. 103 – Mary Evans (*top*); Radio Times Hulton Picture Library (*bottom*). 104 – Radio Times Hulton Picture Library. 105 – Swiss National Tourist Office. 106 – Gerry Cranham. 109 – Central Press. 110-111 – Swiss National Tourist Office. 112 – Camera Press. 113 – Popperfoto (*top*); Associated Press (*bottom*). 114 – Radio Times Hulton Picture Library. 115 – Popperfoto. 117, 118, 119 – Swiss National Tourist Office. 121 – Popperfoto. 123 – Associated Press. 124 – National Film Board of Canada. 125 – Camera Press. 126 – Ski Club of Great Britain. 127 – Swiss National Tourist Office. 130 – Keystone. 132 – Mansell. 133 – Mary Evans. 135 – Swiss National Tourist Office (*top*); Grindelwald Tourist Office (*bottom left*); Radio Times Hulton Picture Library (*bottom right*). 136 – Swiss National Tourist Office (*top*); Grindelwald Tourist Office (*bottom*). 139 – Keystone (*left*); St Moritz Tourist Board (*right*). 141 – Popperfoto. 142 – Radio Times Hulton Picture Library. 143 – Swiss National Tourist Office. 144 – Keystone (*left*); Associated Press (*top right*); Popperfoto (*bottom right*). 145 – Central Press. 147 – Camera Press. 148, 149 – Keystone. 150 – Radio Times Hulton Picture Library (*left*); Keystone (*right*). 151 – Keystone. 152 – Radio Times Hulton Picture Library. 153 – Colorsport. 154 – Tony Duffy. 155 – Gerry Cranham (*top*); Tony Duffy (*bottom*). 156, 157 – Colorsport. 158-9 – Swiss National Tourist Office. 160 – Central Press. 161 – Associated Press. 162 – Peter Fordham. 163 – Gerry Cranham. 165 – Ski Club of Great Britain. 166-7 – Colorsport. 168 – Central Press (*top*); George Konig (*centre*); Popperfoto (*bottom*). 169 – Associated Press. 170 – Gerry Cranham (*top*); Colorsport (*bottom*). 171 – Gerry Cranham. 172 – Camera Press. 173 – Swiss National Tourist Office. 174 – Syndication International (*top*); Peter Fordham (*bottom*). 175 – Peter Fordham. 177 – Gerry Cranham (*top*); Swiss National Tourist Office (*bottom*). 178 – Peter Fordham (*top left and right*); Transworld (*bottom*). 179 – Peter Fordham. 181 – London Express. 182-3 – Colorsport. 184 – Swiss National Tourist Office.